TAKE ME BACK TO THE BALL GAME

Anyone who's ever toed a rubber or snagged a foul pop delights in reliving his days of glory on the diamond. And no people spin better yarns about their exploits—and their opponents—than former major leaguers themselves.

THE "ALL-STARS'" ALL-STAR BASEBALL BOOK

thrusts these ex–big leaguers into the spotlight once more and asks them to name the heroes of their youth. Players from every World Series since 1919 and from every All-Star Game ever played name their fantasy teams, favorite players, and toughest outs—providing a colorful insiders' look at America's favorite sport.

THE "ALL-STARS"

ALL-STAR BASEBALL BOOK

**NICK ACOCELLA AND
DONALD DEWEY**

DISCUS AND FLARE BOOKS

Acknowledgments

The authors wish to thank first and foremost the hundreds of former players—many more than are included here—who gave so enthusiastically of their time by writing and talking to us about their recollections. We would also like to thank several baseball executives and team employees who helped us locate some of the players included in these pages. Among those we would like to mention specifically are Joe Safety and Ann Melia of the Yankees, Jay Horowitz and Patricia Byrne of the Mets, Bill Veeck, Rollie Hemond of the White Sox, Toby Zwikel of the Dodgers, John Sevano of the Angels, Sally O'Leary of the Pirates, Taunee Paur of the Rangers, and Anita Littrell of the Royals.

THE "ALL-STARS' " ALL-STAR BASEBALL BOOK is an original publication of Avon Books. This work has never before appeared in book form.

AVON BOOKS
A division of
The Hearst Corporation
1790 Broadway
New York, New York 10019

First Avon Printing, March 1986

PREFACE

The marketing of nostalgia and fantasy has become as visible a part of baseball as the signing of free agents. Teams hold annual old-timer game promotions. All-star old-timers tour major cities for exhibition contests. Franchise after franchise schedules elaborate ceremonies for retiring the uniform number of a former player. For something like $2500, graying, paunchy fans can fly to Arizona or Florida for a few days and play on the same infield with the diamond heroes of their youth. Baseball card conventions around the country attract thousands of collectors and regularly see tens of thousands of dollars change hands. Bookstore shelves are laden with the reminiscences of sportswriters who covered the Boys of Summer and the daydreams of would-be George Steinbrenners who like to pretend they can cover Dave Winfield's salary. A jock with any fashion consciousness at all owns one of those turn-of-the-century caps originally manufactured for the Pittsburgh Pirates and since copied for just about every team in the major and minor leagues.

In short, we have heard, seen, and read a lot about baseball past, present, and nonexistent in recent years. Just about everybody has had a say about the best, the worst, and the most ideal. Just about everybody has described where he was when it was and how it was. Just about everybody.

Except the players themselves.

As valuable as the insights of the pressbox and the bleachers can be regarding the relative merits of Hank Aaron and Willie Mays, it remains a fact that none of these sportswriters has ever had to paint the outside corner against Aaron and very few fans have ever driven Mays to the center field fence for a long out. Even the most assiduous student of box scores would be hard pressed to measure the psychological impact of a particular player's presence in the lineup, the dugout, or the locker room. Increasingly meticulous statisticians have exposed the insufficiencies of batting and fielding averages in gauging a player's talent, but to what extent did the players believe in those numbers in the first place (or even believe in the new numbers, for that matter)?

The suggestion here is not that only big league players are in a position to offer expert evaluations of what takes place between the white lines. If personal experience were the only criterion for judging ability, a Babe Ruth might have looked at his 14 strikeouts in 25 plate appearances against Hub Pruett and nominated the 29-48 righthander for the Hall of Fame, an Aaron might count his 17 career home runs against Don Drysdale as 17 reasons for denying the Dodger hurler a place in Cooperstown, and several seasons of New York Yankees might vote for Frank Lary as the greatest pitcher of all time. The point, rather, is that by *excluding* the personal and team experiences of those who have done the actual playing, any perspective on baseball history is a necessarily limited one. In providing a forum for the views of hundreds of former major leaguers on the following pages, the present book is an attempt to overcome such a limitation.

—Nick Acocella
Donald Dewey

INTRODUCTION

The first game in the major leagues as we know them today was played between Boston and Philadelphia on Saturday, April 22, 1876. The last time there was anything approaching unanimity in speculating about the greatest possible all-time all-star baseball team was Sunday, April 23, 1876. In the 11 decades since then, thousands of players have jogged through millions of memories and appreciations of what they did or did not accomplish on the diamond. Some of the players have excited the memory to a legendary degree, to the point that we can recall them in the most characteristic of details despite never having actually seen them play. Others have kept our attention through argumentative statistics, fortuitous games, and traumatic at bats. The greats are not only the players we saw, but the players we believe we saw. We are known as fans—as in fanatic, but also as in fancy.

The fan within every ballplayer is subject to the same tempers and prejudices as the rooter sitting in the loge behind home plate. If he can be assumed to have more of an inside professional perspective on the skills of his teammates and opponents, he can likewise be expected to have deeper personal enthusiasms and rancors where his contemporaries are concerned. Also, like the sun-bather in the bleachers, the player has grown up within the lore and myths of the game and perhaps remains even more impressed by a predecessor who had once toed the same mound or stood on the same outfield grass. Not least, the player-as-fan, just like the attorney-as-fan and the secretary-as-fan, would like to be consulted a lot more as such—about who is *truly* entitled to be enshrined at Cooperstown, about who was *really* an underrated player, about what team was *obviously* the best 25-man unit, etc.

In compiling The ''All-Stars' '' All-Star Baseball Book, the authors have addressed themselves to the player-as-fan. The objective was not to conduct an election for certifying the theoretically strongest lineup of all time, but to record first-hand, knowledgeable evaluations of different periods in the evolution of big league baseball in the 20th century. The decision to restrict the survey to former players was based in part on the well-known reluctance of active major leaguers to discuss teammates and opponents who might someday be in reverse roles, in part on the greater definitiveness of the replies of the retired men.

The former players interviewed for The "All-Stars' " All-Star Baseball Book include at least one member of each National and American league all-star team dating back to the inaugural 1933 game in Chicago's Comiskey Park. The following pages also register the views of at least one player from every pennant-winning team from 1919 to 1983 with the exception of teams from which there are no survivors. Included as well are a couple of players who began their careers before there was any such thing as a World Series between National and American leagues. In the cases of some other players, it would admittedly require a stretch of the imagination to think of them as all-stars, but they have been included either because of unusually long service in the big leagues, because of their association with a particularly memorable diamond event, or because of a personal popularity that overshadowed their relatively skimpy skills.

For the most part, The "All-Stars' " All-Star Baseball Book has emerged from personal, written, and telephone interviews conducted specifically for the present work. Other lineups were gathered by one or both of the authors in the course of unrelated newspaper or magazine assignments. A third group of responses—embracing the contributions of such baseball legends as Ty Cobb, Larry Lajoie, Sam Crawford, Fred Clarke, Dazzy Vance, Carl Hubbell, Mickey Cochrane, Hank Greenberg, and Charlie Gehringer—goes back some 25 years when one of the authors, then a teenager, wrote to every member of the Hall of Fame then living and asked each to pick a personal all-time all-star team. For obvious reasons, the presentation of these selections is slightly different from that of the other replies.

Except for the nine lineups elicited 25 years ago, all those interviewed were asked five basic questions:

—aside from yourself, what eight players, righthanded pitcher, and lefthanded pitcher would you want on the field if you had to win one game?

—what player or players deserve election to Cooperstown?

—who was the toughest batter (or pitcher) you ever faced?

—who was the most underrated player you ever played with or against?

—what was the single strongest team you ever saw?

In asking every player for the ideal team he would field if he had to win one game, the stipulation was that the choices be confined to one-time teammates and rivals. (The preference for teammates was particularly blatant among those who played for the Dodgers in the fifties and for the Yankees in the fifties and sixties.) Many players objected to this restriction, however, saying they were as capable of judging talent from a box seat or armchair drawn up in front of a television set as they had been from a dugout. The result is that some lineups span generations, with conspicuous benefit to, among others, Johnny Bench, Brooks Robinson, Luis Aparicio, and Keith Hernandez. Similarly, some players said they would feel uncomfortable leaving out legends like Babe Ruth and Lou Gehrig, even if they had personally never seen them play. Especially understandable was the response of Dick Sisler, who said he felt compelled to choose his father as his all-time first baseman even though he could recall having seen him play only three times. In one of the games, Sisler recounted, Hall of Famer George Sisler was thrown out trying to steal home; in another game he was almost thrown out of the ballpark for an angry shouting match with the opposing pitcher.

Although those responding generally agreed to the ground rule of one player per position, a few indicated that they found it impossible to decide between, say, a Juan Marichal and a Bob Gibson as the best righthanded pitcher and asked that the alternative be mentioned as emphatically as practical. (This has been done either in the actual lineup list or in the comments accompanying the player's choices.) Former Pittsburgh slugger Ralph Kiner had another objection: if he had to win one game, said the veteran New York Mets announcer, there was no way, even theoretically, that he was going to leave himself out of the lineup. Billy Bruton, Bill Werber, Willie Mays, and Roy Campanella responded similarly.

Tempting as it might be for the reader to go through the pages that follow and tote up the preferences received at each position in order to arrive at an overall players' choice team, it should be noted that, because of age, most of the players interviewed were in their prime between 1940 and 1965. While this doesn't depreciate the obvious respect their contemporaries had for players like Vic Power, Gil Hodges, and Bill Mazeroski, in fact might even be interpreted as a forecast of some future balloting at Cooperstown by the Committee on Veterans, it should be taken as a caution against downgrading other first basemen from other eras before and after.

Concerning the question about what player or players deserve election to the Hall of Fame, it should be kept in mind that the survey was conducted in the immediate wake of the controversy over Nellie Fox's failure to gain entrance to Cooperstown by a fraction of a percentage point. The impression is that, but for the timing, Fox, however deserving he might have been, would not have been mentioned so often. On the other hand, resentment over the exclusion of such players as Marty Marion, Bobby Doerr, Ken Keltner, Ernie Lombardi, Phil Rizzuto, and Billy Williams appears to run deep among many ex-players. Worthy of note are the eleven players who nominated themselves for the Hall of Fame. Also worthy of note is the large number of respondents who declined to make any Cooperstown nominations, many of whom described the Hall of Fame as "a joke", "a writers' game", or some other encouragement to indifference.

Where there was no indifference at all, on the other hand, was in the players' recollections of the toughest batters or pitchers they faced. Such relatively obscure names as Russ Bauers, Jesse Flores, Bill Werle, Tom McBride, Skeeter Webb, and Charlie Hollocher came instantly to mind for those who were baffled by them. But if there was one player who dominated the replies to this question, it would be Ewell Blackwell, probably the best pitcher never to win 100 games.

As expected, the question regarding the most underrated player also elicited unusual answers, and not only because of the relatively obscure names advanced. On the contrary, in fact, Cooperstown residents by the names of Aaron, Kaline, Clemente, and Mathews were cited almost as often as classic "gamers" like Jo-Jo Moore, Roy McMillan, and Gil Mc-

Dougald. Perhaps the most pertinent reply to the question about underrated players, however, came from Steve Stone, the American League's 1980 Cy Young Award winner, who explains why he thinks there may never again be a truly underrated player.

As interesting as some of the names advanced by the respondents, of course, are those not put forward with the frequency one might have anticipated. Falling into this category are, among others, Lefty Gomez, Mel Ott, Hank Greenberg, Ralph Kiner, and Pete Rose. The need for defense in a conjectural winner-take-all single game also seems to have cost Stan Musial, Ernie Banks, and Harmon Killebrew and raised the value of the Hodgeses, McMillans, and Powers. (Less frequent was the selection of a strictly offensive player at some position "in order to get his bat in," although one respondent put Rogers Hornsby at third base for just that purpose. Another put Mel Ott at third base. Still another put Hank Aaron at first. And still others put Jimmie Foxx both at third base and in the outfield.) Other beneficiaries of the defense-first philosophy were Jim Hegan, Del Crandall, Paul Blair, Dick Green, and Ozzie Smith.

The single most unusual choice made by anybody? We like Gerry Staley's pick for the best catcher he ever saw. Look it up!

A handful of respondents were willing to answer questions but declined to suggest a team; their remarks are contained in a separate chapter after the alphabetical listing. As for those who refused outright to be part of the survey, several made it clear that they considered their baseball careers an episode in their past and wanted it kept that way. A couple of former stars still connected to the game in a front office capacity begged off on the grounds that they might slight some fellow executive and that this might influence some present or future business negotiation. A few others, including two members of the Hall of Fame, agreed to contribute only if they were paid for it. The authors thought this unnecessary.

As will become clear on the following pages, *The "All-Stars' " All-Star Baseball Book* is as much a record of idiosyncrasy and special moments as it is a confirmation of statistical wisdom and fabled careers. In this sense at least, it is like baseball itself—as much about the Bob O'Farrells and Clem Labines as about the Ty Cobbs and Frank Robinsons.

HANK AARON

Aaron, elected to the Hall of Fame in 1982, has more home runs (755), runs batted in (2262), and total bases (6756) than anyone else who has ever played major league baseball. He is also third on the all-time list in games played (3298), tied for second in runs scored (2174), and third in hits (3771). To recap Aaron's records with the Braves in Milwaukee (1954–65) and in Atlanta (1966–74) and with the Brewers (1975–76) would fill a volume, but some of the highlights of his career include 18 consecutive seasons with 20 or more homers (1954–71), 14 seasons batting over .300, 11 seasons with more than 100 RBI's, 15 seasons with more than 100 runs scored, and a Most Valuable Player Award in 1957 (.322, 44 homers, 132 RBI's, and 118 runs scored). Aaron selects:

    1B—GIL HODGES
    2B—JACKIE ROBINSON
    3B—EDDIE MATHEWS
    SS—ERNIE BANKS
    OF—STAN MUSIAL
    OF—WILLIE MAYS
    OF—ROBERTO CLEMENTE
     C—ROY CAMPANELLA or DEL CRANDALL
    RP—BOB GIBSON or JUAN MARICHAL
    LP—SANDY KOUFAX

Deserves Cooperstown: Billy Williams. "It's a shame he's been passed over."
Toughest Pitchers: Gibson and Don Drysdale. "There wasn't any pitcher I felt I never could get a hit off, but hard throwing righthanders who would brush you back were always tough."
Most Underrated: Williams. "Everyone took him for granted."
Comments: "Banks wasn't the best fielder but he could hit. And Crandall was a hell of a defensive catcher."

JOE ADCOCK

Adcock was a powerful first baseman with the Reds (1950–52), Braves (1953–62), Indians (1963), Dodgers (1964), and Angels (1965–66). He batted .278 with 336 home runs. In 1956 he batted .291, hit 38 homers, and drove in 103 runs. On July 31, 1954, he hit four home runs and a double that missed being the fifth homer by six inches. His 18 total bases that day is still the record for one game. Adcock selects:

> 1B—STAN MUSIAL
> 2B—RED SCHOENDIENST
> 3B—EDDIE MATHEWS
> SS—ROY McMILLAN
> OF—HANK AARON
> OF—JOE DiMAGGIO
> OF—MICKEY MANTLE
> C—DEL CRANDALL
> RP—SAL MAGLIE
> LP—WARREN SPAHN

Toughest Pitcher: "I don't know but I always hit better against the better pitchers than against the poorer ones. I bore down harder."

Most Underrated: Aaron. "That sounds funny but when I was playing with him he always lived in the shadow of Mays and Mantle."

Strongest Teams: 1957–58 Braves. "We should've won the pennant four years in a row. The toughest opponent in the fifties was the Dodgers."

Comments: "Musial was a better outfielder than first baseman so you might want to put McCovey at first. DiMaggio was the greatest ballplayer I ever saw. Crandall is there strictly as a catcher. He couldn't hit with Campanella, but strictly as a catcher he was the best."

DICK ALLEN

Allen played first base, third base, and the outfield for the Phillies (1963–69, 1975–76), Cardinals (1970), Dodgers (1971), White Sox (1972–74), and Athletics (1977). He batted over .300 seven times, compiling a lifetime average of .292. He hit 30 or more home runs six times, with a high of 40 in 1966, led the American League twice in that category (1972 and 1974), and ended his career with 351 homers. In 1972 he was the AL MVP when he led the league in RBI's (113), walks (99), and slugging average (.603) as well as home runs (37). He batted .308 that year. He also had league leading totals in triples once and in slugging average in two seasons other than 1972. The controversial Allen chooses:

   1B—ORLANDO CEPEDA
   2B—BILL MAZEROSKI
   3B—EDDIE MATHEWS, MIKE SCHMIDT, or
       BROOKS ROBINSON
   SS—RUBEN AMARO
   OF—FRANK ROBINSON
   OF—HANK AARON
   OF—ROBERTO CLEMENTE
    C—SMOKEY BURGESS
   RP—BOB GIBSON
   LP—JIM KAAT or SANDY KOUFAX

Toughest Pitcher: Gibson. "No question but that it was Number 45. Everything about him was tough, but especially his competitive attitude."

Most Underrated: Aaron. "Look at the stats, sure. But remember he could beat you a dozen ways. He could steal a base when you needed it. He could beat you with his glove."

Strongest Team: Braves. "They had so much talent but they never got the publicity."

Comments: "Bill White would be my backup at first. Amaro carried no bat at all but he was the best shortstop I've ever seen. Kaat could beat you with his bat or his glove as well as on the mound."

3

FELIPE ALOU

Alou, widely regarded as one of the most underrated players of his era, batted .286 over a 17–year career with the Giants (1958–63), Braves (1964–69), Athletics (1970–71), Yankees (1971–73), Expos (1973), and Brewers (1974). The righthand-hitting outfielder-first baseman's marks included leading the National League in hits, runs, and at bats in 1966, leading the NL in hits and at bats a second time in 1968, and topping the American League in pinch hits in 1972. His single finest year was probably 1966 when he batted .327 with 31 home runs, 32 doubles, and 122 runs scored. Alou, the oldest of the three Alou brothers who once played in the same outfield for the Giants, prefers:

1B—WILLIE McCOVEY
2B—BILL MAZEROSKI
3B—BROOKS ROBINSON
SS—ERNIE BANKS
OF—HANK AARON
OF—WILLIE MAYS
OF—ROBERTO CLEMENTE
C—DEL CRANDALL
RP—JUAN MARICHAL
LP—SANDY KOUFAX

Toughest Pitcher: Fergie Jenkins.
Most Underrated: "Latin players in general never got the recognition they were due in the 1950's and 1960's. I think of players like Orlando Cepeda, Rico Carty, and Julian Javier. Too many times the only interest the press seemed to have in them was to put down quotes that, because of their English, made them sound odd and funny. It has only been in the past few years that I've noticed a more professional attitude by the press toward Latin players."
Strongest Team: 1962 Yankees.

MATTY ALOU

Alou was a lefthanded outfielder with the Giants (1960–65), Pirates (1966–70), Cardinals (1971–72, 1973), Athletics (1972), Yankees (1973), and Padres (1974). He had a .307 lifetime average. In his five seasons with the Pirates he batted .327 and led the NL in batting in 1966 with a .342 average. He also led the NL in hits (231) and doubles (41) in 1968. Alou, who batted .333 in two League Championship Series and appeared in two World Series, chooses:

> 1B—STAN MUSIAL
> 2B—BILL MAZEROSKI
> 3B—BROOKS ROBINSON
> SS—LUIS APARICIO
> OF—HARMON KILLEBREW
> OF—WILLIE MAYS
> OF—ROBERTO CLEMENTE
> C—JOHNNY BENCH
> RP—JUAN MARICHAL
> LP—SANDY KOUFAX

Toughest Pitcher: Koufax.

Strongest Team: Dodgers of the early 1960's. "They had Podres, Drysdale, and Koufax. It was almost impossible to get two runs off them in a game."

LUIS APARICIO

Arguably the greatest defensive shortstop in the history of the American League, Aparicio gained entry to the Hall of Fame in 1984 after an 18–year career with the White Sox (1956–62), Orioles (1963–67), White Sox again (1968–70), and Red Sox (1971–73). A lifetime .262 hitter, he won Rookie of the Year honors in 1956, then went on to lead the AL in stolen bases for nine consecutive years and in fielding at shortstop for eight straight seasons. Among his better offensive years were 1960, when he stole 51 bases, scored 86 runs, and drove in 61 runs as a leadoff hitter, and 1970 when he batted .313 with 29 doubles. Aparicio, the all-time leader in games played at shortstop, picks:

    1B—VIC POWER
    2B—BOBBY RICHARDSON
    3B—BROOKS ROBINSON
    SS—TONY KUBEK
    OF—FRANK ROBINSON
    OF—MICKEY MANTLE
    OF—AL KALINE
     C—BILL FREEHAN
    RP—JIM PALMER
    LP—DAVE McNALLY

Deserves Cooperstown: Phil Rizzuto.
Toughest Pitcher: Camilo Pascual. "Best curveball pitcher I ever saw."
Most Underrated: Tony Oliva and Frank Robinson. "Robinson knew how to beat you a hundred different ways. When he didn't hit, he'd make a big catch or steal a base or kick the ball out of a fielder's glove. He always had something in mind."
Strongest Team: Yankees of the early 1960's.

LUKE APPLING

Appling, who was elected to the Hall of Fame in 1964, spent 20 seasons with the White Sox (1930–43, 1945–50), with whom he became one of the greatest shortstops of all time. A lifetime .310 hitter, he won two batting championships with averages of .388 in 1936 and .328 in 1943. His 1936 mark was the highest batting average ever compiled by a twentieth century shortstop. He batted over .300 in every season except one from 1933 to 1949, his last year as a regular—when he was 42 years old. Appling picks:

1B—JIMMIE FOXX
2B—CHARLIE GEHRINGER
3B—BROOKS ROBINSON
SS—JOE CRONIN
OF—TED WILLIAMS
OF—JOE DiMAGGIO
OF—MICKEY MANTLE
C—MICKEY COCHRANE or BILL DICKEY
RP—BOB FELLER
LP—LEFTY GROVE

Toughest Pitcher: Grove. "Some days you can hit some people, some days you can't. I had some hits off Grove but when I first came up he just blew the ball by me."

RICHIE ASHBURN

Ashburn played center field for a decade and a half with the Phillies (1948–59), Cubs (1960–61), and Mets (1962), compiling a .308 lifetime average. A speedy, slap-hitting leadoff batter, he led the NL in hits three times (221 in 1951, 205 in 1953, and 215 in 1958), in triples twice (14 in 1950 and 13 in 1958), and in batting twice (.338 in 1955 and .350 in 1958). A main cog in the 1950 Phillies pennant-winning Whiz Kids, Ashburn was also a sterling defensive outfielder. Only eight times has an outfielder had as many as 500 putouts in a season—and Ashburn did it four times. Ashburn's choices are:

> 1B—STAN MUSIAL
> 2B—RED SCHOENDIENST
> 3B—EDDIE MATHEWS
> SS—GRANNY HAMNER
> OF—HANK AARON
> OF—WILLIE MAYS
> OF—ROBERTO CLEMENTE
> C—ROY CAMPANELLA
> RP—JUAN MARICHAL
> LP—SANDY KOUFAX

Toughest Pitcher: Sal Maglie. "He wasn't overpowering, but his pitches were hard for me to identify. They came in like fastballs but they broke a little at the plate—just an inch or two."

Most Underrated: Del Ennis. "The guy has better stats than some people in the Hall of Fame. He had one hundred RBI's seven times."

Comments: "I saw the National League most, so my choices come from that league. I took Hamner for all around play even though McMillan was a better fielder. But if you let me play Duke Snider at shortstop I'll take him."

ELDON AUKER

Auker, a big righthander with an underhand delivery, helped pitch the Tigers to two pennants in 1934 and 1935 with records of 15–7 and 18–7. (In the latter year his .720 won-lost percentage was good enough to lead the American League.) Besides the Tigers (1933-38), he pitched for the Red Sox (1939) and the Browns (1940–42). His lifetime record was 130-101. Auker's choices are:

  1B—LOU GEHRIG or HANK GREENBERG
  2B—CHARLIE GEHRINGER
  3B—RED ROLFE
  SS—JOE CRONIN
  OF—TED WILLIAMS
  OF—JOE DiMAGGIO
  OF—AL SIMMONS
   C—MICKEY COCHRANE
  RP—BOB FELLER
  LP—LEFTY GROVE

Toughest Batter: Tommy Henrich.
Most Underrated: Gehringer.
Strongest Team: 1935 Tigers.

BOBBY AVILA

Avila, the second baseman and chief table-setter for the Indians teams of the fifties, batted .281 in 11 major league seasons (1949–59). His finest year was unquestionably 1954, when he contributed to pennant-winning Cleveland's 111 victories by winning the American League batting crown with a .341 average, hitting 27 doubles and 15 home runs, and scoring 112 runs. In 1952 he was the AL leader in triples. Avila, who spent his final big league season in 1959 moving from the Orioles to the Red Sox to the Braves, selects:

1B—FERRIS FAIN
2B—RED SCHOENDIENST
3B—AL ROSEN
SS—PHIL RIZZUTO
OF—JOE DiMAGGIO
OF—WILLIE MAYS
OF—MICKEY MANTLE
C—JIM HEGAN
RP—BOB FELLER
LP—WHITEY FORD

Toughest Pitcher: Ford.
Strongest Teams: "The Yankees dominated the American League year after year in the forties, fifties, and early sixties, but for one team in one season there was nobody better than the Indians in 1954. We weren't just lucky, we were good."

SAL BANDO

Bando was the heart of the Oakland teams that dominated the American League in the early 1970's. A 16-year major leaguer, the third baseman hit .254, with 242 home runs and 1039 runs batted in, in his career with the A's (1966–76) and Brewers (1977–82). His most productive season was probably 1969, when he batted .281 with 31 homers, 113 runs batted in, 106 runs scored, and 111 bases on balls. In 1973 he led the American League in doubles and in six different years hit at least 20 home runs. Bando chooses:

1B—HARMON KILLEBREW
2B—ROD CAREW
3B—BROOKS ROBINSON
SS—RICO PETROCELLI
OF—CARL YASTRZEMSKI
OF—PAUL BLAIR
OF—TONY OLIVA
C—THURMAN MUNSON
RP—JIM PALMER
LP—SAM McDOWELL

Deserves Cooperstown: Oliva.
Toughest Pitcher: Palmer.
Most Underrated: Petrocelli.
Comments: "I'd also have to stick Frank Robinson somewhere in the outfield, probably in left as a righthand-hitting alternative to Yaz."

ERNIE BANKS

Banks, a member of the Hall of Fame since 1977, spent his entire 19-year (1953–71) career with the Cubs, finishing with a .274 average and 572 home runs. His marks include leading the league in home runs and runs batted in twice, belting at least 40 homers five times, and driving in 100 runs eight times. His best years were 1958 (.313, 47 home runs, 23 doubles, 11 triples, 129 runs batted in, 119 runs) and 1959 (.304, 45 home runs, 25 doubles, 143 runs batted in) when he won back-to-back MVP trophies. Banks, who is tied for 11th place among baseball's all-time homer hitters, likes:

1B—GIL HODGES
2B—JACKIE ROBINSON
3B—EDDIE MATHEWS
SS—PEE WEE REESE
OF—HANK AARON
OF—WILLIE MAYS
OF—MICKEY MANTLE
C—ROY CAMPANELLA
RP—ROBIN ROBERTS
LP—SANDY KOUFAX

Toughest Pitchers: Koufax and Stu Miller.
Most Underrated: Billy Williams.
Strongest Team: Dodgers of the 1950's.

FRANKIE BAUMHOLTZ

Outfielder Baumholtz, one of a handful of athletes to have played both baseball and basketball professionally, batted .290 in 10 major league seasons for the Reds (1947–49), Cubs (1949–55), and Phillies (1956–57). A lefty-swinging leadoff man in his prime, he enjoyed his finest season in 1952 with a .325 batting mark that left him only a few points away from the league championship. He led the NL in pinch-hitting in both 1955 and 1956. Baumholtz selects:

> 1B—GIL HODGES
> 2B—JACKIE ROBINSON
> 3B—EDDIE MATHEWS
> SS—ERNIE BANKS
> OF—STAN MUSIAL
> OF—ROBERTO CLEMENTE
> OF—HANK AARON
> C—ROY CAMPANELLA
> RP—ROBIN ROBERTS
> LP—WARREN SPAHN

Toughest Pitchers: Carl Erskine and Sal Maglie.
Most Underrated: Pee Wee Reese.
Strongest Teams: Dodgers of the 1950's, Braves of the 1950's.
Comments: ''Near the end of 1952, I was coming up to bat against the Cardinals when their manager, Eddie Stanky, called time and came out to tell Harvey Haddix to go out to play the outfield and brought Stan Musial in to pitch. When my manager, Phil Cavarretta, saw this, he comes out and says Stanky's trying to make a fool of me. So I turn around to bat righthanded for the only time in my life, line one of Stan's pitches off Solly Hemus at third, and wind up at second. The official scorer called it an error, but Stan was the first one after the game to tell everyone it was as clean a hit as could be.''

GLENN BECKERT

Second baseman Beckert was the guts of the Cubs infield in his nine years (1965–73) in Wrigley Field. A lifetime .283 hitter, he went beyond all offensive expectations in 1971 when he batted .342 and was denied a batting championship only by the even more extraordinary years of Joe Torre (.363) and Ralph Garr (.343). In 1968 he led the National League in runs scored. Beckert, who ended his career with two injury-plagued years in San Diego, chooses:

1B—WILLIE McCOVEY
2B—JOE MORGAN
3B—BROOKS ROBINSON
SS—LUIS APARICIO
OF—HANK AARON
OF—WILLIE MAYS
OF—ROBERTO CLEMENTE
C—JOHNNY BENCH
RP—DON DRYSDALE
LP—SANDY KOUFAX

Deserves Cooperstown: Billy Williams.
Toughest Pitcher: Drysdale.
Most Underrated: Clemente.
Strongest Teams: 1969 Cubs, 1966 Dodgers.

COOL PAPA BELL

Bell, who entered the Hall of Fame in 1974, was a fleet, switch-hitting center fielder in the Negro Leagues between 1922 and 1946. He was a star for such teams as the St. Louis Stars, Homestead Grays, Detroit Wolves, Kansas City Monarchs, Pittsburgh Crawfords, Memphis Red Sox, and Chicago American Giants. At the end of his career he played in Mexico, Cuba, the Dominican Republic, and Puerto Rico until 1950. Records are scanty for the Negro Leagues, but his lifetime batting average is somewhere between .340 and .350 and he once batted .437 in the Mexican League. Bell, who according to legend was so fast he could turn out the lights and be in bed before the room was dark, chooses:

> 1B—OSCAR CHARLESTON
> 2B—SAMMY HUGHES
> 3B—JUDY JOHNSON
> SS—WILLIE WELLS
> OF—MONTE IRVIN
> OF—TURKEY STEARNS
> OF—RAP DIXON
> C—RILEY MACKAY
> RP—THEODORE TRENT
> LP—WILLIE FOSTER

Deserves Cooperstown: "There were a lot of black players who were just as qualified as those they have put in the Hall of Fame."

Toughest Pitcher: "All pitchers are tough when your timing is off, but in general I'd rather face older pitchers. They knew what they were doing. Younger pitchers are too wild."

Strongest Team: 1933 Pittsburgh Crawfords.

Comments: "Norman Stearns, the Detroit center fielder, was the greatest ballplayer I ever saw. Trent died young, of TB, but there was a stretch there of about six years where no white all-star team beat him."

GUS BELL

Bell, considered by many of his contemporaries as the most underrated all-around outfielder of the 1950's, batted .281 in 15 years with the Pirates (1950–52), Reds (1953–61), Mets (1962), and Braves (1962–64). His batting marks include having driven home at least 100 runs in four different seasons, with his single best year probably 1953 when he batted an even .300 with 30 home runs, 105 runs batted in, and 102 runs scored. Bell picks:

1B—STAN MUSIAL
2B—JOE MORGAN
3B—AL ROSEN
SS—MARTY MARION
OF—FRANK ROBINSON
OF—WILLIE MAYS
OF—HANK AARON
C—JOHNNY BENCH
RP—ROBIN ROBERTS
LP—HARVEY HADDIX

Deserves Cooperstown: Ernie Lombardi.
Toughest Pitchers: Haddix and Jim Hearn.
Strongest Team: "For sheer hitting I'll take my own Cincinnati Red teams of the 1950's. We won or lost every game by 12–11 because we had no pitching and great hitting, but we had a lot of fun, and that's what it's supposed to be about, right?"
Comments: "I'm always asked if I regret having had to play in the shadow of Willie Mays and Duke Snider. The answer is no. Sure, both of them got more attention because they played in New York, but I was selected or voted in for six All-Star Games, so how can I ever say that I was ignored?"

WALLY BERGER

Berger, a free-swinging, righthanded center fielder, had his most productive years with the Braves (1930–37). He also played with the Giants (1937–38), Reds (1938–40), and Phillies (1940). Berger had a stunning rookie year (.310, 38 homers, 119 RBI's), followed it with three more .300-plus seasons, led the league in home runs with 34 and RBI's with 130 in 1935, and concluded his career with a .300 average and 242 round-trippers. Berger's selections are:

1B—BILL TERRY
2B—FRANKIE FRISCH
3B—PIE TRAYNOR
SS—WOODY ENGLISH
OF—LLOYD WANER
OF—PAUL WANER
OF—JO-JO MOORE
 C—GABBY HARTNETT or ERNIE LOMBARDI
RP—DAZZY VANCE
LP—CARL HUBBELL

Deserves Cooperstown: Lombardi.
Toughest Pitcher: Hubbell. "His screwball was deceptive. There were bigger screwballs, but his looked just like a fastball."
Most Underrated: Enos Slaughter.
Strongest Team: 1933 Giants. "They had all those pitchers. Besides Hubbell there were Schumacher and Fitzsimmons and Parmalee. They were tough."

YOGI BERRA

One of the most popular figures in baseball history, Berra entered the Hall of Fame in 1971 on the basis of an 18-year (1946–63) career with the Yankees during which he batted .285 with 358 homers and 1430 runs batted in. The lefthand-hitting catcher's marks include having hit at least 20 home runs 11 times and having driven in 100 or more runs in five seasons. His single best years were 1950 (.322, 28 homers, 30 doubles, 116 runs, 124 runs batted in), and his MVP years of 1951, 1954, and 1955. He also holds numerous defensive records for catchers. Berra, who had nine at bats for the Mets in 1965 and who has managed both New York teams (Yankees 1964, 1984–85, Mets 1972–75), prefers:

1B—MICKEY VERNON
2B—JOE GORDON
3B—CLETE BOYER
SS—PHIL RIZZUTO
OF—TED WILLIAMS
OF—JOE DiMAGGIO
OF—MICKEY MANTLE
C—JIM HEGAN
RP—VIC RASCHI
LP—HERB SCORE

Deserves Cooperstown: Rizzuto.
Toughest Pitcher: Alex Kellner.
Most Underrated: Roger Maris. "He wasn't just a home run hitter, he could do everything—hit in the clutch, field, throw, and run."
Strongest Team: 1949–53 Yankees.

OSSIE BLUEGE

Ossie Bluege, the mainstay of the Washington infield for 18 seasons (1922–39), was considered by many of his contemporaries as the best fielding third baseman of his era. Between 1924 and 1931 he never batted below .271 and was usually among the league leaders in doubles. He represented the Senators in the 1935 All-Star Game. After his playing days were over, he managed the club from 1943 to 1947 and then became a scout. His most famous catch for the franchise was Harmon Killebrew.

Bluege's choices:

1B—JOE JUDGE
2B—JOE GORDON
3B—WILLIE KAMM
SS—JOE CRONIN
OF—TRIS SPEAKER
OF—SAM WEST
OF—EARLE COMBS
C—BILL DICKEY
RP—WALTER JOHNSON
LP—LEFTY GROVE

Comments: "Everybody forgets Sam West, but nobody played a ball in center like he did. Cronin was a great hitter, but I made him the shortstop he was because I covered a lot of his territory for him. Tell you the truth, it makes me mad when I see a George Kell or some of these others get into the Hall of Fame. Okay, Kell could hit, but he couldn't hold my glove. John McGraw once told me I was the best he'd ever seen, and that meant a lot to me because he was a third baseman and he knew what he was looking at."

BOBBY BONDS

Bonds had 30 home runs and 30 stolen bases in the same season five times. Over his 14 big league seasons—with the Giants (1968–74), Yankees (1975), Angels (1976–77), White Sox (1978), Rangers (1978), Indians (1979), Cardinals (1980), and Cubs (1981)—he batted .268, hit 332 homers, and stole 461 bases. He hit more than 25 homers nine times and batted in more than 100 runs twice. Bonds, who stole over 40 bases seven times and who also won three Gold Gloves, chooses:

1B—WILLIE McCOVEY or ERNIE BANKS
2B—BILL MAZEROSKI
3B—BROOKS ROBINSON, EDDIE MATHEWS, KEN
    BOYER, or JIM DAVENPORT
SS—GENE ALLEY
OF—HANK AARON
OF—WILLIE MAYS
OF—ROBERTO CLEMENTE
 C—JOHNNY BENCH
RP—BOB GIBSON
LP—STEVE CARLTON

Toughest Pitcher: Andy Messersmith. "He had one of the best change-ups I've ever seen. The remarkable thing about it was that he delivered it with exactly the same arm speed as his fastball."

Most Underrated: Jim Gantner.

Comments: "Robinson, Boyer, and Mathews are obvious, but Davenport belongs right there with them because he was such a clutch hitter. Alley and Maz were the greatest double play combination I've ever seen. Bench was one of the greatest catchers who ever played the game, but as a baserunner I feared Jerry Grote more than any other catcher. He threw the ball on top of the base. The infielders didn't have to tag you. You slid into your own out."

RAY BOONE

Boone was a hard-hitting shortstop-third baseman who had the unenviable task of succeeding Lou Boudreau in Cleveland and George Kell in Detroit. A lifetime .275 hitter, he came up with the Indians in 1948, moved over to the Tigers in 1953, then spent the rest of the decade in stints with the White Sox, Athletics, Braves, and Red Sox before retiring after the 1960 season. His finest seasons were 1954, when he batted .296 with 26 homers, 114 runs batted in, and 94 runs scored, and 1955, when he led the American League in runs batted in (116) while clouting 20 homers and batting .284. Boone chooses:

> 1B—MICKEY VERNON
> 2B—JOE GORDON
> 3B—AL ROSEN
> SS—PHIL RIZZUTO
> OF—JOE DiMAGGIO
> OF—TED WILLIAMS
> OF—MICKEY MANTLE
> C—YOGI BERRA
> RP—ALLIE REYNOLDS
> LP—HAL NEWHOUSER

Deserve Cooperstown: Gordon, Bobby Doerr, and Red Schoendienst.

Toughest Pitcher: Reynolds.

Most Underrated: Pete Runnels and Frank Malzone. "I think of Runnels sometimes when I'm scouting for the Red Sox and I come up against some lefthand-hitting prospect who says he doesn't want to play in Fenway Park because the right-field fence is too far away. And I remind him that until the 1981 strike season, when Carney Lansford did it, the only batting champions the Red Sox have had have been lefties. Runnels, Billy Goodman, Williams, Yaz, going all the way back. Fenway Park never hurt Pete Runnels."

Strongest Team: Yankees of the 1950's.

LOU BOUDREAU

Boudreau, a Hall of Famer since 1970, was a heavy-hitting shortstop for the Indians (1938–50) and Red Sox (1951–52). He batted .295 in his career, led the AL three times in doubles (1941, 1944, and 1947 with 45 each year), and led the league in batting in 1944 with a .327 average. His best season was 1948 when he hit .355, stroked 18 homers, drove in 106 runs, scored 116, and won the Most Valuable Player Award. Boudreau took over as Cleveland's manager in 1942 at the age of 24 and won a pennant and World Series in 1948. He also managed the Red Sox (1952–54), Athletics (1955–57), and Cubs (1960). Boudreau picks:

1B—STAN MUSIAL
2B—ROGERS HORNSBY
3B—MIKE SCHMIDT
SS—OZZIE SMITH
OF—TED WILLIAMS
OF—WILLIE MAYS
OF—HANK AARON
C—YOGI BERRA
RP—BOB FELLER
LP—SANDY KOUFAX

Toughest Pitchers: Hal Newhouser and Red Ruffing. "I could never follow their pitches."

Most Underrated: Ken Keltner. "He was never flashy but he was great with the glove and could hit the long ball."

Comments: "Put Babe Ruth in as the DH."

JIM BOUTON

Bouton had one season in which he looked like a superstar (21–7, 2.53 in 1963) and another in which he looked like a star (18–13, 3.02 in 1964). For the rest of his career—with the Yankees (1962–68), Pilots (1969), and Astros (1969–70)—he looked more like a writer trying to pitch. Which is what he became when he wrote the sensational *Ball Four*, a comic romp through Bouton's career in the big leagues. He later made a comeback with the 1978 Atlanta Braves, winning 1 and losing 3. His lifetime statistics are a 62-63 record and a 3.57 ERA. He was 2–1 with a 1.48 ERA in two World Series. Bouton's picks are:

1B—FRANK ROBINSON
2B—BOBBY RICHARDSON
3B—BROOKS ROBINSON
SS—LUIS APARICIO
OF—MICKEY MANTLE
OF—ROBERTO CLEMENTE
OF—TONY OLIVA
C—ELSTON HOWARD
RP—DON DRYSDALE
LP—WHITEY FORD

Toughest Batters: Oliva and Dick McAuliffe.
Most Underrated: Bill Skowron.
Strongest Team: 1962 Yankees.

CLETE BOYER

Boyer, the best defensive third baseman of his era after Brooks Robinson, batted .242 over 16 years with the Athletics (1955-57), Yankees (1959-66), and Braves (1967-71). Although mainly known for his glove, he had good power, as illustrated by the 18 home runs he hit for the Yankees in two different seasons. Free of Yankee Stadium's Death Valley, he went one better for the Braves in 1967, smashing 26 homers and driving home 96 runs. Boyer, who was the first major leaguer ever traded to Japan and who became one of that country's most popular players, selects:

1B—JOE PEPITONE
2B—JOE MORGAN
3B—KEN BOYER
SS—LUIS APARICIO
OF—HANK AARON
OF—WILLIE MAYS
OF—MICKEY MANTLE
C—JOHNNY BENCH
RP—BOB GIBSON
LP—WHITEY FORD

Deserve Cooperstown: Ken Boyer and Roger Maris. "Maris could do everything before they started playing with his head in New York. He was a great clutch player, fabulous arm, could even outrun Aparicio. I don't know of any better player in the clutch."
Toughest Pitcher: Camilo Pascual.
Most Underrated: Maris.
Strongest Team: 1961 Yankees.

HARRY BRECHEEN

The southpaw known as "The Cat" won 132 and lost 92 with a 2.92 ERA over a 12-year career spent entirely in St. Louis (with the Cardinals in 1940 and from 1943 to 1952, with the Browns in 1953). His best year was 1948, when he posted 20 wins and led the National League in ERA (2.24), winning percentage, shutouts, and strikeouts. It was to be his only 20-game season. Brecheen picks:

1B—GIL HODGES
2B—RED SCHOENDIENST
3B—STAN HACK
SS—MARTY MARION
OF—STAN MUSIAL
OF—TED WILLIAMS
OF—JOE DiMAGGIO
C—ROY CAMPANELLA
RP—JOHNNY SAIN
LP—WARREN SPAHN

Deserve Cooperstown: Schoendienst and Phil Cavarretta.
Toughest Batters: Jackie Robinson and Carl Furillo.
Most Underrated: Enos Slaughter.
Strongest Team: 1942 Dodgers.
Comments: "Like most lefthanders in the National League in the late forties and fifties, I never looked forward to going to Brooklyn. They had Robinson and Furillo and Hodges and Campanella and all those other righties just waiting for you. I think they used to get out to the park early when they heard a lefty was going to start against them. They couldn't wait to get the fun started."

JIM BREWER

Brewer, a southpaw relief specialist, chalked up a record of 69–65 with 132 saves over 17 seasons (1960–76). Originally with the Cubs, he had his greatest years with the Dodgers, turning in such marks for Los Angeles as 7–6 with 24 saves (1970), 6–5 with 22 saves and a 1.89 ERA (1971), and 8–7 with 17 saves and a 1.26 ERA (1972). Brewer, who closed out his career with the Angels, likes:

1B—KEITH HERNANDEZ
2B—JOE MORGAN
3B—MIKE SCHMIDT
SS—MAURY WILLS
OF—TOMMY DAVIS
OF—WILLIE MAYS
OF—ROBERTO CLEMENTE
C—JOHN ROSEBORO
RP—DON DRYSDALE
LP—SANDY KOUFAX

Deserves Cooperstown: Billy Williams. "If he hit everybody like he hit me, he would have been voted in unanimously the first year he was eligible."

Toughest Batter: Dick Groat. "He was probably the only player who actually confused me as a pitcher. He hit everything, no matter where it was pitched, no matter the count. After a while I'd just throw and hope for the best."

Most Underrated: Dave Lopes. "He didn't have the close relations with the Los Angeles media that Steve Garvey and others had, so he had to break records as a runner to be noticed at all. But I always thought he was the core of the Dodgers."

Strongest Team: Giants of the mid-1960's.

JIM BROSNAN

Brosnan is probably as well known for his writing as for his classy relief pitching in the late 1950's and early 1960's. The author of *The Long Season*, a diary of the 1959 season, and of numerous articles, Brosnan pitched for the Cubs (1954, 1956–58), Cardinals (1958–59), Reds (1959–63), and White Sox (1963). He won 55 and lost 47 with 67 saves. In 1960 he was 7–2 with 12 saves and a 2.36 ERA and the following year he was 10–4, 16 saves, 3.04. He also appeared in the 1961 World Series. Brosnan's selections are:

> 1B—GIL HODGES
> 2B—BILL MAZEROSKI
> 3B—KEN BOYER
> SS—PEE WEE REESE
> OF—WILLIE MAYS
> OF—FRANK ROBINSON
> OF—ROBERTO CLEMENTE
> C—YOGI BERRA
> RP—BOB GIBSON
> LP—SANDY KOUFAX

Deserve Cooperstown: Nellie Fox and Lindy McDaniel.
Toughest Batter: Frank Thomas.
Most Underrated: Boyer.
Strongest Team: 1961 Yankees.
Comments: "If I had to pick the best I have ever seen rather than the best I played with or against, I would have Mike Schmidt at third, Ozzie Smith at short, Johnny Bench behind the plate, and Tom Seaver as the righty pitcher."

BILLY BRUTON

Bruton was the center fielder on the great Braves teams of the late fifties. A lifetime .273 hitter, the lefty batter played for the Braves from 1953 to 1960 and finished his career with the Tigers (1961–64). He led the NL in stolen bases in three consecutive seasons, beginning with his rookie year. He also led the NL in triples in 1956 and 1960 and in runs scored in 1960. Defying the sophomore jinx, he had one of his best years in 1954 when he batted .284 and stole 34 bases. He batted .289 in 1959 and .286 in 1960. Bruton, who missed the 1957 World Series because of injuries but batted .333 in the 1958 Series, chooses:

1B—GIL HODGES
2B—RED SCHOENDIENST
3B—EDDIE MATHEWS or KEN BOYER
SS—ERNIE BANKS
OF—FRANK ROBINSON
OF—BILLY BRUTON
OF—HANK AARON
C—ROY CAMPANELLA
RP—ROBIN ROBERTS
LP—WARREN SPAHN or JOHNNY ANTONELLI

Toughest Pitchers: Vinegar Bend Mizell and Curt Simmons. "They both had unorthodox moves."

Most Underrated: Aaron. "In the fifties, until people realized he was creeping up on Babe Ruth's record."

Strongest Teams: Dodgers of the 1950's, Braves of the late 1950's. "We should have won four pennants in a row."

BOB BUHL

Buhl was a mainstay of the great Milwaukee Braves pitching staff of the late 1950's. His lifetime record of 166–132 and 3.55 ERA were compiled with the Cubs (1962–66) and Phillies (1966–67) as well as the Braves (1953–62). As a rookie he won 13 and lost 8 with a 2.97 ERA. He won 18 games twice, in 1956 and 1957, leading the NL in won-lost percentage (.720) in the latter year. His four shutouts in 1959 were good enough to tie for the league lead. Buhl's picks are:

1B—GIL HODGES
2B—RED SCHOENDIENST
3B—EDDIE MATHEWS
SS—ALVIN DARK
OF—HANK AARON
OF—WILLIE MAYS
OF—STAN MUSIAL
C—WALKER COOPER
RP—ROBIN ROBERTS
LP—WARREN SPAHN

Toughest Batter: Musial.
Most Underrated: Billy Bruton.
Strongest Team: "The Dodgers in Ebbets Field."

TOMMY BYRNE

Byrne was a hard-throwing southpaw whose best years were with the Yankees. He began his career in New York (1943, 1946–51) and ended it there (1954–57) as well. In between he stopped with the Browns (1951–52) and the White Sox (1953). His lifetime stats include 85 wins, 69 losses, and a 4.11 ERA. His best year was 1955 when he led the AL in won-lost percentage (.762 on the basis of a 16–5 record) and had a 3.15 ERA. Byrne selects:

> 1B—BILL SKOWRON
> 2B—JOE GORDON
> 3B—BILLY JOHNSON
> SS—PHIL RIZZUTO
> OF—JOE DiMAGGIO
> OF—MICKEY MANTLE
> OF—CHARLIE KELLER
> C—YOGI BERRA or BILL DICKEY
> RP—ALLIE REYNOLDS or VIC RASCHI
> LP—WHITEY FORD

Most Underrated: Keller.

Toughest Hitters: Bob Dillinger and Al Rosen. "I had a great curve but Dillinger would always hit line drives off me. Once when he was with the Browns he got a base hit past my ear. Yogi picked up the bat to get it out of the way and found out it was shaved down on one side. No wonder he could hit that curve ball. For two years I couldn't get Rosen out. Then one day when a ball he hit foul by two feet was called a home run, so I just gave up and started telling him what I was going to throw and after that he couldn't get a hit. I can still hear him mumbling after he popped up."

DOLF CAMILLI

Camilli batted .277 and walloped 239 home runs in a 12-year career spent with the Cubs (1933–34), Phillies (1934–37), Dodgers (1938–43), and Red Sox (1945). His most productive season was 1941, when he hit .285, led the National League in both homers (34) and runs batted in (120), and won the Most Valuable Player Award. The southpaw swinger hit at least 20 home runs eight times, drove in at least 100 runs five times, scored at least 100 runs four times, and walked at least 100 times four times. He was also a fine gloveman at first base. Camilli's picks:

1B—BILL TERRY
2B—BILLY HERMAN
3B—BROOKS ROBINSON
SS—PEE WEE REESE
OF—PAUL WANER
OF—TED WILLIAMS
OF—JOE DiMAGGIO
C—GABBY HARTNETT
RP—DIZZY DEAN
LP—CARL HUBBELL

Deserve Cooperstown: Ernie Lombardi and Dick Bartell.
Toughest Pitcher: Dean.
Most Underrated: Chick Hafey.
Strongest Teams: Yankees of the 1930's, 1941 Dodgers.
Comments: ''I think everything has gotten out of proportion in baseball. When I was playing, we always took a licking from the owners when it came to money and other contract things. Now it's the players giving it to the owners, mainly because of free agency. I think free agency will eventually kill all professional sports.''

ROY CAMPANELLA

Campanella, a member of the Hall of Fame since 1969, was the Dodgers' catcher from 1948 to 1957 after a brief but outstanding career in the Negro Leagues. Hampered by injuries for much of his career—which ended in an automobile accident that left him in a wheelchair for life—Campanella was, nevertheless, a great defensive catcher and a feared hitter. His .276 lifetime average and 242 home runs are impressive, but in the years when Campy was healthy he was more than impressive, he was incomparable. In 1951 he hit .325 with 33 homers, 33 doubles, and 108 RBI's. In 1953 he batted .312 with 41 homers, 103 runs scored, and a league-leading 142 RBI's. And in 1955 he hit .318 with 32 homers and 107 RBI'S. In all three years he won the NL Most Valuable Player Award. Campanella chooses:

<pre>
          1B—GIL HODGES
          2B—JACKIE ROBINSON
          3B—BILLY COX
          SS—PEE WEE REESE
          OF—WILLIE MAYS
          OF—DUKE SNIDER
          OF—CARL FURILLO
           C—ROY CAMPANELLA
          RP—DON NEWCOMBE
          LP—SANDY KOUFAX
</pre>

Toughest Pitchers: Satchel Paige, Ewell Blackwell, Robin Roberts, and Sal Maglie. "Paige threw hard and had outstanding control. Blackwell's ball moved *so* much; he didn't throw anything straight. Roberts had excellent control and hit the spots. Maglie had that tremendous curve that he could throw at different speeds."

Most Underrated: Hank Aaron.

Strongest Team: "Do you have to ask?"

GEORGE CASE

Case was the premier base stealer in the American League in the 1940's. He led the league in thefts six times, reaching a high of 61 in 1943. He played primarily for the Senators (1937–45, 1947) and put in one year (1946) with the Indians. A .282 lifetime hitter, he once collected nine hits in a double-header and still holds the record for circling the bases in the shortest time, 13.5 seconds. Case selects:

1B—HANK GREENBERG
2B—BOBBY DOERR
3B—KEN KELTNER
SS—LOU BOUDREAU
OF—JOE DiMAGGIO
OF—TED WILLIAMS
OF—TOMMY HENRICH
C—BILL DICKEY
RP—BOB FELLER
LP—HAL NEWHOUSER

Deserve Cooperstown: Henrich and Newhouser.
Toughest Pitcher: Feller. "If the war hadn't interfered, Bob would have been the best who ever lived."
Most Underrated: Stan Spence. "I never saw Stan make a mistake in the outfield and he had the most accurate throwing arm of my time."
Strongest Team: 1938–42 Yankees.

PHIL CAVARRETTA

Cavarretta, a lefty first baseman who also played a considerable number of games in the outfield, batted .293 in 20 seasons with the Cubs (1934–53) and two with the White Sox (1954–55). In 1935, at the age of 19, he became the youngest regular first baseman ever and batted .275. Cavarretta led the NL in hits (197) in 1944 and in batting (.355) the following year, when he was chosen the NL's MVP. He was also player-manager of the Cubs from 1951 to 1953. Cavarretta picks:

1B—BILL TERRY
2B—BILLY HERMAN
3B—PIE TRAYNOR
SS—PEE WEE REESE
OF—STAN MUSIAL
OF—JOE DiMAGGIO
OF—JOE MEDWICK
 C—GABBY HARTNETT
RP—DIZZY DEAN
LP—CARL HUBBELL

Deserves Cooperstown: Stan Hack.
Toughest Pitcher: Harry Brecheen. ''I just couldn't hit him. He had a sharp, fast-breaking curve, a slower, bigger-breaking ball, and a good screwball. The funny part is that every time he pitched against us the first time up against him he'd knock me on my seat. I'd ask him why. I'd tell him I couldn't hit him anyway. And he'd just say the ball slipped. Every time.''
Most Underrated: Hack.
Comments: ''Dean was outstanding. His fastball moved. It rose. And he had tremendous control.''

ORLANDO CEPEDA

From his Rookie-of-the-Year debut with the Giants in 1958, Cepeda went on to become one of the National League's preeminent power hitters for most of his career, winding up with a .297 batting average that included 379 home runs. After leaving the Giants in 1966 in an unpopular trade for Ray Sadecki, he went on to productive seasons with the Cardinals (1966–68) and Braves (1969–72), before winding down in the American League with the Athletics (1972), Red Sox (1973), and Royals (1974). The righthand-hitting first baseman's finest years were 1961 (.311, 46 home runs, 142 runs batted in) and 1967 (NL MVP with .325, 25 home runs, 111 runs batted in). Cepeda, who at various times led the NL in home runs, runs batted in, and doubles, likes:

> 1B—WILLIE McCOVEY
> 2B—JULIAN JAVIER
> 3B—CLETE BOYER
> SS—JOSE PAGAN
> OF—HANK AARON
> OF—WILLIE MAYS
> OF—CURT FLOOD
> C—TIM McCARVER
> RP—JUAN MARICHAL
> LP—STEVE CARLTON

Toughest Pitchers: Fergie Jenkins and Don Drysdale.
Most Underrated: "Flood was certainly overlooked, although he was one of the best defensive outfielders of his time and was also the man who made it possible for Lou Brock to steal so many bases. Billy Williams was another who suffered from playing in somebody else's shadow, in his case that of Ernie Banks."
Strongest Team: Giants of the early 1960's.

DEAN CHANCE

Chance, a hard throwing and sometimes wild righthander, was the best pitcher the Angels had in the first decade of their existence. He pitched for the Angels from 1961 to 1966 before moving to the Twins (1967–69), Indians (1970), Mets (1970), and Tigers (1971). In 1964 Chance won the Cy Young Award on the basis of a 20–9 record (which placed him in a tie for the AL lead in wins), a league leading 1.65 ERA and 11 shutouts, and 207 strikeouts. Chance, who also won 20 games in 1967, picks:

     1B—BOOG POWELL
     2B—ROD CAREW
     3B—BROOKS ROBINSON
     SS—LUIS APARICIO
     OF—FRANK ROBINSON
     OF—MICKEY MANTLE
     OF—AL KALINE
      C—JOHNNY BENCH
     RP—BOB GIBSON
     LP—SANDY KOUFAX or WHITEY FORD

Toughest Batter: Tony Oliva. "I was righthanded and he was lefthanded and he hit the ball to left."

Most Underrated: Dick McAuliffe. "No one was more competitive."

Strongest Team: Yankees of the early 1960's.

Comments: "The best manager was Billy Martin. No manager was as sharp as that boy."

SPUD CHANDLER

Chandler pitched his entire career for the Yankees (1937–47) and won 109 games while losing only 43. This gives him the record for the highest won-lost percentage (.717) of all pitchers with 100 or more wins. In 1943 Chandler was selected the AL's Most Valuable Player on the basis of a 20–4 (.833) record. He also led the league in wins, percentage, ERA (1.64), and shutouts (five). He led the league in ERA (2.46) again in 1947. He was 2–2 in World Series competition, both wins coming in 1943 against the Cardinals. Chandler picks:

1B—LOU GEHRIG
2B—CHARLIE GEHRINGER
3B—GEORGE KELL
SS—PHIL RIZZUTO
OF—TED WILLIAMS
OF—JOE DiMAGGIO
OF—HANK GREENBERG
C—BILL DICKEY
RP—RED RUFFING
LP—HAL NEWHOUSER

Toughest Batter: Joe Cronin.
Most Underrated: Tommy Henrich.
Strongest Teams: Yankees of the late 1930's and early 1940's, Tigers of the mid-1940's.

FRED CLARKE

Clarke was the player-manager of the Louisville Sluggers (1897–99) and the Pirates (1900–11, 1913–15). As an outfielder he batted .315 for 21 years and tied for the NL lead in doubles in 1903 (32) and in triples in 1906 (13). As a manager he won four pennants (1901–03, 1909). His best seasons were 1895 (.354), 1897 (.406), 1899 (.347) and 1903 (.351). Clarke, who was elected to the Hall of Fame in 1945, chooses:

> 1B—HAL CHASE
> 2B—EDDIE COLLINS
> 3B—JIMMY COLLINS
> SS—HONUS WAGNER
> OF—TRIS SPEAKER
> OF—TY COBB
> OF—BABE RUTH
> C—JOHNNY KLING
> RP—CHRISTY MATHEWSON
> LP—RUBE WADDELL

Wagner and Waddell—only briefly—are the only selections who played with and for Clarke. Jimmy Collins, a Hall of Famer, hit .294 between 1895 and 1908. Waddell, also in the Hall of Fame, pitched for only 13 years (1897, 1899–1910), but led the Athletics pitching staff in the pennant-winning years of 1902 and 1905 and struck out 349 batters in 1904, a major league record that stood for over 60 years. The biggest surprise here, however, is Kling. Only a .271 hitter over 13 years (1900–08, 1910–13), mostly with the Cubs, Kling was the receiver of the great Tinker-to-Evers-to-Chance pennant winners of 1906–08 and 1910. In those years he handled a pitching staff that included Three Finger Brown, Orval Overall, and Jack Pfiester.

HARLOND CLIFT

Clift, a righthand-hitting third baseman, played for the Browns between 1934 and 1943 and then for the Senators through the 1945 season. His best years were in 1937 (29 home runs, 118 runs batted in, .306) and 1938 (34 home runs, 118 runs batted in, .290). In seven of his nine full seasons with the Browns he scored at least 100 runs, his high coming in 1936 when he crossed the plate 145 times. A fine glove man as well, Clift's relative lack of recognition is largely due to the fact that he played for the colorless Brownies. Clift's choices:

1B—LOU GEHRIG
2B—JOE GORDON
3B—JIMMIE FOXX
SS—JOE CRONIN
OF—TED WILLIAMS
OF—JOE DiMAGGIO
OF—BOB JOHNSON
C—BILL DICKEY
RP—BOB FELLER
LP—LEFTY GOMEZ

Deserves Cooperstown: "You're darn right. Me!"

Toughest Pitchers: "Feller was the toughest pitcher I ever faced. Gomez was right up there, but the truth is that I always hit the Yankees pretty good, so their pitchers' reputations didn't mean too much to me."

Foxx was, of course, primarily a first baseman, but he played 135 games at third and what would be sacrificed in defense by placing him there would probably be more than compensated for by his .325 lifetime average and 534 home runs.

TY COBB

Cobb was perhaps the greatest player in the history of base-ball and became a charter member of the Hall of Fame in 1936. His .367 lifetime average and 12 batting champion-ships have survived as records for almost seven decades. His aggressive style of play won him many enemies but even more respect. The lefthanded outfielder hit over .300 23 times in his career with the Tigers (1905–26) and Athletics (1927–28). He led the AL in homers once, in doubles three times, in triples and RBI's four times each, in runs scored five times, in stolen bases six times, and in hits eight times. His 96 stolen bases in 1915 and career 4191 career base hits endured as records until 1962 and 1985, respectively. His re-cord of three .400–plus batting averages (.420 in 1911, .410 in 1912, and .401 in 1922) is in no danger of being surpassed. Cobb chooses:

    1B—GEORGE SISLER
    2B—EDDIE COLLINS
    3B—PIE TRAYNOR
    SS—HONUS WAGNER
    OF—JOE JACKSON
    OF—TRIS SPEAKER
    OF—BABE RUTH
     C—MICKEY COCHRANE or BILL DICKEY
    RP—WALTER JOHNSON, CHRISTY MATHEWSON,
        or GROVER CLEVELAND ALEXANDER
    LP—EDDIE PLANK or LEFTY GROVE

   Cobb, who made these selections about five years before he died in 1961, chose all contemporaries. His note suggests that the doubtful "Look up hitting, baserunning, fielding as-sists and putouts."
   Cobb often said that the pitcher who gave him the most trouble was Carl Weilman, a lefty who had an 84–94 record and a 2.67 ERA with the Browns in eight seasons (1912–17, 1919–20).

MICKEY COCHRANE

Cochrane, one of the greatest catchers of all time, had a lifetime average of .320 and hit 119 home runs. He broke in with a .331 average with the Athletics in 1925. He stayed with the A's through 1933 and went to the Tigers as player-manager from 1934 until 1937 when his career was abruptly ended when he was beaned by Yankee pitcher Bump Hadley. He managed one more season after that. His best years were with the pennant-winning A's of 1929–31 when he batted .331, .357, and .349. He also led the Tigers to—and played in— the 1934 and 1935 World Series. Elected to the Hall of Fame in 1947, Cochrane died in 1962. Cochrane selects:

    1B—GEORGE SISLER
    2B—EDDIE COLLINS
    3B—PIE TRAYNOR
    SS—JOE CRONIN
    OF—TY COBB
    OF—BABE RUTH
    OF—TRIS SPEAKER
     C—BILL DICKEY or GABBY HARTNETT
    RP—WALTER JOHNSON
    LP—LEFTY GROVE

Comments: "I didn't see Honus Wagner."

ROCKY COLAVITO

Colavito was a power-hitting righthanded outfielder with the Indians (1955–59, 1965–67), Tigers (1960–63), Athletics (1964), White Sox (1967), Dodgers (1968), and Yankees (1968). He stroked 374 homers to go with his .266 lifetime average. Three times he had more than 40 homers (41 in 1958, 42 to lead the AL in 1959, and 45 in 1961.) He also led the AL with 108 RBI's in 1965 (his sixth 100-plus RBI season) and with a .620 slugging average in 1958. Colavito's choices are:

    1B—VIC POWER
    2B—BOBBY RICHARDSON
    3B—BROOKS ROBINSON
    SS—LUIS APARICIO
    OF—TED WILLIAMS
    OF—WILLIE MAYS
    OF—MICKEY MANTLE
     C—YOGI BERRA
    RP—BOB LEMON
    LP—WHITEY FORD

Deserve Cooperstown: Ernie Lombardi, Phil Rizzuto, Roger Maris, Nellie Fox, and Richardson.
Toughest Pitcher: Ryne Duren.
Most Underrated: Maris.
Strongest Team: 1961 Yankees.

JERRY COLEMAN

Coleman spent nine seasons (1949–57) with the Yankees, mostly as a second baseman, and during those nine years the Yankees won eight pennants. A lifetime .263 hitter, he had his two best years in 1949 and 1950 when he hit .275 with 21 doubles, and .287 with 19 doubles and 69 RBI's. He is currently an announcer for the Padres and also managed San Diego for one season (1980). Coleman's choices are:

1B—KEITH HERNANDEZ
2B—JOE GORDON
3B—BROOKS ROBINSON
SS—OZZIE SMITH
OF—JOE DiMAGGIO
OF—MICKEY MANTLE
OF—AL KALINE
C—JOHNNY BENCH
RP—BOB GIBSON
LP—SANDY KOUFAX

Deserves Cooperstown: Joe Gordon.
Toughest Pitcher: Virgil Trucks.
Most Underrated: Gil McDougald.
Strongest Teams: "The best team I played for was the 1950 Yankees; the best one I played against was the 1954 Cleveland Indians."
Comments: "My all-time team is selected on the basis of two factors: skill in performance and attitude toward team effort."

JOCKO CONLAN

Conlan was the fourth umpire elected to the Hall of Fame (1974). He played only two years in the major leagues, batting .263 in 128 games as an outfielder for the White Sox in 1934 and 1935. He joined the National League umpiring staff in 1941 and retired after the 1964 season. He officiated in six World Series, six All-Star Games, and four National League playoffs. Conlan selects:

1B—LOU GEHRIG or BILL TERRY
2B—CHARLIE GEHRINGER
3B—PIE TRAYNOR
SS—HONUS WAGNER
OF—BABE RUTH
OF—TRIS SPEAKER
OF—TY COBB
C—GABBY HARTNETT
RP—WALTER JOHNSON
LP—LEFTY GROVE

Most Underrated: Arky Vaughan.

Comments: "No one was more graceful at first than Hal Chase. He could throw guys out at third on a bunt. But I don't want him on my team because he was a crook. Buck Weaver wasn't a crook. Commissioner Kenesaw Landis threw him out of baseball because he knew about throwing the World Series, not because he threw games. Joe Dugan, a pretty good third baseman with the Yankees, once told me, 'We all learned to play third base watching Weaver.' Neither Johnson nor Grove had a curve and neither one ever had a sore arm. There are only two men in baseball I didn't like, Durocher and Jackie Robinson, because of the bad language they used. Durocher knew the game but couldn't handle men. The best manager I knew was George Stallings. He was the most brilliant man I ever met in baseball. I threw twenty-seven guys out of games in my first year, and everybody got the message."

JOHNNY COONEY

Cooney practically divided his 20-year (1921–30, 1935–44) career evenly into a first phase as a pitcher and a second phase as an outfielder. As a moundsman who did most of his hurling for the Braves between 1921 and 1930, he won 34 and lost 44, turning in his best season in 1925 when he won 14 games for the mediocre Bostonians. After a trip to the minors to sharpen his batting prowess, he returned as an outfielder to the Dodgers in 1935, then moved back to the Braves in 1938, back again to the Dodgers in 1943, and finally to the Yankees for the tail end of 1944. A .286 lifetime hitter, Cooney hit over .300 three times as an outfielder and batted at least .270 for seven consecutive years. He was considered a good leadoff man with little power (only two career homers). Cooney picks:

    1B—BILL TERRY
    2B—ROGERS HORNSBY
    3B—PIE TRAYNOR
    SS—LUIS APARICIO
    OF—EDD ROUSH
    OF—TERRY MOORE
    OF—HANK AARON
     C—GABBY HARTNETT
    RP—GROVER CLEVELAND ALEXANDER
    LP—WARREN SPAHN

Toughest Pitcher: Dazzy Vance.
Strongest Team: Giants managed by Bill Terry.
Comments: "Every ballplayer likes to think he belongs in the Hall of Fame, and that's kind of crazy. But it's also true that the selection committee tends to favor the big home run hitters and forget about other players who are just as responsible—if not more so—for a game being won or a pennant being taken. It's players like Nellie Fox who suffer from that attitude."

WALKER COOPER

Cooper, a hulking catcher whose size belied his agility behind the plate, hit .285 in an 18-year (1940–57) National League career. With the Cardinals from 1940 to 1945, he then moved on to the Giants, Reds, Braves, Pirates, Cubs, and Cardinals again. In eight different seasons he batted over .300, enjoying his finest year in 1947 when he terrorized pitchers with 24 doubles, 35 home runs, eight triples, 122 runs batted in, and a .305 average. Cooper prefers:

1B—GIL HODGES
2B—LONNY FREY
3B—BROOKS ROBINSON
SS—MARTY MARION
OF—STAN MUSIAL
OF—TERRY MOORE
OF—ENOS SLAUGHTER
C—BILL DICKEY
RP—MORT COOPER
LP—CARL HUBBELL

Deserves Cooperstown: Marion.
Toughest Pitcher: Hubbell.
Most Underrated: Marion.
Mort Cooper, the other half of baseball's most famous battery, compiled a record of 128–75 (2.97 ERA) in 11 seasons with the Cardinals (1938–45), Braves (1945–47), Giants (1947), and Cubs (1949). With his brother Walker on the receiving end, he won 65 games between 1942 and 1944, leading the league in ERA in 1942 and in winning percentage in 1943. He died in 1958.

ROGER CRAIG

Craig's lifetime mark of 74–98 over 12 seasons (1955–66) barely tells the story of one of the game's all-time hard-luck righthanders. An important factor in the Brooklyn team's last two pennants in 1955 and 1956, he stayed with the Dodgers until he was drafted by the expansion Mets in 1962. Later travels included stops with the Cardinals, Reds, and Phillies. While with the inept Mets, Craig rewrote the book on pitching woes, losing 24 games in 1962 and 22 in 1963, and at one point dropping 18 in a row, tying the NL record. In contrast was 1959 for the Dodgers, when he posted a mark of 11–5 and a 2.06 ERA and led the league in shutouts. It is quite possible that Craig's most enduring legacy to baseball will be the split-fingered fastball. Since his success in teaching the pitch to hurlers on the world champion Tigers in 1984, he has become a model instructor for pitching coaches in both leagues. Craig, who managed the Padres in 1978 and 1979, and who took over the Giants in 1985, chooses:

1B—WILLIE McCOVEY
2B—JOE MORGAN
3B—GEORGE BRETT
SS—ALAN TRAMMELL
OF—WILLIE MAYS
OF—MICKEY MANTLE
OF—HANK AARON
C—JOHNNY BENCH
RP—BOB GIBSON
LP—SANDY KOUFAX

Toughest Batter: Eddie Mathews.
Most Underrated: Ken Boyer.
Strongest Team: 1955 Dodgers.

DOC CRAMER

Cramer was a lefthand-hitting outfielder with the Athletics (1929–35), Red Sox (1936–40), Senators (1941), and Tigers (1942–48). A fine defensive outfielder and an outstanding leadoff hitter, Cramer led the American League in at bats seven times. He batted over .300 eight times, hit as high as .336 in 1932 and .332 in 1935, and finished with a .296 lifetime average. Cramer's choices:

1B—JIMMIE FOXX or LOU GEHRIG
2B—EDDIE COLLINS or CHARLIE GEHRINGER
3B—OSSIE BLUEGE
SS—LUKE APPLING
OF—BABE RUTH
OF—TY COBB
OF—TRIS SPEAKER
C—MICKEY COCHRANE or BILL DICKEY
RP—GEORGE EARNSHAW or TED LYONS
LP—LEFTY GROVE

Deserves Cooperstown: "There are a lot of people who don't belong in the Hall of Fame, but I won't venture to say who they are."

Toughest Pitcher: Lyons. "He just had everything. Perfect control. Everything."

Strongest Teams: 1936–39 Yankees, 1931 Athletics.

DEL CRANDALL

Crandall was a superior defensive catcher who batted .254 and hit 179 home runs in his 16 seasons in the big leagues. Most of his career was spent with the Braves—in Boston in 1949 and 1950 and in Milwaukee from 1953 to 1963. His last three seasons (1964–66) were in San Francisco, Pittsburgh, and Cleveland. He batted as high as .297 (1962) and hit as many as 26 homers (1955). He is credited with masterful handling of the Milwaukee pitching staff on the pennant-winning teams of 1957 and 1958 and won four Gold Gloves (1958–60, 1962). Crandall later managed the Milwaukee Brewers for part of 1972 and all of 1973, 1974, and 1975, and the Seattle Mariners for part of 1983 and 1984. Crandall picks:

> 1B—ERNIE BANKS
> 2B—RED SCHOENDIENST
> 3B—EDDIE MATHEWS
> SS—PEE WEE REESE
> OF—HANK AARON
> OF—WILLIE MAYS
> OF—STAN MUSIAL
> C—ROY CAMPANELLA
> RP—DON DRYSDALE
> LP—WARREN SPAHN

Toughest Pitchers: Bob Friend and Larry Jackson. "A lot of guys are going to say that I couldn't hit them either, but Friend and Jackson had these funky deliveries and good breaking balls that I couldn't pick up."

Most Underrated: Eddie Stanky.

Strongest Team: 1956–59 Braves.

Comments: "Gil Hodges was better defensively than Banks and no one was better than Joe Adcock with his foot on the bag. Alvin Dark is a close second to Reese. Juan Marichal and Lew Burdette, who was the most fun to catch, are right behind Drysdale. And Spahn over Sandy Koufax because he lasted so much longer."

SAM CRAWFORD

Crawford, who played in the same outfield with Ty Cobb for 13 seasons, was a lifetime .309 hitter and fleet defensive outfielder with the Reds (1899–1902) and Tigers (1903–17). He led the league triples six times and still holds the career record for most triples (312). He also led the AL in doubles once, runs scored once, homers twice, and RBI's three times. His hometown, Wahoo, Nebraska, gave him his colorful nickname, "Wahoo-Sam." He appeared in three World Series (1907-09) and was elected to the Hall of Fame in 1957. Crawford's best are:

1B—HAL CHASE
2B—LARRY LAJOIE
3B—BILL BRADLEY
SS—HONUS WAGNER
OF—TRIS SPEAKER
OF—TY COBB
OF—JOE JACKSON
C—RAY SCHALK
RP—WALTER JOHNSON
LP—EDDIE PLANK

Some surprises here. Chase was the fanciest fielding first baseman of his day (1905–19) and a lifetime .291 hitter whose career ended under a cloud because of his connections with gamblers and a probable involvement in the Black Sox scandal. Bradley was the premier third baseman of the early years of this century; he batted .271 lifetime and was an anchor of the Cleveland infield from 1901 to 1910. Although Schalk has had a plaque at Cooperstown since 1955, he is usually not considered in the same class with Mickey Cochrane and Bill Dickey, but even though he hit only .253 in his career (1912–29) he was one of the leaders of the great White Sox teams in those years.

TONY CUCCINELLO

One of the more forgotten players of his era, second baseman Cuccinello batted .280 over a 15-year (1930–45) career that saw him holding together the infield for the Reds, Dodgers, Braves, Giants, Braves again, and White Sox. Always a fine glove man, he also hit over .300 five times, enjoying a particularly fine year for Cincinnati in 1931 with 39 doubles, 11 triples, 93 runs batted in, and a .315 average. Cuccinello suffered one of baseball's foulest blows in 1945 when, with only a week left in the season, he was informed by his team, the White Sox, that he would not be invited back to spring training the following year. At the time, the infielder was leading the AL in hitting! He eventually lost the batting championship to Snuffy Stirnweiss by less than one point. Cuccinello picks:

> 1B—BILL TERRY
> 2B—FRANKIE FRISCH
> 3B—PIE TRAYNOR
> SS—TRAVIS JACKSON
> OF—JOE DiMAGGIO
> OF—TED WILLIAMS
> OF—CHICK HAFEY
> C—GABBY HARTNETT
> RP—DIZZY DEAN
> LP—CARL HUBBELL

Deserves Cooperstown: Ernie Lombardi.
Toughest Pitcher: Dean.
Most Underrated: Glenn Wright.
Strongest Team: Cubs of the early 1930's.

MIKE CUELLAR

Southpaw Cuellar put together a record of 185–130 (3.14 ERA) in 15 seasons with the Reds (1959), Cardinals (1964), Astros (1965–68), Orioles (1969–76), and Angels (1977). A four-time 20-game winner, he led the American League in winning percentage in both 1970 (when he was 24–8) and 1974. In his first year as an Oriole, in 1969, he was named the AL's Cy Young Award winner for leading Baltimore into the World Series with a mark of 23–11 (2.38). Cuellar picks:

1B—BOOG POWELL
2B—DAVE JOHNSON
3B—BROOKS ROBINSON
SS—MARK BELANGER
OF—DON BUFORD
OF—PAUL BLAIR
OF—FRANK ROBINSON
C—ELLIE HENDRICKS
RP—JIM PALMER
LP—DAVE McNALLY

Toughest Batters: Eric Soderholm, Rod Carew, and Tony Oliva. "I didn't like any of those Twins. They all knew how to hit."

Most Underrated: Roger Maris. "The man hits sixty-one home runs and all people are worried about is what that does to Babe Ruth's reputation. Maris was a damn good player."

Strongest Team: 1969–71 Orioles. "Of course I pick all Orioles for my team. I won with them on the field. I can't imagine anything better."

TOMMY DAVIS

Davis, a righthand-hitting outfielder who also played some third and first, batted .294 in one of the most ubiquitous careers in baseball history. In 18 years between 1959 and 1976 he played for the Dodgers, Mets, White Sox, Pilots, Astros, Athletics, Cubs, Athletics again, Cubs again, Orioles, Angels, and Royals. His best year was 1962 when he led the National League in batting, hits, and runs batted in. Davis, who was also the NL batting champion in 1963, picks:

1B—GIL HODGES
2B—BILL MAZEROSKI
3B—BROOKS ROBINSON
SS—ROY McMILLAN
OF—HANK AARON
OF—WILLIE MAYS
OF—ROBERTO CLEMENTE
C—ROY CAMPANELLA
RP—JUAN MARICHAL
LP—SANDY KOUFAX

Deserves Cooperstown: Billy Williams.

Toughest Pitchers: Larry Jackson and Don Cardwell.

Most Underrated: Williams, McMillan, Curt Flood, and Tony Oliva.

Comments: ''There's no question in my mind that moving around so much affected my career. I got a lot more defensive, for one thing, because when you're always being traded, you start hitting to stay rather than hitting to play. I also don't think it's a coincidence I had my best years with the Dodgers and Orioles, the two teams I played with for the longest stretches.''

BUCKY DENT

Dent played shortstop for the White Sox (1973–76), Yankees (1977–82), Rangers (1982–83), and Royals (1984). He batted .247 in his career, with a season high of .274 in 1974. He played in three AL Championship Series and batted .349 in two World Series, including a .417 average in the 1978 Series. Dent is probably best remembered for his dramatic three-run homer in the seventh inning that put the Yankees ahead of the Red Sox in their one-game playoff for the 1978 AL East title. Dent selects:

1B—DICK ALLEN
2B—FRANK WHITE
3B—BROOKS ROBINSON
SS—MARK BELANGER
OF—JIM RICE
OF—PAUL BLAIR
OF—REGGIE JACKSON
C—THURMAN MUNSON
RP—JIM PALMER
LP—RON GUIDRY

Toughest Pitcher: Nolan Ryan. "He threw so hard and had such a good curve."

Most Underrated: Mark Belanger. "He didn't hit for a high average but he glued the Baltimore infield together for a long time."

Strongest Team: 1978 Yankees.

BILL DICKEY

Dickey spent his entire career with the Yankees as the hard-hitting, lefty-swinging catcher of Murderers' Row (1928–43, 1946). He also managed the Yankees for part of the 1946 season and was a longtime coach at Yankee Stadium. His .313 average, 202 homers, and defensive skills make him a popular choice as the best catcher of all time. He holds numerous records, and his .362 average in 1936 is the highest ever by an American League catcher. He was elected to the Hall of Fame in 1954. Dickey picks:

> 1B—LOU GEHRIG
> 2B—CHARLIE GEHRINGER
> 3B—PIE TRAYNOR
> SS—JOE CRONIN
> OF—BABE RUTH
> OF—JOE DiMAGGIO
> OF—AL SIMMONS
> C—YOGI BERRA
> RP—BOB FELLER
> LP—LEFTY GROVE

Toughest Pitcher: Johnny Allen. "He had good control and would come straight sidearm or overhand. And he was as difficult to catch as he was to hit." Allen pitched for five teams in 13 seasons (1932–44), winning 142 and losing 75 with a 3.75 ERA.

Most Underrated: Allen.

Strongest Team: 1936–37 Yankees.

Comments: "If I couldn't have Feller and Grove, I'd take Red Ruffing and Lefty Gomez."

LARRY DIERKER

Dierker, the first successful pitcher in Houston history, had a record of 139–123 (3.30 ERA) over 13 years with the Astros (1964–76) and a final season with the Cardinals (1977). The righthander's best year was undoubtedly 1969, when he won 20, lost 13, struck out 240 batters, and turned in an ERA of 2.33. Dierker's choices:

> 1B—LOU GEHRIG
> 2B—JOE MORGAN
> 3B—MIKE SCHMIDT
> SS—OZZIE SMITH
> OF—HANK AARON
> OF—WILLIE MAYS
> OF—BABE RUTH
> C—JOHNNY BENCH
> RP—TOM SEAVER
> LP—WARREN SPAHN

Deserve Cooperstown: Nellie Fox, Tony Perez, and Billy Williams.

Toughest Batters: Roy McMillan and Matty Alou.

Most Underrated: Gene Tenace. ''The thing about Tenace is that people were always criticizing him for not being a good defensive catcher and for not hitting for a high enough average. Well, when I saw him with the Padres, he never looked like a defensive embarrassment to me. And as far as his hitting is concerned, this was a guy who always walked one hundred times a year and was among the leaders in slugging average and on-base percentage. To me, slugging and on-base averages are the real gauges to offense, and very few catchers, certainly, have been as good as Tenace in the history of the game.''

BOB DILLINGER

Dillinger, a speedy third baseman, played for the Browns (1946–49), Phillies (1950), Pirates (1950–51), and White Sox (1951). His lifetime average was .306 and he led the American League in stolen bases for three consecutive years (1947–49). Two of those seasons were his best. In 1948 he led the league in base hits and batted .321. The following year he batted .324. Dillinger's choices are:

1B—FERRIS FAIN
2B—JOE GORDON
3B—GEORGE KELL
SS—VERN STEPHENS
OF—JOE DiMAGGIO
OF—MICKEY MANTLE
OF—TED WILLIAMS
C—YOGI BERRA
RP—JIM PALMER
LP—SANDY KOUFAX

Deserves Cooperstown: Stephens. "There are a lot of shortstops in there who couldn't hit with him."

Toughest Pitcher: Virgil Trucks. "He threw so hard and I wasn't that good a fastball hitter.

Most Underrated: Chuck Stevens. "He was one of the better fielding first basemen and never got credit because he didn't hit a lot."

Strongest Team: Yankees.

DOM DiMAGGIO

DiMaggio, "The Little Professor," patrolled center field for the Red Sox for 11 seasons (1940–42, 1946–53). Primarily a leadoff batter, he batted .298 in his career and led the American League in runs scored twice (with 131 in 1950 and 113 in 1951). His best season was 1950 when he batted .328, led the AL in stolen bases with 15, and tied for the lead in triples with 11. In the 1946 World Series he batted .259, hit 3 doubles, and drove in 3 runs. DiMaggio's choices are:

1B—JIMMIE FOXX
2B—BOBBY DOERR
3B—KEN KELTNER
SS—LUKE APPLING or JOE CRONIN
OF—TED WILLIAMS
OF—JOE DiMAGGIO
OF—MICKEY MANTLE
C—BILL DICKEY
RP—BOB FELLER
LP—HAL NEWHOUSER or LEFTY GROVE

Deserve Cooperstown: Lefty O'Doul and Ernie Lombardi.

Toughest Pitcher: Dizzy Trout.

Most Underrated: Doerr.

Strongest Team: Yankees of the 1940's.

BOBBY DOERR

Doerr played more games exclusively at second base (1852) than anyone else—and he played them all for the Red Sox (1937–44, 1946–51). A sterling defensive player and an important part— and later captain—of the slugging Boston lineups of the 1940's, he batted .288 and hit 223 home runs. He hit over .300 three times, clouted more than 15 homers 10 times, and drove in more than 100 runs six times. His best year was 1944 when he hit .325 and led the AL in slugging with .528. In the 1946 World Series he batted .409. Doerr's selections are:

> 1B—LOU GEHRIG
> 2B—CHARLIE GEHRINGER
> 3B—BROOKS ROBINSON
> SS—JOE CRONIN
> OF—TED WILLIAMS
> OF—JOE DiMAGGIO
> OF—BABE RUTH
> C—BILL DICKEY
> RP—BOB FELLER
> LP—LEFTY GROVE

Deserve Cooperstown: Mel Harder, Ernie Lombardi, Joe Gordon, Ken Keltner, Phil Rizzuto, and Billy Williams.

Toughest Pitcher: Feller.

Most Underrated: Keltner. "He was a steady if unspectacular third baseman with a good accurate arm. And he hit with power in the clutch."

Strongest Teams: 1946 Red Sox, 1949 Yankees.

PETE DONOHUE

The righthanded Donohue has remained one of baseball's better kept secrets after a 12-year (1921–32) career in which he won 134 and lost 118. Despite the fact that he played for mediocre teams (Reds, 1921–30; Giants, 1930–31; Indians, 1931; Red Sox, 1932), he accomplished many league-leading feats, including: best winning percentage in 1922, most wins in 1926, most games started in both 1925 and 1926, most complete games in 1925, most innings pitched in both 1925 and 1926, and most shutouts in 1926. In both 1923 and 1925 he won 21 games, while coming up with 20 victories in 1926 and 18 in 1922. Donohue picks:

1B—BILL TERRY
2B—CHARLIE GEHRINGER
3B—PIE TRAYNOR
SS—LUIS APARICIO
OF—ROBERTO CLEMENTE
OF—TRIS SPEAKER
OF—ROSS YOUNGS
C—GABBY HARTNETT
RP—WALTER JOHNSON
LP—LEFTY GROVE

Deserves Cooperstown: Pete Donohue.

Toughest Batter: Charlie Hollocher. "Hollocher usually hit about .300 every season, and it always seemed like .290 of that came off me." Hollocher was the Cubs shortstop from 1918 to 1924, batting .304.

Most Underrated: Dolf Luque. "Luque won almost two hundred games and was completely overlooked by everybody. And I can't help believing that that was in good part due to the fact that he was Cuban."

DICK DONOVAN

The righthanded Donovan compiled a record of 122–99 over a 15-year career that started slowly with the Braves in 1950, but then began to pick up steam when he went to the American League in 1954. In the junior circuit he pitched for the Tigers (1954), White Sox (1955–60), Senators (1961), and Indians (1962–65). In 1957 he led the AL in both winning percentage (16–6, .727) and complete games (16); in 1961 he was the league leader in ERA (2.40). His only 20-game season was for the mediocre Indians in 1962. Donovan's choices:

                1B—EARL TORGESON
                2B—NELLIE FOX
                3B—BROOKS ROBINSON
                SS—LUIS APARICIO
                OF—WILLIE MAYS
                OF—MICKEY MANTLE
                OF—HANK AARON
                 C—YOGI BERRA
                RP—BOB LEMON
                LP—BILLY PIERCE

Deserves Cooperstown: Fox.
Toughest Batters: Al Kaline and Joe Collins.
Most Underrated: Fox.
Strongest Team: 1962 Giants.
Comments: "Obviously, there were players who had better numbers than guys like Torgeson. At first, for instance, I think right away of Orlando Cepeda. But the thing with a Torgeson was that he could go 0–5 in a game and still be a great player because of something he would do on the field or on the bench. He was *always*—and I mean always—in the game."

AL DOWNING

Downing threw a lot of pitches in his 17-year career with the Yankees (1961–69), Athletics (1970), Brewers (1970), and Dodgers (1971–77), but he is probably destined to be remembered most for the 715th gopher pitch served up to Hank Aaron. Nevertheless, the southpaw racked up a respectable record of 123–107 (3.22 ERA), being especially effective in 1963 for New York (13–5, 2.56) and in 1971 for Los Angeles (20–9, 2.68). He also led the American League in strikeouts (and walks) in 1964 and the National League in shutouts in 1971. Downing prefers:

1B—WILLIE McCOVEY
2B—JOE MORGAN
3B—MIKE SCHMIDT
SS—LUIS APARICIO
OF—HANK AARON
OF—WILLIE MAYS
OF—ROBERTO CLEMENTE
C—ELSTON HOWARD
RP—JUAN MARICHAL
LP—SANDY KOUFAX

Deserve Cooperstown: Howard, Roger Maris, and Maury Wills.
Toughest Batter: Clemente.
Most Underrated: Jim Gilliam.
Strongest Team: 1961 Yankees.
Comments: "The toughest pick for me is at second base. I think you also have to keep Davey Lopes in mind, but I'll stick with Morgan because he was better at turning the double play."

WALT DROPO

Dropo, nicknamed "The Moose," was a powerful right-handed hitting first baseman for 13 big league seasons with the Red Sox (1949–52), Tigers (1952–54), White Sox (1955–58), Reds (1958–59) and Orioles (1959–61). His remarkable rookie season, 1950—in which he hit .322 with 34 home runs and a league-leading 144 RBI's—won him Rookie of the Year honors. He still holds the American League record for most consecutive hits (12). His lifetime statistics are a .270 average and 152 homers. Dropo selects:

        1B—GIL HODGES
        2B—BOBBY DOERR
        3B—BROOKS ROBINSON
        SS—LUIS APARICIO
        OF—TED WILLIAMS
        OF—JOE DiMAGGIO
        OF—WILLIE MAYS
         C—YOGI BERRA
        RP—BOB LEMON
        LP—SANDY KOUFAX

Deserve Cooperstown: Phil Rizzuto and Doerr.
Toughest Pitcher: Lemon.
Most Underrated: Nellie Fox.
Strongest Team: 1950 Red Sox.

DON DRYSDALE

Drysdale, a Hall of Famer since 1984, teamed up with Sandy Koufax in the 1960's to give Los Angeles one of the most potent righty-lefty pitching tandems in the history of the game. A Dodger from 1956 to 1969, Drysdale won 209 games against 166 losses, struck out 2486 batters, and wound up with a 2.95 ERA. His achievements included establishing a major league record for most consecutive scoreless innings pitched (58), winning 20 games twice, leading the league in strikeouts three times and in games started four years in a row, winning the Cy Young Award in 1962, and compiling an earned run average under 3.00 in nine different seasons. He also had 29 career home runs, including seven in 1965. Drysdale's picks:

> 1B—GIL HODGES
> 2B—JACKIE ROBINSON
> 3B—EDDIE MATHEWS
> SS—PEE WEE REESE
> OF—DUKE SNIDER
> OF—WILLIE MAYS
> OF—HANK AARON
> C—ROY CAMPANELLA
> RP—BOB GIBSON
> LP—SANDY KOUFAX

Deserve Cooperstown: Nellie Fox, Billy Williams, and Willie McCovey.

Toughest Batter: "Too many to mention."

Most Underrated: Carl Furillo.

Strongest Team: Dodgers of the 1950's.

Comments: "I suppose I'm betraying my Brooklyn beginnings by mentioning Hodges, Robinson, Reese, Snider, Campanella, and Furillo, but they were the nucleus of an awesome team. The only team that came close to them were the Braves in the late 1950's."

RYNE DUREN

Duren was a big fireballing righthanded relief pitcher who wore eyeglasses so thick he frightened batters as much as he overpowered them. He struck out more than a batter per inning (630 in 589⅓ innings) in his 10 years in the major leagues. He pitched for the Orioles (1954), Athletics (1957), Yankees (1958–61), Angels (1961–62), Phillies (1963–64, 1965), Reds (1964), and Senators (1965). For two years, 1958 and 1959, he was virtually untouchable, posting ERA's of 2.02 and 1.88 and striking out 87 in 75⅔ innings and 96 in 76⅔ innings. His lifetime record was 27–44 with a 3.83 ERA. Duren's selections are:

1B—VIC POWER
2B—BOBBY RICHARDSON
3B—CLETE BOYER
SS—WILLIE MIRANDA
OF—ROGER MARIS
OF—MICKEY MANTLE
OF—TED WILLIAMS
C—ELSTON HOWARD
RP—ALLIE REYNOLDS
LP—SANDY KOUFAX

Toughest Batters: Pete Runnels and Nellie Fox. "They always hit me inside out. I could pitch around the guys who could hit the fastball."

Most Underrated: Andy Carey and Bill Skowron.

Strongest Teams: "The 1958 Yankees for talent but the 1962 Angels for team effort."

Comments: "Defensively Boyer was ahead of Brooks Robinson for a few years and he had a better arm. Miranda is there just for picking it. Maris was sensational defensively as well as with the bat. And give honorable mention to Willie Mays and Roberto Clemente in the outfield."

FRANK ELLERBE

Ellerbe batted .268 in six years as an American League third baseman with the Senators (1919–21), Browns (1921–24), and Indians (1924). He was the regular third baseman on the 1922 Browns, who battled the Yankees for the pennant into the final days of the season. His best years with the bat were 1920 (.292) and 1921 (.286). Ellerbe's selections are:

    1B—GEORGE SISLER
    2B—ROGERS HORNSBY or EDDIE COLLINS
    3B—JOE DUGAN
    SS—CHICK GALLOWAY
    OF—TY COBB
    OF—TRIS SPEAKER
    OF—JOE JACKSON or BABE RUTH
     C—HANK SEVEREID
    RP—WALTER JOHNSON
    LP—HARRY HARPER

Toughest Pitchers: Walter Johnson and Carl Mays.
Most Underrated: Sisler. "I haven't heard enough about George."
Strongest Team: 1919–20 White Sox.
Comments: "The toughest man to play third base against was Ty Cobb."
Galloway played for the Athletics (1919–27) and Tigers (1928), batted .264 in his career, and hit as high as .324 in 1922. Severeid, a fine defensive catcher with the Reds (1911–13), Browns (1915–25), Senators (1925–26), and Yankees (1926), hit .289 in his 15 years in the majors. He batted over .300 for five consecutive seasons (1921–25). Harper won only 59 and lost 76 but he compiled a lifetime ERA of 2.87 in 10 seasons with the Senators (1913–19), Red Sox (1920), Yankees (1921), and Dodgers (1923).

WOODY ENGLISH

English was a slim infielder for the Cubs (1927–36) and Dodgers (1937–38). He played primarily at shortstop (more than 800 games) but appeared in 400 games at third base as well. A lifetime .286 hitter, he batted .335 with 14 homers, 100 walks, and 152 runs scored in 1930. He appeared in both the 1929 and 1932 World Series for the Cubs. English's selections are:

1B—BILL TERRY
2B—ROGERS HORNSBY
3B—PIE TRAYNOR
SS—TRAVIS JACKSON
OF—RIGGS STEPHENSON
OF—LLOYD WANER
OF—PAUL WANER
C—GABBY HARTNETT
RP—VAN LINGLE MUNGO
LP—CARL HUBBELL

Toughest Pitcher: Ed Brandt. "He was very fast and threw a difficult change-up. It's strange because he was a lefty and I could usually hit lefties." Brandt won 121 and lost 146 for the Braves, Dodgers, and Pirates between 1928 and 1938. Pitching mostly for dismal Boston teams, he won 18 games twice and 16 twice and had a 3.86 career ERA.

Most Underrated: Stephenson.

Strongest Team: 1932 Yankees.

DEL ENNIS

Ennis, a slugging righthanded outfielder, was the big bat in the Philadelphia Phillies lineup from 1946–56. He batted over .300 three times, stroked more than 20 homers nine times, and drove in more than 100 runs in seven seasons. In 1950, his best season, he led the Whiz Kids to a pennant with a batting average of .311 and career highs in homers (31), and RBI's (126, a league-leading figure). He also played for the Cardinals (1957–58), Reds (1959), and White Sox (1959). Ennis chooses:

1B—EDDIE WAITKUS
2B—RED SCHOENDIENST
3B—WILLIE JONES
SS—PEE WEE REESE
OF—STAN MUSIAL
OF—WILLIE MAYS
OF—TED WILLIAMS
C—WALKER COOPER
RP—ROBIN ROBERTS
LP—WARREN SPAHN

Toughest Pitcher: Ewell Blackwell.
Strongest Team: 1950 Phillies.
Waitkus and Jones were teammates of Ennis on the pennant-winning 1950 Phillies. The former hit .285 in 11 seasons (1941, 1946–55), with a career high .304 with the 1946 Cubs. The latter hit .258 in 15 seasons (1947–61), batting as high as .285 with the 1951 Phils.

CARL ERSKINE

Erskine, probably the most popular pitcher on the Boys of Summer staffs, won 122 and lost 78 in his 12 years (1948–59) with the Dodgers. An overhand curve specialist whose career was shortened by arm miseries, he enjoyed his best seasons in 1952, when he was 14–6 with a 2.70 ERA, and 1953, when he was 20–6 and struck out 187 batters. Erskine, who pitched no-hitters against the Cubs and Giants during his career, prefers:

           1B—GIL HODGES
           2B—JACKIE ROBINSON
           3B—BROOKS ROBINSON
           SS—DAVE CONCEPCION
           OF—DUKE SNIDER
           OF—WILLIE MAYS
           OF—JOE DiMAGGIO
            C—ROY CAMPANELLA
           RP—ROBIN ROBERTS
           LP—WARREN SPAHN

Deserves Cooperstown: Hodges. "I think he should be in the Hall of Fame both as a player and as a manager."

Toughest Batter: Stan Musial.

Most Underrated: Don Newcombe. "Newcombe had great years, some of the greatest years any Dodger pitcher ever had. But he had an abrasive personality back in his playing days and didn't get on too well with the writers. Put that together with the fact that he didn't win when he pitched in the World Series, and the writers weren't exactly falling over themselves to give him credit."

Strongest Teams: 1955 Dodgers, 1953 Yankees.

ROY FACE

Face did a great deal to publicize the cause of the relief pitcher in 1959 when he put together a record mark of 18 wins and 10 saves against only one loss (2.70 ERA) out of the bullpen. Overall, the 16-year veteran (Pirates, 1953, 1955–68; Tigers, 1968; Expos, 1969) won 104 games, lost 95, and saved 193. In three different seasons he led the NL in saves, and on two other occasions in mound appearances. Face was called on to start only one game over the last 13 years of his career. Face's picks:

> 1B—GIL HODGES
> 2B—BILL MAZEROSKI
> 3B—KEN BOYER
> SS—GRANNY HAMNER
> OF—HANK AARON
> OF—WILLIE MAYS
> OF—MICKEY MANTLE
> C—ROY CAMPANELLA
> RP—ROBIN ROBERTS
> LP—WARREN SPAHN

Deserves Cooperstown: "A pitcher named Face."
Toughest Batters: Stan Musial and Richie Ashburn.
Most Underrated: Mazeroski.
Strongest Team: 1960 Yankees.
Comments: "I always thought Hamner got the short end when people talked about shortstops. Not to take anything away from Pee Wee Reese and some of the others, but Hamner could do it just as well as they could. I also think he was a little stronger at the plate."

FERRIS FAIN

Fain, a lefthanded first baseman, batted .290 in his nine-year
career with the Athletics (1947–52), White Sox (1953–54),
Tigers (1955), and Indians (1955). He won back-to-back batting championships in 1951 and 1952 with averages of .344
and .327, respectively. Fain, who also led the AL with 43
doubles in 1952, chooses:

>   1B—MICKEY VERNON
>   2B—JOE GORDON
>   3B—GEORGE KELL
>   SS—PHIL RIZZUTO
>   OF—TED WILLIAMS
>   OF—JOE DiMAGGIO
>   OF—AL KALINE
>   C—BIRDIE TEBBETTS
>   RP—BOB FELLER
>   LP—MEL PARNELL or WHITEY FORD

Toughest Pitcher: Parnell. ''The righthanders were pie à
la mode for me, but when those lefthanders walked out there
I wanted to drink a warm glass of iodine. And Parnell was
the worst of them. He just wouldn't throw the ball where I
was swinging.''

Most Underrated: Eddie Joost. ''He was a hell of a shortstop and he always got the important base hit.''

Comments: ''I'll make myself the designated runner and
anyone who remembers how slow I was will know how funny
that is. That Tebbetts was the smartest catcher I ever saw. He
had a lot to do with Parnell's success against me. Lefty
O'Doul of the San Francisco Seals was the best manager I
ever saw for getting the most out of his players.''

RON FAIRLY

Fairly batted .266 in 21 seasons with the Dodgers (1958–69), Expos (1969–74), Cardinals (1975–76), Athletics (1976), Blue Jays (1977), and Angels (1978). A particularly reliable hitter in clutch situations, the lefty-swinging first baseman-outfielder usually hit between .275 and .300 and drove in 70-odd runs in the prime of his career. His best years offensively were 1961, when he batted .322 for Los Angeles, and 1977, when he clouted 19 home runs for Toronto. Fairly, the only player to represent both Canadian teams at the All-Star Game, likes:

        1B—GIL HODGES
        2B—JIM GILLIAM
        3B—EDDIE MATHEWS
        SS—ERNIE BANKS
        OF—FRANK ROBINSON or BILLY WILLIAMS
        OF—WILLIE MAYS
        OF—HANK AARON or ROBERTO CLEMENTE
         C—JOHNNY BENCH
        RP—BOB GIBSON
        LP—SANDY KOUFAX

Deserve Cooperstown: "Shortstops in general. Just because most of them haven't hit a lot of home runs, they've been overlooked."

Toughest Pitchers: Juan Marichal and Bob Veale. "Against Veale I went three-for-nine—three hits in nine years."

Most Underrated: Jim Davenport. "In the late innings of a game, he became as dangerous as Mays or McCovey."

Strongest Team: 1963 Dodgers.

RICK FERRELL

Ferrell, elected to the Hall of Fame in 1984, caught more games (1806) than any other American Leaguer. His 18-year career was spent primarily with second-division clubs—the Browns (1929–33, 1941–43), Red Sox (1933–37), and Senators (1937–41, 1944–45, 1947)—but he batted .281 in his career, with a season high of .315 in 1932. Over six seasons (1931–36) he batted .303. From 1934 to 1938 he teamed with his brother, Wes, to form an all-star sibling battery for the Red Sox and Senators. Ferrell's selections are:

> 1B—LOU GEHRIG
> 2B—CHARLIE GEHRINGER
> 3B—BROOKS ROBINSON
> SS—JOE CRONIN
> OF—TED WILLIAMS
> OF—JOE DiMAGGIO
> OF—BABE RUTH
>   C—MICKEY COCHRANE
> RP—BOB FELLER
> LP—LEFTY GROVE

Toughest Pitcher: Feller.
Most Underrated: Jimmie Foxx.
Strongest Team: 1929–31 Athletics.
Comments:''There were so many great players in my playing days that I always hesitate to name an all-star team. Since I spent my entire career in the American League, my selections are of course strictly American League.''

BOO FERRISS

Ferriss burst upon the American League scene with two consecutive 20-win seasons. In 1945, his rookie year, he was 21–10 for the Red Sox with a 2.96 ERA. The following year the big righthander helped pitch Boston to a pennant with a 25–6 record (for a league-leading .806 percentage) and a 3.25 ERA. He also won a game in the World Series. Injuries plagued him for his remaining four seasons in Boston, and he slipped to 12–11 in 1947 and 7–3 in 1948. His lifetime record was 65–30, with a 3.64 ERA. Ferriss chooses:

1B—HANK GREENBERG
2B—BOBBY DOERR
3B—GEORGE KELL
SS—LUKE APPLING
OF—TED WILLIAMS
OF—JOE DiMAGGIO
OF—CHARLIE KELLER
C—YOGI BERRA
RP—BOB FELLER
LP—HAL NEWHOUSER

Deserves Cooperstown: Doerr.
Toughest Batter: Keller.
Most Underrated: Dom DiMaggio.
Strongest Team: 1946 Red Sox.
Comments: "I have always thought that the late forties was a great era for major league baseball. There were many, many great players."

ED FIGUEROA

Figueroa is the only Puerto Rican to win 20 games in a season. The righthander pitched for the Angels (1974–75), Yankees (1976–80), Rangers (1980), and Athletics (1981). He was 20–9 in 1978 with a 2.99 ERA, won more games (55) for Yankees in their 1976–78 pennant winning seasons than any other pitcher, and won eight in a row late in 1978 to help the Yankees catch the Red Sox in their dramatic pennant race. His career record was 80–67 with a 3.51 ERA. Figueroa selects:

> 1B—GEORGE SCOTT
> 2B—BOBBY GRICH
> 3B—GRAIG NETTLES
> SS—MARK BELANGER
> OF—CHET LEMON
> OF—PAUL BLAIR
> OF—RICK MANNING
> C—THURMAN MUNSON
> RP—JIM PALMER
> LP—MICKEY LOLICH

Deserve Cooperstown: Munson, Palmer, Catfish Hunter, Reggie Jackson, and Rod Carew.
Toughest Batter: George Brett.
Most Underrated: Chris Chambliss.

ELBIE FLETCHER

Fletcher was a lefty first baseman with a sharp eye and a fancy glove. He won a newspaper contest as the best high school prospect in the Boston area and was invited to the Braves spring training camp in 1934. He played for Boston in 1934–35 and 1937–39, was traded to Pittsburgh (1939–43, 1946–47), went to Cleveland, was injured in spring training and missed the 1948 season, and played one final season (1949) for the Braves. Fletcher batted .271 with 79 homers and batted .290 with 12 homers in 1939 and .273 with 16 homers and 104 RBI's the following year. He also led the NL in walks in 1940 and 1941. Fletcher selects:

1B—DOLF CAMILLI
2B—BILLY HERMAN
3B—STAN HACK
SS—PEE WEE REESE
OF—LLOYD WANER
OF—ENOS SLAUGHTER
OF—MEL OTT
C—AL LOPEZ
RP—DIZZY DEAN
LP—JOHNNY VANDER MEER

Deserve Cooperstown: Ken Keltner and Terry Moore. "Moore was remarkable. I once saw him dive for a ball and catch it barehanded."

Toughest Pitchers: Cliff Melton and Bill Werle. "Melton had a breaking ball that was always on your hands." Werle's 29–39 lifetime record with three teams between 1949 and 1954 probably make him a bad memory for few other hitters.

Most Underrated: Bob Elliott.

Strongest Teams: Cardinals and Dodgers of the late 1930's and early 1940's.

Comments: "And the best manager I played for was Bill McKechnie, a perfect gentleman who took care of all his players like a father."

JIM FREGOSI

Although mainly infamous to New Yorkers as the man the Mets received from the Angels in exchange for Nolan Ryan, Fregosi was actually one of the dominant players of the American League for much of the 1960's. A .265 hitter over 18 big league seasons, the righthand-hitting shortstop was with California from 1961 to 1971, with the Mets in 1972 and 1973, with the Rangers from 1973 to 1977, and with the Pirates in 1977 and 1978. In 1968 Fregosi led the AL in triples. His single best year was probably 1970, when he batted .278 with 22 homers, 82 runs batted in, and 95 runs scored. Fregosi, who came back to manage the Angels to a divisional championship in 1979, picks:

1B—WILLIE McCOVEY
2B—BILL MAZEROSKI
3B—BROOKS ROBINSON
SS—ROBIN YOUNT
OF—BILLY WILLIAMS
OF—MICKEY MANTLE
OF—AL KALINE
C—JOHNNY BENCH
RP—DEAN CHANCE
LP—SANDY KOUFAX

Deserve Cooperstown: McCovey and Williams.
Toughest Pitcher: Sam McDowell.
Most Underrated: Roger Maris.
Strongest Teams: Yankees of the early 1960's, Athletics of the 1970's.
Comments: ''I don't think I ever played behind anyone as overpowering as Dean Chance in 1964, when he won twenty. As for Maris, everyone remembers the sixty-one home runs, but he also had one of the best outfield arms I ever saw and always seemed to be in position for a play.''

LARRY FRENCH

French was a star southpaw starter for three National League teams, the Pirates (1929–34), Cubs (1935–41), and Dodgers (1941–42). He never won 20 games in a season. (His high was 18, a figure he reached three times). But he racked up 197 career victories against 171 losses with a 3.44 ERA. He tied for the NL lead in shutouts twice and led in winning percentage (.789, 15–4) in his last season. In three World Series (1935, 1938, and 1941) he lost two games without winning any, but his ERA was only 3.00. French picks:

1B—BILL TERRY
2B—FRANKIE FRISCH
3B—PIE TRAYNOR
SS—PEE WEE REESE
OF—JOE MEDWICK
OF—PAUL WANER
OF—PETE REISER
 C—GABBY HARTNETT
RP—DIZZY DEAN
LP—SANDY KOUFAX

Deserves Cooperstown: Larry French. "I believe with one hundred ninety-seven wins in fourteen years with forty shutouts that I should be in the Hall of Fame. I led the league in 1942 and went to war never to return to get my two hundred-plus wins."

Toughest Batters: Medwick and Terry.

Strongest Team: 1935 Cubs.

BOB FRIEND

Although his lifetime record was a sub-.500 mark of 197–230, Friend was one of the dominant pitchers of the National League for most of his 16 years (1951–66). His main problem was that he spent a good part of his career with Pittsburgh teams that rank among the worst of all time. The righthander's best years were 1958, when he won 22 for the finally improving Pirates, and 1955, when he led the league in earned run average (2.83). In addition to his 20-game season, he won at least 17 games four times. Friend, who finished up his pitching in 1966 in a season split between the Yankees and Mets, picks:

> 1B—GIL HODGES
> 2B—BILL MAZEROSKI
> 3B—EDDIE MATHEWS
> SS—PEE WEE REESE
> OF—ROBERTO CLEMENTE
> OF—HANK AARON
> OF—WILLIE MAYS
> C—ROY CAMPANELLA
> RP—ROBIN ROBERTS
> LP—WARREN SPAHN

Deserves Cooperstown: Mazeroski.
Toughest Hitter: Aaron.
Strongest Team: 1952 Dodgers. "Or maybe it just seems like the 1952 Dodgers were the greatest because they had practically an all-star team on the field and won the pennant, while the Pirates were losing one hundred twelve. I myself had seventeen losses that year, and Murry Dickson lost more than I did!"

WOODY FRYMAN

The southpaw Fryman pitched in the majors for 18 seasons (1966–83), first as a starter and then as an increasingly effective reliever. Holder of a 141–155 lifetime record, he came up with the Pirates in 1966, then traveled to the Phillies (1968), Tigers (1972), Expos (1975), Reds (1977), Cubs (1978), and back to the Expos (1978). His best seasons were in Montreal near the end of his career, especially in 1980 when he saved 17 games. Fryman chooses:

1B—WILLIE STARGELL
2B—BILL MAZEROSKI
3B—BROOKS ROBINSON
SS—GENE ALLEY
OF—WILLIE MAYS
OF—ROBERTO CLEMENTE
OF—AL KALINE
C—JOHNNY BENCH
RP—JUAN MARICHAL
LP—SANDY KOUFAX

Toughest Batter: Billy Williams.
Strongest Team: 1972 Reds.
Comments: "Talking about who belongs in Cooperstown and who was an underrated player is pretty much the same thing because both categories are determined a great deal by the media. For instance, even though they're both in the Hall of Fame, I think of Clemente and Hank Aaron as having played most of their careers as underrated players. And the reason for that is neither of them played in New York or Los Angeles, where the media have their headquarters."

CARL FURILLO

Furillo, the clutch-hitting and rocket-armed right fielder for Brooklyn's Boys of Summer teams, batted .299 in 15 seasons (1946–1960) as a Dodger. His finest years at the plate were 1953, when he won the batting crown with a .344 mark, and 1955, when he batted .314 with 26 homers and 95 runs batted in. In both 1949 and 1950 he drove in more than 100 runs, and only once in his career (when he had an eye ailment in 1952) did he bat below .289 as a regular. Furillo, who also led the National League in at bats in 1951, chooses:

    1B—GIL HODGES
    2B—JIM GILLIAM or JACKIE ROBINSON
    3B—JACKIE ROBINSON or BILLY COX
    SS—PEE WEE REESE
    OF—HANK AARON
    OF—WILLIE MAYS
    OF—DUKE SNIDER
     C—ROY CAMPANELLA
    RP—SAL MAGLIE
    LP—WARREN SPAHN

Deserve Cooperstown: Red Schoendienst and Phil Rizzuto.

Toughest Pitchers: Maglie and Bob Rush.

Most Underrated: Schoendienst.

Strongest Team: Dodgers of the 1950's. "The Brooklyn teams weren't just good on the field, but in the head, too. We didn't need a manager. We had seven or eight guys who were managers. All we needed was somebody to walk up to home plate with the lineup card or to yank a pitcher every once in a while. When Walter Alston took over in 1954, he didn't seem to know that and was always afraid of using the hit-and-run and played everything close to the vest. With guys like Robinson, Reese, and Hodges around, that was just being as greenhorn as you could be."

MIKE GARCIA

Garcia, "The Big Bear," was one-fourth of the 1954 Cleveland Indians starting rotation. The other three—Bob Lemon, Early Wynn, and Bob Feller—are all in the Hall of Fame, but it was Garcia who led the league in ERA, with a 2.64, that year. Garcia spent all but two years of his 14-year career from 1948 to 1961 with the Indians. The last two years were with the White Sox and Senators. Garcia had two 20-win seasons and finished up at 142–97 with a 3.27 ERA. In his only World Series in 1954, he lost one game without winning any. Garcia's choices are:

```
1B—MICKEY VERNON
2B—BOBBY DOERR
3B—KEN KELTNER
SS—LOU BOUDREAU
OF—JOE DiMAGGIO
OF—TED WILLIAMS
OF—MICKEY MANTLE
 C—JIM HEGAN or YOGI BERRA
RP—BOB FELLER
LP—MEL PARNELL
```

Toughest Batter: Berra. "Everybody says he was a bad ball hitter. He wasn't. He hit everything. And he was so damn strong."

Most Underrated: Al Rosen.

Strongest Team: 1949 Red Sox. "I was only a rookie at the time and all those guys with those big bats frightened me."

RALPH GARR

Garr, a lefthanded slap hitter, batted a hefty .306 in 13 seasons with the Braves (1968–75), White Sox (1976–79), and Angels (1979–80). In three different years he collected at least 200 hits, enjoying his finest season in 1974, when he won the National League batting crown with a .353 average and also led in hits and triples. The outfielder also ravaged NL pitchers in 1971 for a .343 mark. Garr, whose .386 average in 1970 stands as the highest in International League history, goes with:

            1B—ORLANDO CEPEDA
            2B—BILL MAZEROSKI
            3B—BROOKS ROBINSON
            SS—DAVE CONCEPCION
            OF—PETE ROSE
            OF—WILLIE MAYS
            OF—HANK AARON
             C—JOHNNY BENCH
            RP—CATFISH HUNTER
            LP—JERRY KOOSMAN

Toughest Pitchers: Tom Seaver and Steve Carlton.

Most Underrated: Al Oliver. "Someday somebody is going to wake up and notice that he bats .300 every year. Too bad he's never played for a winning team or one that gets a lot of media attention."

Strongest Teams: Braves of the late 1960's, Reds of the 1970's.

NED GARVER

Garver had the misfortune to labor for truly dreary teams for most of his career. The righthander pitched for the Browns (1948–52), Tigers (1952–56), Athletics (1957–60), and Angels (1961). He won 129 and lost 157 despite a quite respectable 3.73 ERA. His best year was 1951, when he was 20–12 with a 3.73 ERA. The remarkable thing about his achievements that season was that the Browns finished a dismal last, winning only 52 games. Thus, Garver won almost 40 percent of his team's games. Garver selects:

1B—ROY SIEVERS or FERRIS FAIN
2B—JOE GORDON
3B—GEORGE KELL
SS—LUKE APPLING
OF—AL KALINE
OF—TED WILLIAMS
OF—JOE DiMAGGIO
C—YOGI BERRA
RP—BOB FELLER
LP—HAL NEWHOUSER

Deserves Cooperstown: Newhouser.
Toughest Batter: Williams.
Most Underrated: Bill Tuttle. Tuttle played center field for three AL clubs in the fifties and early sixties. He batted .259 in his career and as high as .300 in 1958.
Strongest Team: Red Sox of the late 1940's and early 1950's.

CHARLIE GEHRINGER

Gehringer, "The Mechanical Man," spent his entire career (1924–42) with the Tigers. A .320 lifetime hitter, 13 times in 14 years he hit over .300, with a high of .371 to lead the AL in batting and win an MVP Award in 1937. He had seven seasons with over 200 base hits, leading the league twice in that category. He also topped the American League twice in doubles (with a high of 60 in 1936), once in triples, twice in runs scored, and once in stolen bases. He even hit 184 home runs, reaching double numbers 11 times. He batted .321 in three World Series (1934, 1935, 1940). One of the greatest of all second basemen, Gehringer was enshrined in Cooperstown in 1949. His choices are:

1B—LOU GEHRIG
2B—ROGERS HORNSBY
3B—PIE TRAYNOR
SS—JOE CRONIN
OF—BABE RUTH
OF—JOE DiMAGGIO
OF—TED WILLIAMS
C—BILL DICKEY
RP—WALTER JOHNSON
LP—LEFTY GROVE

Toughest Pitcher: Grove.
Gehringer picked the above team 30 years ago. Today he says: "There is no way anyone can pick an all-star team. Perhaps every ten years you could pick one. It's impossible to sort out players after witnessing baseball for sixty years because so many things change such as speeded-up baseballs, big gloves, Astroturf, expanded leagues, high salaries, etc."

HANK GREENBERG

Greenberg was inducted into the Hall of Fame in 1956 on the basis of a 13-year career (1930, 1933–41, 1945–47) with the Tigers and Pirates over which he batted .313, swatted 331 home runs, and compiled a slugging average of .605. Highlights of his career include hitting 58 homers in 1938; driving in 183 runs in 1937; leading the league in homers four times, in runs batted in four times, and in doubles twice; and being named the American League's Most Valuable Player in 1935 and 1940. Greenberg chooses:

> 1B—JIMMIE FOXX
> 2B—CHARLIE GEHRINGER
> 3B—HARLOND CLIFT
> SS—ROBIN YOUNT
> OF—TED WILLIAMS
> OF—JOE DiMAGGIO
> OF—BABE RUTH
> C—MICKEY COCHRANE
> RP—BOB FELLER
> LP—LEFTY GROVE

Asked to fill out a similar lineup some years ago, Greenberg made other choices for first, third, short, and one of the outfield spots. Formerly he had preferred Lou Gehrig to Foxx, Pie Traynor to Clift, Honus Wagner to Yount, and Ty Cobb to Williams. Either way, it isn't a bad lineup.

JIM GREENGRASS

Jim Greengrass, a power-hitting outfielder for one of the earlier versions of Cincinnati's Big Red Machine, played for the Reds between 1952 and 1955, then another two seasons for the Phillies. His career was ended abruptly by a knee injury that was ultimately diagnosed as phlebitis. His best years were 1953 (20 home runs, 100 runs batted in, .285) and 1954 (27 home runs, 95 runs batted in, .280). Greengrass's choices:

> 1B—STAN MUSIAL
> 2B—JOHNNY TEMPLE
> 3B—KEN BOYER
> SS—ROY McMILLAN
> OF—WILLIE MAYS
> OF—CARL FURILLO
> OF—MONTE IRVIN
> C—ROY CAMPANELLA
> RP—ROBIN ROBERTS
> LP—WARREN SPAHN

Comments: "Temple and McMillan were the greatest double play combination I ever saw, and that's what you're looking for in middle infielders. There was an outfielder around at the time by the name of Glen Gorbous who had the most powerful arm I've ever seen, but for a combination of power and accuracy nobody was better than Furillo. For backup players I'd have to mention Ted Kluszewski, Brooks Robinson, Pee Wee Reese, Duke Snider, Don Mueller, and Del Rice. After Spahn would be Harvey Haddix."

BURLEIGH GRIMES

Righthander Grimes was elected to the Hall of Fame in 1964 after a 19-year (1916–34) career during which he posted a record of 270–212. One of Cooperstown's more conspicuous vagabonds, he entered the major leagues with the Pirates, then went on to the Dodgers, Giants, back to the Pirates, Braves, Cardinals, Cubs, Cardinals again, Pirates for a third time, and Yankees. His marks include winning 20 games five times and leading the league in complete games four times and in strikeouts once. His single best year was probably for the Pirates in 1928, when he won 25 games and had a 2.99 ERA, but he didn't embarrass Brooklyn in 1920 (23 wins, 2.22) or 1921 (22 wins, 2.83), either. One of the game's great rubber arms, Grimes pitched 4179 ⅔ innings in the big leagues. He was also a fine hitter, collecting 42 safeties in 1928 and at least 30 in three other seasons. Grimes, who managed the Dodgers in 1937 and 1938, prefers:

> 1B—BILL TERRY
> 2B—ROGERS HORNSBY
> 3B—PIE TRAYNOR
> SS—HONUS WAGNER
> OF—ZACK WHEAT
> OF—CHICK HAFEY
> OF—BABE RUTH
> C—JIMMIE WILSON
> RP—GROVER CLEVELAND ALEXANDER
> LP—WARREN SPAHN

Comments: "My alternates are George Sisler, Frankie Frisch, Freddie Lindstrom, Charley Gelbert, Paul Waner, Mel Ott, Ross Youngs, Gabby Hartnett, Dazzy Vance, and Rube Marquard. For righthand pitchers you also have to mention Dizzy Dean, Babe Adams, Charlie Root, and Allie Reynolds; for lefties, Carl Hubbell, Wilbur Cooper, and Lefty Gomez." Wilson caught for three NL teams between 1923 and 1940. He batted .284 and starred in the 1940 World Series, his fourth, hitting .353 at the age of 40.

DICK GROAT

Shortstop Groat batted .286 over a 14-year (1952, 1955–67) major league career with the Pirates, Cardinals, Phillies, and Giants. As the spark plug for the pennant-winning Pirates in 1960, he was named the league's Most Valuable Player and also picked up a silver bat as the league's leading hitter (.325). In 1963 he had another fine year, this time for the Cardinals, batting .319 with a league-leading 43 doubles, 11 triples, 73 runs batted in, and 85 runs scored. The following season he was one of the major reasons St. Louis won the pennant. Groat, who also played professional basketball in the NBA, chooses:

> 1B—GIL HODGES
> 2B—BILL MAZEROSKI
> 3B—KEN BOYER
> SS—ALVIN DARK
> OF—STAN MUSIAL
> OF—ROBERTO CLEMENTE
> OF—HANK AARON
> C—ROY CAMPANELLA
> RP—DON DRYSDALE
> LP—SANDY KOUFAX

Deserve Cooperstown: Mazeroski and Roy Face.
Toughest Pitcher: Koufax.
Most Underrated: Don Hoak.
Strongest Team: 1952–56 Dodgers.
Comments: "Honorable mention in the outfield to Curt Flood."

STEVE GROMEK

Gromek pitched for 17 years in the American League with the Indians (1941–53) and Tigers (1953–57). He won 123 and lost 108 and compiled a 3.41 ERA. In 1945 he was 19–9 with a 2.55 ERA. In the 1948 World Series he won the only game he pitched, a seven-hit, 2–1 victory over Johnny Sain in the fourth game. Gromek selects:

> 1B—MICKEY VERNON
> 2B—JOE GORDON
> 3B—KEN KELTNER
> SS—LOU BOUDREAU
> OF—JOE DiMAGGIO
> OF—TED WILLIAMS
> OF—CHARLIE KELLER
> C—JIM HEGAN
> RP—BOB FELLER
> LP—HAL NEWHOUSER

Deserve Cooperstown: Nellie Fox and Newhouser.

Toughest Batters: Eddie Lake and Skeeter Webb. "One year Lake went twenty for twenty off me and Webb choked up and just stroked the ball to right." Webb batted .219 in 12 seasons (1932, 1938–48) with five teams.

Most Underrated: Hegan. "In ten years I saw him drop only one pop fly. If he could've hit .300, he'd have been the greatest catcher of all time.

Strongest Team: 1948 Indians.

Comments: "I'll take Keltner over Pete Rose. Backup pitchers would be Bob Lemon, Allie Reynolds, Early Wynn, Herb Score, Bobby Shantz, and Whitey Ford."

JERRY GROTE

Grote, equalled only by Johnny Bench as a defensive catcher at the height of his career, batted .252 in 16 major league seasons with the Astros (1963–64), Mets (1966–77), Dodgers (1977–78), Royals (1981), and Dodgers again (1981). Known mainly for his handling of the Seaver-Koosman-McGraw-Matlack pitching staffs in New York, he could also deliver timely hits, as attested to by the fact that he batted above .270 seven times. His single best year at the plate was probably 1975, when he hit .295. Grote chooses:

```
1B—WES PARKER
2B—MANNY TRILLO
3B—MIKE SCHMIDT
SS—ROY McMILLAN or BUD HARRELSON
OF—HANK AARON
OF—WILLIE MAYS
OF—ROBERTO CLEMENTE
 C—RANDY HUNDLEY
RP—TOM SEAVER or DON DRYSDALE
LP—STEVE CARLTON or SANDY KOUFAX
```

Toughest Pitcher: Drysdale.
Most Underrated: Harrelson, Aaron, and Pete Rose. "I don't care how many stories they write about Rose; I still don't get the feeling people understand that he's been an all-star at every position he's played."
Strongest Team: 1969 Orioles.
Comments: "The lineup I chose is a defensive one because that's the way you win. As for Hundley over Bench, all I know is that in the early 1970's the Mets were this close to trading me to Cincinnati. They told me I would've been the catcher and Bench would've been moved to another position. I don't know why the deal never happened."

HARVEY HADDIX

Haddix, "The Kitten," was a crafty southpaw with the Cardinals (1952–56), Phillies (1956–57), Reds (1958), Pirates (1959–63), and Orioles (1964–65). He won 136 and lost 113 with a 3.63 ERA in his 14-year career. But there were times when he was near perfect. In 1953 he was 20–9 with a 3.06 ERA and led the NL with 6 shutouts. In the 1960 World Series he was 2–0 with a 2.45 ERA. And, of course, on May 26, 1959 he pitched 12⅓ perfect innings against the Braves before losing the game on an error, an intentional walk, and a home run that was turned into a double by sloppy baserunning. Haddix picks:

```
1B—STAN MUSIAL or GIL HODGES
2B—BILL MAZEROSKI or RED SCHOENDIENST
3B—EDDIE MATHEWS or BILLY COX
SS—DICK GROAT or DAVE CONCEPCION
OF—FRANK ROBINSON
OF—WILLIE MAYS or MICKEY MANTLE
OF—HANK AARON
 C—YOGI BERRA or JOHNNY BENCH
RP—ROBIN ROBERTS
LP—WARREN SPAHN or SANDY KOUFAX
```

Toughest Batter: Mays. "He just hit everything I threw."
Most Underrated: Bill Virdon. "He was such a good defensive ball player. And he would be hitting .270 going into August and then would slump."
Strongest Team: 1960 Pirates.

MEL HARDER

Harder pitched for the Cleveland Indians for 20 years (1928–47) and won 223 while losing 186 for the Tribe. His lifetime ERA was 3.80. His best season was 1934, when he led the American League in shutouts with six and compiled a 20–12 record and a 2.61 earned run average. He also won 22 (and lost 11) the following year. Harder, a longtime coach with the Indians, managed them for one game in 1961. Harder's selections are:

1B—LOU GEHRIG
2B—ROGERS HORNSBY
3B—PIE TRAYNOR
SS—JOE CRONIN
OF—TED WILLIAMS or HANK AARON
OF—JOE DiMAGGIO or WILLIE MAYS
OF—BABE RUTH or TY COBB
C—BILL DICKEY
RP—WALTER JOHNSON
LP—WARREN SPAHN

Harder's choices cross leagues and generations. He would be willing to live with any three of the outfielders he names.

BUD HARRELSON

Despite batting a mere .236 in 16 seasons with the Mets (1965–77), Phillies (1978–79), and Rangers (1980), shortstop Harrelson was the glue of the New York infield for more than a decade, including the pennant-winning years of 1969 and 1973. Among the Gold Glover's defensive accomplishments was tying the National League record in 1970 for most games (54) by a shortstop without committing an error. In the same year that he achieved that feat, he proved a particularly pesky eighth-place hitter for the Mets, drawing 95 walks and scoring 72 runs. Harrelson goes with:

1B—KEITH HERNANDEZ
2B—JOE MORGAN
3B—MIKE SCHMIDT
SS—OZZIE SMITH
OF—HANK AARON
OF—WILLIE MAYS
OF—ROBERTO CLEMENTE
C—JOHNNY BENCH
RP—TOM SEAVER
LP—STEVE CARLTON

Deserves Cooperstown: "Without getting into names, I think we will see a lot more players with defensive skills getting in. Part of the reason for this, I think, is the designated hitter, which has ironically accented the importance of one-dimensional players defensively as well as offensively."

Toughest Pitchers: Carlton and Bob Gibson.

Most Underrated: Ted Sizemore "He always gave himself up for Lou Brock."

Strongest Team: 1971 National League All-Star Team. "Are you kidding? I walked out on that field and saw Aaron, Mays, Clemente, and all the others hitting batting practice shots into Detroit's upper deck, so I just walked straight out to the field for a few grounders. I felt like a Little Leaguer."

MIKE HEGAN

Hegan was a fancy fielding first baseman who established a major league record (since surpassed by Steve Garvey) for most consecutive games without an error (178 between 1970 and 1973). He played for the Yankees (1964, 1966–67, 1973–74), Pilots (1969), Brewers (1970–71, 1974–77), and Athletics (1971–73). A .242 hitter over his career, he batted .329 as a pinch-hitter and late-inning defensive replacement in 1972. He also appeared in two World Series (1964 and 1972). Hegan's choices are:

> 1B—CARL YASTRZEMSKI
> 2B—ROD CAREW
> 3B—BROOKS ROBINSON
> SS—ROBIN YOUNT
> OF—FRANK ROBINSON
> OF—HANK AARON
> OF—REGGIE JACKSON
> C—BILL FREEHAN
> RP—CATFISH HUNTER
> LP—TOMMY JOHN

Deserve Cooperstown: Phil Rizzuto and Hunter.
Toughest Pitchers: Nolan Ryan and Sam McDowell.
Most Underrated: Dick Green.
Strongest Team: 1972 Athletics.
Comments: "It may be time for those who pick all-time teams to begin adding the categories of righthanded and left-handed relief pitchers, since that area has become so important over the last fifteen to twenty years. Also, as an American League player, I believe the DH is a key factor in a team's offensive capabilities. Many players have performed well in that highly specialized and difficult role. My candidates for these three roles are Rollie Fingers, Sparky Lyle, and Hal McRae."

BABE HERMAN

Herman, who will always be synonymous with the Daffy Dodgers of the late 1920's, was one of the National League's most feared hitters over a 13-year career that started with Brooklyn in 1926 and ended in Ebbets Field 20 years later when he returned for a brief wartime appearance. In between the Dodger years he played for the Reds (1932), Cubs (1933), Pirates (1935), Reds again (1935), and Tigers (1937). He throttled pitchers for a lifetime batting average of .324 and 181 home runs. His .300 seasons (nine of them) included marks of .381 in 1929 and .393 in 1930. In the latter year he also crushed 35 homers and 48 doubles, and drove home 130 runs. He led the NL in triples in 1932. Herman picks:

     1B—LOU GEHRIG
     2B—ROGERS HORNSBY
     3B—PIE TRAYNOR
     SS—TRAVIS JACKSON
     OF—TED WILLIAMS
     OF—TY COBB
     OF—BABE RUTH
      C—GABBY HARTNETT
     RP—GROVER CLEVELAND ALEXANDER
     LP—CARL HUBBELL

Deserve Cooperstown: Carl Furillo and Bullet Rogan. "Rogan was a pitcher for the Kansas City Monarchs in the Negro Leagues and he was better than Satchel Paige, than any of them."

Toughest Pitcher: Bill Hallahan. "Hallahan was always wild enough to keep me off balance at the plate."

Most Underrated: Johnny Frederick. "Before Frederick broke his leg and became known as a pinch-hitter, he was the best outfielder I played with. I always knew where he was. We lost the pennant in 1930 because he got hurt."

Strongest Team: 1930 Dodgers.

BILLY HERMAN

Billy Herman was elected to the Hall of Fame in 1975 on the basis of a 15-year playing career in which he batted .304 as a second baseman for the Cubs (1931–41), Dodgers (1941–43, 1946), Braves (1946), and Pirates (1947). His best season was in 1935, when he led the National League in hits and doubles and batted .341. In 1947 he was player-manager of the Pirates, and between 1964 and 1966 he managed the Red Sox. Herman's choices are:

> 1B—LOU GEHRIG
> 2B—CHARLIE GEHRINGER
> 3B—BROOKS ROBINSON
> SS—PEE WEE REESE
> OF—STAN MUSIAL
> OF—JOE DiMAGGIO
> OF—BABE RUTH
> C—GABBY HARTNETT
> RP—DIZZY DEAN
> LP—CARL HUBBELL

Reese, Hartnett, and Dean were Herman's teammates at one time or another. The same three, plus Musial and Hubbell, were opponents in various seasons. Ruth's fadeout in the National League in 1935 also corresponded with Hermans' career. The only member of the team not active during Herman's playing days is Robinson. ''But I saw enough of him when I was managing and coaching in the American League. Never any better,'' he says.

BILLY HOEFT

Hoeft's 15-year career falls into two parts. In the beginning he was a starting pitcher for the Tigers (1952–59) and Red Sox (1959). Then he moved to the bullpen for the Orioles (1959–62), Giants (1963, 1966), Braves (1964), and Cubs (1965–66). His best seasons were 1955 (16–7) and 1956 (20–14). He led the AL in shutouts in 1955. Hoeft picks:

> 1B—BILL SKOWRON
> 2B—BILLY MARTIN
> 3B—BROOKS ROBINSON
> SS—HARVEY KUENN
> OF—WILLIE MAYS
> OF—MICKEY MANTLE
> OF—TED WILLIAMS
> C—YOGI BERRA
> RP—JIM BUNNING
> LP—WARREN SPAHN

Deserves Cooperstown: Nellie Fox.
Toughest Batter: Fox. ''No matter what I threw him he'd hit a sandiron wedge out to short left field and into the same ten-foot circle just out of reach of everyone.''
Most Underrated: Bill Tuttle.
Strongest Team: 1963 Giants.
Comments: ''Like all pitchers, the thing I remember best was hitting, and I hit two home runs against Baltimore once. Also, I remember being jokingly nominated for an Emmy after pitching a sixteen-inning game in Yankee Stadium in the second end of a Sunday doubleheader. The game went on so long we knocked Walt Disney off the air. Unfortunately I lost 4–3.''

TOMMY HOLMES

Holmes, a lefthand-hitting outfielder, batted .302 in 11 seasons with the Braves (1942–51) and Dodgers (1952). Although always a solid hitter, he had a dream year in 1945—leading the National League in hits, doubles, home runs, total bases, and slugging, batting .352, driving in 117 runs, scoring 125 runs, and striking out only nine times. In the same year, he set a new NL record for hitting in consecutive games (37), eclipsed only 33 years later by Pete Rose. Holmes, who served as a player-manager for the Braves in 1951 and 1952, goes with:

    1B—STAN MUSIAL
    2B—JACKIE ROBINSON
    3B—BOB ELLIOTT
    SS—MARTY MARION
    OF—DUKE SNIDER
    OF—RICHIE ASHBURN
    OF—ENOS SLAUGHTER
     C—ROY CAMPANELLA
    RP—EWELL BLACKWELL
    LP—WARREN SPAHN

Deserves Cooperstown: "Start with me. You look up all the statistics about batting average, strikeouts per at bats, and fielding, and then look up the records of Snider, Willie Mays, Mickey Mantle, and Terry Moore."

Toughest Pitcher: Blackwell.

Most Underrated: Elliott. "In 1948 he was the greatest RBI man I ever saw."

Strongest Team: 1948 Braves.

JOHNNY HOPP

Hopp, a scrappy lefthanded outfielder-first baseman, batted .296 over 14 seasons with the Cardinals (1939–45), Braves (1946–47), Pirates (1948–49, 1950), Dodgers (1949), Yankees (1950–52), and Tigers (1952). His best years were 1944, when he batted .336, 1946, when he hit .333, and 1950, when he hit .339. He appeared in five World Series—1942, 1943, and 1944 with the Cardinals and 1950 and 1951 with the Yankees. Hopp's picks are:

1B—JOHNNY MIZE
2B—JACKIE ROBINSON
3B—STAN HACK
SS—MARTY MARION
OF—STAN MUSIAL
OF—DUKE SNIDER
OF—ENOS SLAUGHTER
C—ERNIE LOMBARDI
RP—MORT COOPER or WHITLOW WYATT
LP—WARREN SPAHN

Toughest Pitcher: Monte Kennedy. "He hit me more than I hit him. He could throw the ball through a brick wall. Once he hit me in the head. Another time he hit the peak of my cap and turned the cap around on my head." Kennedy won 42 and lost 55 for the Giants (1946–53). He had a 3.84 lifetime ERA but he won more than he lost in only one season.

Most Underrated: Terry Moore and Johnny Hopp.

Strongest Team: 1942 Cardinals.

Comments: "These selections are based on my eleven years in the National League. I didn't spend enough time in the American to say. Mize over Gil Hodges although Hodges was a better fielder. Hack did a good job every day. Marion had an extremely accurate arm and his throws to first were light as a feather. I didn't see enough of Willie Mays but he certainly was a superstar. I'll take Lombardi for his arm, defense, and bat over Roy Campanella, Walker Cooper, and Harry Danning."

WILLIE HORTON

Horton batted .273 over an 18-year career that was generally divided into stardom for the Tigers (1963–77) and journeying around the American League for five other teams (1977–81). A righthand-hitting outfielder with a lot of power, he was one of the main reasons for Detroit's pennant-winning 1968 season, when he clouted 36 home runs and hit :285. Even toward the end of his career, in 1979 for Seattle, he had enough pop left to hit 29 homers and drive in 106 runs. Horton, who also played for the Rangers, Indians, Athletics, and Blue Jays, picks:

                1B—NORM CASH
                2B—DICK McAULIFFE
                3B—BROOKS ROBINSON
                SS—LUIS APARICIO
                OF—CARL YASTRZEMSKI
                OF—MICKEY STANLEY
                OF—REGGIE JACKSON
                 C—BILL FREEHAN
                RP—DENNY McLAIN
                LP—MICKEY LOLICH

Toughest Pitchers: Luis Tiant and Dave McNally.
Most Underrated: Stanley. "Best center fielder defensively I ever saw. Better than Paul Blair, Mickey Mantle, all of them."
Strongest Team: 1970 Orioles.

FRANK HOWARD

Nobody has ever been more suited to the role of home run slugger than the gigantic Howard, who slammed 382 balls out of the park in a 16-year career with the Dodgers (1958–64), Senators-Rangers (1965–72), and Tigers (1972–73). A lifetime .273 hitter, his best season was undoubtedly 1969, when he clouted 48 homers, drove in 111 runs, scored 111, and batted .296. Other marks include winning Rookie of the Year honors in 1960, leading the American League in homers twice, in runs batted in and walks once, and enjoying three straight seasons (1968–70) of at least 44 home runs. In May 1968 the righthand-batting outfielder put himself in the record books by hitting 10 home runs in 20 at bats. Howard, who has managed both the Padres and the Mets, chooses:

1B—WILLIE McCOVEY
2B—BILL MAZEROSKI
3B—EDDIE MATHEWS
SS—LUIS APARICIO
OF—WILLIE MAYS
OF—HANK AARON
OF—MICKEY MANTLE
C—ELSTON HOWARD
RP—JUAN MARICHAL
LP—SANDY KOUFAX

Toughest Pitcher: Jim Maloney.
Most Underrated: Bobby Richardson. "Most people seem to remember those Yankee teams of the early 1960's in terms of Mantle, Roger Maris, and Whitey Ford. They were all great, but Richardson and Howard always struck me as the glue that held them together."
Strongest Team: 1962 Giants.

CARL HUBBELL

Hubbell, the Giants' meal ticket in the 1930's, spent his entire career (1928–43) with the Polo Grounders. He won 20 games or more five years running (1933–37), and in that span he led the NL in victories three times, won-lost percentage twice, ERA three times, strikeouts once, and shutouts once. He was the National League MVP in 1933 and 1936. In six World Series appearances in three Series Hubbell won four and lost two and had a 1.79 ERA. His remarkable screwball made "King Carl" the dominant pitcher of the thirties. A longtime Giants executive in both New York and San Francisco, he was elected to the Hall of Fame in 1947. Hubbell selects:

1B—LOU GEHRIG
2B—CHARLIE GEHRINGER
3B—PIE TRAYNOR
SS—JOE CRONIN
OF—BABE RUTH
OF—WILLIE MAYS
OF—MEL OTT
C—GABBY HARTNETT
RP—GROVER CLEVELAND ALEXANDER
LP—LEFTY GROVE

Comments: "I can only judge the players that I have seen." Hubbell wrote that about 30 years ago. Perhaps he has seen better since, but no one would be embarrassed by this combination.

TEX HUGHSON

Hughson was a big righthander who won 96 and lost only 54 in an eight-year career with the Red Sox (1941–44, 1946–49). His lifetime ERA of 2.94 was exceptional. Hughson won a league-leading 22 games in 1942, lost only six, and gave up only 2.59 earned runs per nine innings pitched. He also led the American League that year in complete games, innings pitched, and strikeouts. In 1944 he was 18–5 (2.26) when he was drafted in late August, but he still topped all AL pitchers in won-lost percentage (.783). In Boston's pennant-winning season of 1946, he won 20 and lost 11 with a 2.75 ERA. Hughson selects:

1B—JOHNNY MIZE
2B—BOBBY DOERR
3B—GEORGE KELL
SS—PHIL RIZZUTO
OF—TED WILLIAMS
OF—JOE DiMAGGIO
OF—STAN MUSIAL
C—YOGI BERRA
RP—BOB FELLER
LP—HAL NEWHOUSER

Deserve Cooperstown: Doerr and Rizzuto.
Toughest Batters: Nellie Fox and Johnny Pesky. "I had the most trouble with lefthanded hitters who hit to the opposite field."
Most Underrated: Doerr.
Strongest Team: 1946 Red Sox.

RANDY HUNDLEY

Although he batted only .236 in 14 seasons with the Giants (1964–65), Cubs (1966–73), Twins (1974), Padres (1975), and Cubs a second time (1976–77), Hundley was one of the finest defensive catchers of his era. Among the records he set behind the plate were for most games caught by a rookie, most games with fewest errors (four in 150 games), and most appearances in a season by a catcher. He could also hit the long ball on occasion, as evidenced by the 19 home runs he blasted in 1966 and the 18 he hit in 1969. Hundley, who retired with a lifetime fielding average of .990, likes:

1B—ERNIE BANKS
2B—BILL MAZEROSKI
3B—RON SANTO
SS—DON KESSINGER
OF—BILLY WILLIAMS
OF—WILLIE MAYS
OF—HANK AARON
C—JERRY GROTE
RP—BOB GIBSON
LP—SANDY KOUFAX

Deserve Cooperstown: Santo and Williams. "I'm not saying Santo was a better fielder than Brooks Robinson, but take a look at their offensive statistics."

Toughest Pitchers: Gibson, Jim Bunning, and Don Drysdale.

Most Underrated: Bill Hands. "Nobody ever realized how good he was because he was always overshadowed by Fergie Jenkins and Ken Holtzman."

Strongest Teams: 1968 Cardinals, Dodgers of the 1960's and 1970's.

RON HUNT

Hunt, the holder of most records in the hit-by-pitch category, batted .273 in 12 seasons with the Mets (1963–66), Dodgers (1967), Giants (1968–70), Expos (1971–74), and Cardinals (1974). One of his best seasons at the plate was his debut year of 1963, when he barely lost out as Rookie of the Year to Pete Rose by batting .272 with 10 homers and 28 doubles. Although he was later to hit over .300 twice and became recognized as a capable defensive second baseman, he will always be most associated with such black-and-blue records as most times hit by a pitch in a career (243), most times hit by a pitch in a season (50 times in 1971), and seven-time leader in the National League of hit batsmen. Hunt likes:

1B—GIL HODGES
2B—BILL MAZEROSKI
3B—BROOKS ROBINSON
SS—ROY McMILLAN
OF—TED WILLIAMS
OF—WILLIE MAYS
OF—ROBERTO CLEMENTE
C—JOHNNY BENCH
RP—DON DRYSDALE
LP—SANDY KOUFAX

Toughest Pitcher: Drysdale.
Most Underrated: Bobby Wine.
Strongest Team: Braves of the early 1960's.

MONTE IRVIN

Irvin, who was elected to the Hall of Fame in 1973, played first base and the outfield for only eight major league seasons, seven with the Giants (1949–55) and one with the Cubs (1956). But he had an impressive career in the old Negro Leagues before entering the majors. He batted .293 in his big league career. His personal season highs were a .329 average in 1953, 24 homers in 1951, and 121 RBI's to lead the NL in 1951. In the 1951 World Series he batted .458 with 11 hits in 24 at bats. Irvin's selections are:

> 1B—LOU GEHRIG
> 2B—JACKIE ROBINSON
> 3B—EDDIE MATHEWS
> SS—ERNIE BANKS
> OF—WILLIE MAYS
> OF—JOE DiMAGGIO
> OF—MICKEY MANTLE
>   C—ROY CAMPANELLA
> RP—BOB GIBSON
> LP—SANDY KOUFAX

Deserve Cooperstown: Phil Rizzuto and Marty Marion.
Toughest Pitcher: Ewell Blackwell.
Most Underrated: Larry Doby and Richie Ashburn.
Strongest Teams: 1954 Giants, 1951 Yankees.
Comments: "The Negro League Players comparable to the players I've picked are, in the same order: Buck Leonard, Sammy Hughes, Ray Dandridge, Willie Wells, Cool Papa Bell, Oscar Charleston, Martin Dihigo, Josh Gibson, Satchel Paige, and Willie Foster."

LARRY JACKSON

Jackson was a star righthander for three National League teams: the Cardinals (1955–62), Cubs (1963–66), and Phillies (1966–68). He won 10 or more games in all but the first two of his 14 seasons. His best record was in 1964, when he led the NL with 24 wins while losing only 11. But twice he posted ERA's better than his 1964 mark of 3.14. In 1963 he was 2.55 (with a 14–18 record), and in 1968 he had a 2.77 ERA (with a 13–17 record). In 1966 he tied for the NL lead in shutouts with five. Lifetime he was 194–183 with a 3.40 ERA. Jackson selects:

1B—STAN MUSIAL
2B—RED SCHOENDIENST
3B—RON SANTO
SS—ERNIE BANKS
OF—HANK AARON
OF—WILLIE MAYS
OF—ROBERTO CLEMENTE
C—JOHNNY BENCH
RP—BOB GIBSON
LP—WARREN SPAHN

Deserves Cooperstown: Larry Jackson. "That's not a facetious statement."

Toughest Batter: Harry Anderson. "He just had confidence against me. Hitting, just like pitching, is to a great extent mental. A pattern develops. A guy hits good pitches off me, then he expects to hit the good ones." Anderson was a .264 hitter in five NL seasons. In 1958 he batted .301 with 23 homers.

Most Underrated: Pee Wee Reese, Roy McMillan, and Banks. "Ernie was a better hitter with men on base than anyone else in baseball."

Strongest Team: Braves of the late 1950's.

Comments: "I'll take Santo over Ken Boyer, but just barely."

TRAVIS JACKSON

Jackson, inducted into the Hall of Fame in 1982, played his entire 15-year (1922–36) career with the Giants. A lifetime .291 hitter, the righthand-batting shortstop topped the .300 mark six times while contributing some of the best infield defense in the National League. His most productive season at the plate was 1929 when he hit .294 with 21 home runs, 94 runs batted in, and 92 runs scored. In 1934 he batted in 101 runs. Jackson selects:

1B—BILL TERRY
2B—ROGERS HORNSBY
3B—PIE TRAYNOR
SS—JOE CRONIN
OF—JOE DiMAGGIO
OF—MICKEY MANTLE
OF—STAN MUSIAL
C—MICKEY COCHRANE
RP—WALTER JOHNSON
LP—CARL HUBBELL

Toughest Pitcher: Charlie Root.

Root, who died in 1970, was tough on more batters than Jackson. In his 17-year career with the Browns (1923) and Cubs (1926–41), he won 201 games against 160 losses. The righthander's finest season was 1927, when he led the league with 26 wins.

Strongest Team: 1927 Yankees.

LARRY JANSEN

Jansen was a mainstay of the Giants pitching staff in the late 1940's and early 1950's. He led the National League in wins in the pennant-winning 1951 season with 23, and topped all NL pitchers in won-lost percentage (.808, 21–5) in his rookie year of 1947. His career record with the Giants (1947–54) and Reds (1956) was 122–89, with a 3.78 ERA. Jansen's choices:

1B—WHITEY LOCKMAN
2B—RED SCHOENDIENST
3B—KEN BOYER
SS—ROY McMILLAN
OF—WILLIE MAYS
OF—STAN MUSIAL
OF—DEL ENNIS
 C—ROY CAMPANELLA
RP—SAL MAGLIE
LP—WARREN SPAHN

Toughest Batters: "Del Ennis hit a ton off me, but the one who wore me out was Hank Greenberg, even though he only played in the National League one year. Later he told me how he used to set me up. He knew I had a great curve and he knew that I would throw that curve whenever I had two strikes on him. He was just smarter than I was."

Most Underrated: McMillan. "When I went over to Cincinnati for six weeks in 1956 I realized how much ground he could cover."

Strongest Team: 1951 Giants. "As a team we did so many things to help one another. It was a real team effort."

FERGIE JENKINS

Jenkins pitched for 19 seasons in both leagues with the Phillies (1965–66), Cubs (1966–73, 1982–83), Rangers (1974–75, 1978–81), and Red Sox (1976–77). He was a 20-game winner in six consecutive seasons (1967–72) with the Cubs and led the NL with 24 victories to win the Cy Young Award in 1971. He also led the AL in wins with 25 in 1974. He is the only pitcher in history to strike out more than 3000 batters (3192) and walk fewer than 1000 (997), a combination which gives him the second highest strikeouts to bases on balls ratio. Jenkins, who finished his career with 284 wins and 226 losses with a 3.34 ERA, selects:

1B—LEE MAY
2B—DAL MAXVILL
3B—DICK ALLEN
SS—MAURY WILLS
OF—BOB ALLISON
OF—JIM WYNN
OF—TOMMIE AGEE
C—JERRY GROTE
RP—PHIL REGAN
LP—JOHN HILLER

Deserves Cooperstown: Billy Williams.
Toughest Batter: Pete Rose.
Most Underrated: Williams.
Strongest Team: Giants of the 1960's.

DAVE JOHNSON

Second baseman Johnson batted .261 in 13 seasons with the Orioles (1965–72), Braves (1973–75), Phillies (1977–78), and Cubs (1978). After contributing mightily to Baltimore pennants in the late 1960's and 1970's, he moved over to the National League where he won Comeback Player of the Year honors in 1973 for belting 43 home runs and 25 doubles, driving in 99 runs, walking 81 times, and averaging .270. (The 43 homers gave him the all-time power mark for second basemen with Rogers Hornsby.) After being released by the Braves in 1975, he wound his way to Japan for a couple of years, subsequently returning in 1977 to Philadelphia where he became the first player ever to hit two pinch-grand slams in one season. Johnson, who has been managing the Mets since 1984, prefers:

```
1B—KEITH HERNANDEZ
2B—JOE MORGAN
3B—BROOKS ROBINSON
SS—CAL RIPKEN
OF—FRANK ROBINSON
OF—MICKEY MANTLE
OF—HANK AARON
 C—GARY CARTER
RP—BOB GIBSON or DWIGHT GOODEN
LP—STEVE CARLTON or SANDY KOUFAX
```

Toughest Pitcher: Bruce Sutter.
Most Underrated: Paul Blair.
Strongest Teams: 1969–71 Orioles, 1977–78 Phillies.
Comments: ''There seemed to be a lot of raised eyebrows when I hit all those homers in Atlanta, but in 1971, when I was still with Baltimore, I think I would've hit just as many if I hadn't gotten hurt. It was around that time that I stopped being a defensive hitter, going to right field all the time. Certainly, I never thought of that year with the Braves as any kind of fluke.''

CLEON JONES

Jones, one of baseball's rare righthanded batters who threw from the left side, batted .281 over 12 years (1963, 1965–75) with the Mets and a final season (1976) with the White Sox. The clutch-hitting outfielder's single finest year was 1969, when he led the "Miracle Mets" to the World Championship with a .340 average that included 25 doubles, 92 runs scored, and 75 runs driven in. Jones, whose key hits in the final two months of the 1973 season helped produce another New York pennant, chooses:

> 1B—WILLIE McCOVEY
> 2B—BILL MAZEROSKI
> 3B—KEN BOYER
> SS—ERNIE BANKS
> OF—HANK AARON
> OF—WILLIE MAYS
> OF—ROBERTO CLEMENTE
> C—JOHNNY BENCH
> RP—TOM SEAVER
> LP—SANDY KOUFAX

Deserves Cooperstown: Billy Williams.
Toughest Pitchers: Koufax and Bob Gibson.
Most Underrated: Williams and Jerry Grote.
Strongest Teams: 1969–70 Orioles, Pirates of the late 1960's and early 1970's. "The Orioles didn't have any weaknesses. I know most people think the Big Red Machine teams in Cincinnati were the best in those days, but they had nothing over those Clemente-Mazeroski-Stargell teams. The Pirates also had better pitchers than the Reds."

BUCK JORDAN

Jordan, a righthanded throwing, lefty swinging first baseman, played for the Giants (1927, 1929), Senators (1931), Braves (1932–37), Reds (1937–38), and Phillies (1938). He batted as high as .323 (with 66 RBI's) in 1936, and finished his career with a .299 average. Jordan's selections are:

1B—BILL TERRY
2B—ROGERS HORNSBY
3B—PIE TRAYNOR
SS—JOE CRONIN
OF—BABE RUTH
OF—JOE DiMAGGIO
OF—MEL OTT
C—GABBY HARTNETT
RP—DIZZY DEAN
LP—CARL HUBBELL

Deserves Cooperstown: Ernie Lombardi.
Toughest Pitcher: Hubbell.
Most Underrated: Lloyd Waner.
Strongest Team: ''The Gas House Gang St. Louis Cardinals.''
Comments: ''I think Ruth had more natural ability than any other ballplayer. With the playing records of the above, I wonder what the salaries of this group would be.''

JIM KAAT

Lefthander Kaat, the most durable pitcher in the history of big league baseball, compiled a record of 283–237 over an astonishing 25 years with the Senators-Twins (1959–73), White Sox (1973–75), Phillies (1976–79), Yankees (1979–80), and Cardinals (1980–83). His marks include winning 20 games three times and placing sixth on the list of game appearances by a pitcher. His finest season was 1966 when he posted a record of 25–13 (2.75 ERA) for the Twins. Kaat, whose fielding prowess earned him a Gold Glove 16 times in his career, likes:

1B—KEITH HERNANDEZ
2B—BOBBY RICHARDSON
3B—BROOKS ROBINSON
SS—OZZIE SMITH
OF—PETE ROSE
OF—MICKEY MANTLE
OF—GEORGE HENDRICK
C—THURMAN MUNSON
RP—DEAN CHANCE
LP—STEVE CARLTON

Toughest Batter: Al Kaline.
Most Underrated: Tony Oliva.
Strongest Team: Yankees of the early 1960's.
Comments: "I'd also want Harmon Killebrew as a designated hitter and Bruce Sutter as a reliever."

AL KALINE

Kaline, a Hall of Fame member since 1980, hit .297 with 399 home runs in 22 years (1953–74) for the Tigers. Among the righthand-hitting outfielder's numerous offensive accomplishments were collecting 3007 hits during his career; leading the American League in batting (1955), hits (1955), slugging percentage (1959), and doubles (1961). His best years were undoubtedly 1955 (27 home runs, 102 runs batted in, 121 runs scored, .340) and 1956 (27 home runs, 128 runs batted in, 96 runs scored, .314). Kaline, who also won ten Gold Gloves, chooses:

1B—HARMON KILLEBREW
2B—NELLIE FOX
3B—BROOKS ROBINSON
SS—LUIS APARICIO
OF—FRANK ROBINSON
OF—MICKEY MANTLE
OF—CARL YASTRZEMSKI
C—YOGI BERRA
RP—BOB LEMON
LP—MICKEY LOLICH

Toughest Pitchers: Lemon, Early Wynn, and Nolan Ryan. "I would distinguish between Lemon and Wynn, on the one hand, and Ryan, on the other, however. I considered the first two the toughest pitchers in a period when I was a good hitter. By the time Ryan came into the league I was well past it."

Most Underrated: Aparicio and Norm Cash.

Strongest Team: 1984 Tigers.

WILLIE KAMM

Kamm was a slick fielding third baseman for the White Sox (1923–31) and Indians (1931–35). He impressed everyone by starting a groundball triple play against the Giants in spring training of his rookie year. But he could also handle a bat. His lifetime average of .281 includes marks of .292 (1923), .294 (1926), .308 (1928), and .290 (1931). Never a power hitter, he did stroke 30 or more two-base hits seven times and 10 or more three-base hits three times. Kamm selects:

1B—LOU GEHRIG
2B—CHARLIE GEHRINGER
3B—OSSIE BLUEGE
SS—JOE CRONIN
OF—BABE RUTH
OF—TY COBB
OF—AL SIMMONS
C—MICKEY COCHRANE
RP—GEORGE EARNSHAW
LP—LEFTY GROVE

Toughest Pitcher: Earnshaw.
Comments: ''I only played in the American League so my opinions are biased toward that league and my best team includes only players from my day.''

GEORGE KELL

Kell, who was inducted into Cooperstown in 1983, had a 15-year American League career that included stints with the Athletics (1943–46), Tigers (1946–52), Red Sox (1952–54), White Sox (1954–56), and Orioles (1956–57). A lifetime .306 batter, he won the AL batting title in 1949 with a .343 mark and hit at least .300 for eight consecutive seasons between 1946 and 1953. He also led the league in both hits and doubles in 1950 and 1951. Kell's choices:

1B—MICKEY VERNON
2B—BOBBY DOERR
3B—BROOKS ROBINSON
SS—LUIS APARICIO
OF—JOE DiMAGGIO
OF—TED WILLIAMS
OF—MICKEY MANTLE
C—YOGI BERRA
RP—BOB LEMON
LP—HAL NEWHOUSER

Deserve Cooperstown: Newhouser and Phil Rizzuto.

Toughest Pitchers: Lemon, "followed by Bob Feller and the entire Cleveland staff of the early 1950's."

Most Underrated: Gil McDougald.

Strongest Teams: "The 1950 Tigers were the best team I ever played with and the Yankees of that era were the toughest to play against."

Comments: "I think I played in the very best of times because we had only sixteen teams. Individually, the players might not have been better than those today, but we didn't have expansion diluting the leagues as a whole either."

CHARLIE KELLER

Keller was a stocky lefthand-hitting outfielder for the Yankees (1939–43, 1945–49, 1952) and Tigers (1950–51) with a keen eye and considerable power. He walked more than 100 times in five different seasons, leading the AL twice. And he hit over 20 homers in every season in which he played over 100 games. His lifetime average was .286 (with a high of .334 as a rookie), and he hit 189 homers. He missed all of 1944 and much of 1945 while in the merchant marines, and suffered a crippling back injury in 1947 that limited him to part-time duty and pinch-hitting in his last six seasons. Keller batted .306, hit five home runs, and drove in 18 runs in 19 World Series games. In the 1939 Series against the Reds he pounded Cincinnati pitchers for a .438 average, three homers, and six RBI's in four games. Keller's choices are:

1B—STAN MUSIAL
2B—JOE GORDON
3B—BROOKS ROBINSON
SS—JOE CRONIN
OF—TED WILLIAMS
OF—JOE DiMAGGIO
OF—MICKEY MANTLE
C—BILL DICKEY
RP—BOB FELLER
LP—WHITEY FORD

Toughest Pitcher: "When you're in a streak you can hit any of them."

Comments: "For four or five years there never was a second baseman like Gordon. Phil Rizzuto, when he first came up, was right up there with the best of them."

KEN KELTNER

Keltner, a .276 hitter as a third baseman with the Indians from 1937 to 1949 and the Red Sox in 1950, was a steady if unspectacular star performer. He was spectacular, however, the day he made two circus catches to rob Joe DiMaggio of two hits and end his 56-game hitting streak. His highest season batting average was .325 in 1939 and the most home runs he hit in a season was 31 in 1948. He had two 100-plus RBI seasons and eight seasons with more than 10 home runs. He appeared in the 1948 World Series. Keltner's choices are:

1B—LOU GEHRIG
2B—CHARLIE GEHRINGER
3B—RED ROLFE
SS—LOU BOUDREAU
OF—JOE DiMAGGIO
OF—TED WILLIAMS
OF—TOMMY HENRICH
C—BILL DICKEY
RP—TED LYONS
LP—LEFTY GOMEZ

Deserve Cooperstown: Mel Harder and Joe Gordon.
Most Underrated: Gordon.
Strongest Team: 1936–39 Yankees. "They didn't make mistakes."

DON KESSINGER

Kessinger, a switch-hitting shortstop with the Cubs (1964–75), Cardinals (1976–77), and White Sox (1977–79), batted .252 over 16 seasons. His best year was 1969, when he batted .273, scored 109 runs, hit 38 doubles, and won the first of two successive Gold Gloves. Kessinger, who also managed the White Sox in 1979, selects:

 1B—ERNIE BANKS
 2B—JOE MORGAN or GLENN BECKERT
 3B—RON SANTO or BROOKS ROBINSON
 SS—LUIS APARICIO
 OF—BILLY WILLIAMS or WILLIE STARGELL
 OF—WILLIE MAYS
 OF—HANK AARON or ROBERTO CLEMENTE
  C—JOHNNY BENCH
 RP—BOB GIBSON, TOM SEAVER, JUAN
   MARICHAL, or DON DRYSDALE
 LP—SANDY KOUFAX or STEVE CARLTON

Toughest Pitcher: Gaylord Perry. "He had that 'super sinker.' You know what I mean. He never blew me away. I just kept beating the ball into the ground right at infielders."

Most Underrated: Williams. "I don't know why, probably because he was never on a pennant winner."

Strongest Team: 1969 Cubs. "We were as good as I ever saw that year. But it was the best of times and the worst of times. We had the biggest thrills and the worst disappointments—for us and for the fans. And we are still a closely knit group, perhaps closer because we didn't win."

Comments: "Everybody knew that Santo could hit, but I never realized how good a defensive third baseman he was until he was gone. Then everyone started saying that I had lost range. I hadn't lost any range. It was just that now I had to get to balls I'd never had to worry about before because Bill Madlock was on my right and not Ronnie."

HARMON KILLEBREW

The greatest righthanded home run hitter in the history of the American League, Killebrew was admitted into the Hall of Fame in 1984 on the strength of a 22-year (1954–75) career that saw him accumulate 573 home runs and a .256 average. His numerous batting accomplishments for the Senators-Twins between 1954 and 1974 include leading the league in home runs six times, in runs batted in three times, and in slugging percentage twice. The first baseman-third baseman-outfielder hit at least 40 home runs eight times, drove in 100 runs nine times, and drew at least 100 walks seven times. His single best season was 1969, when he was named American League MVP for clubbing 49 homers, driving in 140 runs, scoring 106 runs, walking 145 times, and batting .276. He also ranks third behind Babe Ruth and Ralph Kiner for the best ratio of home runs per at bats. Killebrew, who spent his final season as a designated hitter for the Royals, chooses:

    1B—VIC POWER
    2B—NELLIE FOX
    3B—BROOKS ROBINSON
    SS—LUIS APARICIO
    OF—TED WILLIAMS
    OF—MICKEY MANTLE
    OF—AL KALINE
    C—YOGI BERRA
    RP—JIM PALMER
    LP—WHITEY FORD

Deserves Cooperstown: Fox.
Toughest Pitcher: Stu Miller.
Most Underrated: Cesar Tovar. "The man was a dream to hit behind. A great leadoff man."
Strongest Team: 1969 Twins.

RALPH KINER

Kiner, elected to the Hall of Fame in 1975, played only 10 seasons, but he hit 369 home runs and led the NL or tied for the lead in homers in each of his first seven seasons (1946–52). For those seven seasons and part of an eighth, the big righthanded outfielder was the Pittsburgh franchise, which finished with a winning record only in that time. He also led the NL in RBI's once, in walks three times, and in slugging three times. His best season was 1949, when he batted .310, hit 54 homers, drove in 127 runs, and had a .658 slugging average. He closed his career with a lifetime .279 average after a season and a half with the Cubs (1953–54) and one year with the Indians (1955). Kiner picks:

1B—TED KLUSZEWSKI
2B—JACKIE ROBINSON
3B—EDDIE MATHEWS
SS—ERNIE BANKS
OF—WILLIE MAYS
OF—HANK AARON
OF—RALPH KINER
C—JOHNNY BENCH
RP—EWELL BLACKWELL
LP—WARREN SPAHN

Deserves Cooperstown: Billy Williams.
Toughest Pitcher: Blackwell. "His delivery was unorthodox. He looked like a man falling out of a tree. It was hard to pick the ball up and since you only have about two-fifths of a second to react, it was impossible to find the ball."
Most Underrated: Williams and Mickey Vernon. "Stars with bad teams never get the credit they deserve."
Strongest Team: Dodgers of the early 1950's.
Comments: "I want Banks as much for his spirit as for his bat. It's hard to pick Bench over Campanella, but I'd have to. I want Blackwell in his prime of course. And if I have to win one ball game with this team, then I want something to say about it so I'll put myself in there."

TED KLUSZEWSKI

Kluszewski, a muscular lefthand-hitting first baseman, averaged a solid .298 over 15 years with the Reds (1947–57), Pirates (1958–59), White Sox (1959–60), and Angels (1961). His batting achievements include leading the National League in both home runs and runs batted in in 1954, leading in hits in 1955, clubbing at least 40 homers three straight years (1953–55), and driving in 100 runs five times. His best year was 1954, when he batted .326 with 49 home runs, 141 runs batted in, and 104 runs scored. Kluszewski, who rarely struck out despite his power-hitting image, likes:

1B—STAN MUSIAL
2B—BILL MAZEROSKI
3B—BOB ELLIOTT
SS—ROY McMILLAN
OF—TED WILLIAMS
OF—WILLIE MAYS
OF—DUKE SNIDER
C—ROY CAMPANELLA
RP—ROBIN ROBERTS
LP—WARREN SPAHN

Toughest Pitcher: Roberts.
Most Underrated: McMillan.
Strongest Team: Dodgers of the 1950's.

MARK KOENIG

Koenig was the shortstop on the great New York Yankees team of 1927. (Along with Ray Morehart and George Pipgras, he is one of only three surviving members of that fabled team.) He played 12 years in the majors (1925–36), appearing also with the Tigers, Cubs, Reds, and Giants. A lifetime .279 hitter, Koenig was one of very few players to appear in the World Series with three different clubs (Yankees, 1926–28, Cubs, 1932, and Giants, 1936). Koenig's selections are:

> 1B—LOU GEHRIG
> 2B—ROGERS HORNSBY
> 3B—JOE DUGAN
> SS—LUKE APPLING
> OF—BABE RUTH
> OF—TY COBB
> OF—HARRY HEILMANN
> C—MICKEY COCHRANE
> RP—GEORGE UHLE
> LP—HERB PENNOCK

Deserve Cooperstown: Bob Meusel and Tony Lazzeri.

Toughest Pitcher: Uhle. "George had a wonderful fastball, a cracking good curve, a wicked change-up, and good control. If you look up his record, you'll see that he beat us more often than not." Uhle had a 200-166 record and a 3.99 ERA in 17 seasons (1919-34, 1936), primarily with the Tigers and Indians.

Most Underrated: Meusel.

Strongest Team: "They all pick the 1927 Yankees as the greatest team of all time, but I have to mention those Athletics of 1929, 1930, and 1931. They were tough."

Comments: "My greatest thrill in baseball was joining the Yankees and being a teammate of Babe Ruth, who was just a big overgrown kid."

ED KRANEPOOL

Kranepool, a lefty-swinging first baseman-outfielder, spent his entire 18-year career (1962–79) with the Mets after joining the team in its first year of existence. A lifetime .261 batter who topped the .300 mark twice, he spent most of his later years as a pinch-hitter, leading the National League in safeties in that category in 1974. Kranepool's choices:

1B—ORLANDO CEPEDA
2B—PETE ROSE
3B—MIKE SCHMIDT
SS—ERNIE BANKS
OF—WILLIE MAYS
OF—MICKEY MANTLE
OF—FRANK ROBINSON
C—JOHNNY BENCH
RP—JUAN MARICHAL
LP—SANDY KOUFAX

Deserve Cooperstown: Nellie Fox and Phil Rizzuto.
Toughest Pitcher: Curt Simmons.
Most Underrated: Billy Williams.
Strongest Team: Braves of late 1960's. "It's not a slight of the Mets of 1969 to say that the Braves around the same period were stronger on paper. They had Hank Aaron, Rico Carty, and all those other hitters capable of getting up there and smacking at least twenty to twenty-five homers a year. There just never seemed to be a big enough lead against them."
Comments: "I pick Marichal narrowly over Tom Seaver."

TONY KUBEK

Kubek, a Yankee for all of his nine years (1957–65) in the majors, batted .266 and played excellent shortstop for most of his career, although he also filled in at third and in the outfield. As Rookie of the Year in 1957 he played all three positions. A lefthanded hitter, he had his best season in 1960, when he batted .273 with 14 homers and 62 RBI's. He batted only .240 in six World Series, but he hit two home runs in the third game of the 1957 Series, the first ever in his hometown of Milwaukee. In the seventh game of the 1960 Series Kubek was hospitalized when he was struck in the throat by a ground ball off the bat of Bill Virdon that took a bad hop and cost the Yankees a world championship. Kubek, currently a network broadcaster, selects:

      1B—STAN MUSIAL
      2B—RED SCHOENDIENST
      3B—BROOKS ROBINSON
      SS—LUIS APARICIO
      OF—MICKEY MANTLE
      OF—WILLIE MAYS
      OF—HANK AARON or TED WILLIAMS
      C—YOGI BERRA
      RP—DEAN CHANCE
      LP—HERB SCORE

Deserve Cooperstown: Schoendienst, Marvin Miller, and Bowie Kuhn.
Toughest Pitcher: Chance.
Most Underrated: Roger Maris and Clete Boyer.
Strongest Team: 1960–61 Yankees.

HARVEY KUENN

One of the finest contact hitters of his era, Kuenn batted .303 over 15 years with the Tigers (1952–59), Indians (1960), Giants (1961–65), Cubs (1965–66), and Phillies (1966). A shortstop when he was named Rookie of the Year in 1953 but later converted to the outfield, he led the American League in hits four times and in doubles three times, rising to special heights in 1959 when he won the batting championship with a .353 average that included 42 doubles. Kuenn, who managed the Brewers into the World Series in 1982, likes:

1B—WILLIE McCOVEY
2B—NELLIE FOX
3B—EDDIE MATHEWS
SS—LUIS APARICIO
OF—HANK AARON
OF—WILLIE MAYS
OF—MICKEY MANTLE
C—YOGI BERRA
RP—ALLIE REYNOLDS
LP—SANDY KOUFAX

Deserves Cooperstown: Reynolds.
Toughest Pitchers: Reynolds and Koufax.
Most Underrated: Ray Boone. "He was one of the best power hitters of my day, but he had two things going against him. The first was that they were always moving him around—from catching to shortstop to third base and then to first. The second thing was that he was forced to replace George Kell in Detroit, and Kell had been a very popular player."
Strongest Team: Yankees of the 1950's.

CLEM LABINE

Although others like Joe Black and Jim Hughes may have had single great seasons, Labine was the most constant of Brooklyn's relief aces in the Boys of Summer era. With the Dodgers from 1950 to 1960, and then briefly with the Tigers, Pirates, and Mets, the 13-year big league veteran won 77, lost 56, and saved 96. His best years were in 1956 and 1957, when he led the National League in saves, and in 1955, when he led in pitching appearances. An occasional starter in crucial situations (the second game of the 1951 playoffs, the next to last game of the 1956 season with the pennant on the line), he finished in double figures in wins three times. Labine selects:

1B—GIL HODGES
2B—JACKIE ROBINSON
3B—BILLY COX
SS—PEE WEE REESE
OF—HANK AARON
OF—WILLIE MAYS
OF—DUKE SNIDER
C—ROY CAMPANELLA
RP—DON DRYSDALE
LP—SANDY KOUFAX

Deserve Cooperstown: Nellie Fox and Carl Furillo. "I've never quite been able to figure out the voting procedure at Cooperstown. For instance, how can people who never saw a Nellie Fox play decide whether or not he was great, good, or mediocre? Just by looking at numbers? I don't think so. But of course if that *is* the only criterion, then it's inevitable that home run stats are going to leap out at you."

Toughest Batters: Aaron and Mays.

Most Underrated: Bill Virdon and Bobby Thomson.

Strongest Teams: Dodgers and Yankees of the 1950's.

LARRY LAJOIE

Lajoie, elected to the Hall of Fame in 1937, was the greatest second baseman before Rogers Hornsby. His career with the Phillies, Athletics, and Indians spanned 21 seasons (1896–1916) during which he batted .339. His .422 average with the A's in 1901 is the highest ever recorded by an American Leaguer and second only to Hornsby's .424 in 1924. He also led the AL in batting in 1903 and 1904; in doubles four times; in hits four times; and in homers once. He managed the Indians for five seasons (1905–09). Lajoie's selections:

    1B—HAL CHASE
    2B—ROGERS HORNSBY
    3B—BILL BRADLEY
    SS—HONUS WAGNER
    OF—TY COBB
    OF—GINGER BEAUMONT
    OF—JIMMY McALEER
     C—MICKEY COCHRANE
    RP—CHRISTY MATHEWSON or WALTER JOHNSON

Beaumont and McAleer are truly idiosyncratic choices. The former, a forgotten star with the Pirates, Braves, and Cubs (1899–1910), batted .311 in his career and led the National League in hitting with a .357 average in 1902. McAleer, only a .255 hitter, was a superlative fielder who sparked the old National League Cleveland Spiders in the 1890's.

EDDIE LAKE

Lake was a nimble fielding shortstop who rarely hit for a high average (.231 lifetime) but who frequently ended up among league leaders in runs scored because of all the walks he drew. Originally a member of the Cardinals (1939–41), he had his most productive seasons when he moved to the American League to play for the Red Sox (1943–45) and Tigers (1946–50). His best year was for Boston in 1945 when he hit .279 with 11 home runs, 27 doubles, and 106 walks. In 1946 he drew more than 100 walks and scored more than 100 runs, and in 1947 he again strolled to first base more than 100 times despite a batting average no higher than .211. Lake's choices:

1B—LOU GEHRIG
2B—BOBBY DOERR
3B—KEN KELTNER
SS—FRANK CROSETTI
OF—TED WILLIAMS
OF—JOE DiMAGGIO
OF—CHARLIE KELLER
C—BILL DICKEY
RP—BOB FELLER
LP—LEFTY GROVE

Deserves Cooperstown: Ernie Lombardi. "It's a rotten shame that Lombardi hasn't been elected to the Hall of Fame. Some people say he was slow, but so what? To me that means all those .300 years he had were due to real hits, not dribblers he beat out. And he was a great defensive catcher. The only thing keeping him out is politics."

Toughest Pitcher: Feller.

Most Underrated: Lombardi.

Strongest Team: Cardinals of early 1940's.

MAX LANIER

Lanier compiled a record of 108–82 and an earned run average of 3.01 over a 14-year major league career that began with the Cardinals in 1938. After the 1946 season he jumped from St. Louis to the Mexican League, not returning to the majors until 1949. Three mediocre seasons with the Cardinals were followed by even worse years with the Giants and Browns. Lanier's best seasons were 1943, when he won 15 games and had a 1.90 ERA, and 1944, when he won 17 and came in with a 2.65 ERA. His picks:

1B—JOHNNY MIZE
2B—RED SCHOENDIENST
3B—BOB ELLIOTT
SS—MARTY MARION
OF—TED WILLIAMS
OF—WILLIE MAYS
OF—STAN MUSIAL
C—GABBY HARTNETT
RP—DIZZY DEAN
LP—CARL HUBBELL

Toughest Batter: Bob Elliott.
Most Underrated: Terry Moore.
Strongest Teams: "The toughest teams I ever saw were the Cardinals and Dodgers of 1942. As far as comparing that era with this one, I'd have to say that there are as many good individual players around now as then but that they're spread thinner over a lot more teams. I also think some of the players today are overpaid. You can't blame them for it, but they are in a lot of cases."

DON LARSEN

Larsen, a sometimes overpowering fastball pitcher, is remembered today almost exclusively for one game—the fifth game of the 1956 World Series in which he pitched the only perfect game in World Series history. The big righthander pitched for the Browns-Orioles (1953–54), Yankees (1955–59), Athletics (1960–61), White Sox (1961), Giants (1962–64), Colts .45's-Astros(1964–65), Orioles again (1965), and Cubs (1967). He won 81 while losing 91, but posted a 3.78 ERA in his career. In World Series play with the Yankees and Giants he won four and lost two. Larsen's selections are:

1B—MICKEY VERNON
2B—BOBBY AVILA
3B—ANDY CAREY
SS—GIL McDOUGALD
OF—MICKEY MANTLE
OF—AL KALINE
OF—WILLIE MAYS
C—YOGI BERRA
RP—DON DRYSDALE
LP—WHITEY FORD

Deserves Cooperstown: "Well *I* don't. The perfect game was just my day. We all have to have one day."

Toughest Batters: Harvey Kuenn, Billy Goodman, and Pete Runnels. "I always had fair luck against the big guys like Ted Williams. It was the guys who just put the ball in play who drove me nuts."

Most Underrated: Nellie Fox.

Strongest Teams: Yankees of the 1950's, 1956 Dodgers, and 1957–58 Braves.

Comments: "I might put Jim Davenport at third. And how can you leave Williams out of the outfield? For other pitchers you have to take Sandy Koufax and Jim Bunning. And Jack Sanford; nobody was better than Sanford in 1962."

FRANK LARY

Lary compiled a 128–116 record over a 12-year career with the Tigers (1954–64), Mets (1964), Braves (1964), Mets again (1965), and White Sox (1965). Known for his special ability for defeating the power-laden Yankees, the right-hander had two 20-win seasons—1956, when he was 21–13 with 20 complete games and a 3.15 ERA, and 1961, when he was 23–9 with 22 complete games and a 3.24 ERA. Lary selects:

```
1B—LARRY DOBY
2B—FRANK BOLLING
3B—BROOKS ROBINSON
SS—LUIS APARICIO
OF—MICKEY MANTLE
OF—AL KALINE
OF—WILLIE MAYS
 C—JOHNNY BENCH
RP—ROBIN ROBERTS
LP—WARREN SPAHN
```

Toughest Batters: Mantle and Stan Musial.
Most Underrated: Kaline.
Strongest Team: Yankees of the 1950's and early 1960's.
Comments: "The whole Hall of Fame business has to be rethought. There are too many there who don't belong there. Mediocre pitchers with good clubs get there, but good pitchers with mediocre clubs don't. In my time, for instance, there was a lefthander who won regularly because of the team he was on. Today he's in Cooperstown, but if he'd been on the Washington Senators he wouldn't be. Same thing with managers. Casey Stengel was great because he managed the Yankees, but in my opinion Al Lopez and Paul Richards were far better."

COOKIE LAVAGETTO

Lavagetto's dramatic 1947 World Series hit off Bill Bevens
has tended to overshadow his solid 10-year career as a third
baseman for the Pirates (1934–36) and Dodgers (1937–41,
1946–47). A lifetime .269 hitter, he had his finest season in
1939, when he batted .300, drove in 87 runs, and scored 93.
He managed the Washington-Minnesota franchise from 1957
to 1961. Lavagetto's choices:

> 1B—BILL TERRY
> 2B—BILLY HERMAN
> 3B—STAN HACK
> SS—PEE WEE REESE
> OF—ROBERTO CLEMENTE
> OF—PAUL WANER
> OF—JOE MEDWICK
> C—ERNIE LOMBARDI
> RP—DIZZY DEAN
> LP—SANDY KOUFAX

Deserves Cooperstown: Lombardi.
Toughest Pitchers: Dean, Bill Lee, and Bucky Walters.
Lee, with a 169–157 record in 14 seasons (1934–47), pitched
for the Cubs, Phillies, and Browns. In 1938 he was 22–9, with
a 2.66 ERA and nine shutouts.
Most Underrated: Hack.
Strongest Teams: 1949–64 Yankees, 1952–56 Dodgers.
Comments: "There are little things you always remember
about great players. Terry, for example, was an artist at pick-
ing up a grounder and throwing out a runner at home or third.
Nobody hit behind a runner better than Jackie Robinson. And
Koufax was not only the greatest pitcher I ever saw, but I
don't think he ever lost in the final weeks of the season. Once
September came, he seemed to be invulnerable."

VERN LAW

Righthander Law spent his entire 16-year (1950–51, 1954–67) career with the Pirates, winning 162 and losing 147 for a franchise that he helped convert from one of the worst in baseball history to World Series victors. In the championship year of 1960 he was particularly brilliant, contributing 18 complete games with his 20–9 record and winning the Cy Young Award. In 1965 he posted a mark of 17–9 with a 2.15 ERA. Law's selections are:

> 1B—GIL HODGES
> 2B—BILL MAZEROSKI
> 3B—BROOKS ROBINSON
> SS—PEE WEE REESE
> OF—WILLIE MAYS
> OF—ROBERTO CLEMENTE
> OF—DUKE SNIDER
> C—ROY CAMPANELLA
> RP—BOB GIBSON
> LP—SANDY KOUFAX

Deserves Cooperstown: Mazeroski. "The thing about Mazeroski was that, as great as he was in the field, he had a bad period in the beginning as a hitter because Bobby Bragan would always yank him for a pinch-hitter in a key situation. Then Danny Murtaugh came in to manage the Pirates and things changed. There was a game when Maz started looking over his shoulder to the bench from the on-deck circle, expecting to be waved in for a hitter. But Murtaugh told him, 'No, sir. You're the one who has to drive in the run.' And from then on Maz started to become a great clutch hitter."

Toughest Batter: Mays.

Strongest Team: Dodgers of the 1950's.

THORNTON LEE

Lee was the lefthanded ace of the White Sox in the late 1930's and early 1940's. He came to the Chisox (1937–47) from the Indians (1933–36) and played one final season (1948) with the Giants. Lee had several winning seasons with the Sox and in 1941 was truly exceptional, winning 22 and losing 11 and leading the American League in ERA (2.37). Lifetime he was 117–124 with 3.56 ERA. Lee's choices are:

                1B—LOU GEHRIG
                2B—CHARLIE GEHRINGER
                3B—JIMMIE FOXX
                SS—LUKE APPLING
                OF—BABE RUTH
                OF—JOE DiMAGGIO
                OF—TED WILLIAMS
                 C—BILL DICKEY
                RP—TED LYONS
                LP—LEFTY GROVE

Deserve Cooperstown: Wally Berger, Mel Harder, Charlie Grimm, and Jimmy Dykes.

Toughest Batter: Rogers Hornsby.

Most Underrated: Rollie Hemsley and Floyd Baker. Hemsley caught almost 1500 games for seven teams in both leagues between 1928 and 1947. He batted .262 and was a superior defensive catcher. Baker was a lefty swinging AL third baseman from 1943 to 1955. He batted .251 in his career.

Strongest Team: 1936–67 Yankees.

BOB LEMON

Lemon, a Hall of Famer since 1976, played his entire career (1941–42, 1946–58) with the Indians. A third baseman before World War II, Lemon switched to the mound in 1946 and went on to win 207 while losing only 128 for a .618 won-lost percentage. His lifetime ERA was 3.23. A 20-game winner six times, he led the AL in victories three times, complete games five times, innings pitched three times, strikeouts once, and shutouts once. In 1954, his best season, he was 23–7 with a 2.72 ERA. In the 1948 World Series he won two games and in the 1954 Series he lost two. Lemon, who later managed the Yankees to a pennant and also piloted the Royals and White Sox, selects:

1B—LOU GEHRIG
2B—JOE GORDON
3B—KEN KELTNER
SS—LOU BOUDREAU
OF—TED WILLIAMS
OF—JOE DiMAGGIO
OF—TOMMY HENRICH
C—JIM HEGAN
RP—ALLIE REYNOLDS
LP—WHITEY FORD

Toughest Batter: Minnie Minoso. ''It was the way he stood on top of the plate.''
Most Underrated: Keltner.

JIM LEMON

Lemon spent 12 years menacing major league pitchers with his hefty righthanded cuts that produced 164 homers and as many as 138 strikeouts in a season. Lemon played for the Indians in 1950 and 1953, went to the Senators in 1954, began playing regularly in 1956, moved with the franchise to Minnesota in 1961, and spent his last season (1963) with the Phillies and White Sox as well as the Twins. Lemon's highest season average was .284 in 1957. (Lifetime he was .262.) His highest season total in homers was 38 in 1960. He managed the Texas Rangers in 1968. Lemon's choices are:

1B—HARMON KILLEBREW
2B—NELLIE FOX
3B—BROOKS ROBINSON
SS—LUIS APARICIO
OF—TED WILLIAMS
OF—JOE DiMAGGIO
OF—MICKEY MANTLE
C—JIM HEGAN
RP—BOB LEMON
LP—HERB SCORE

Toughest Pitcher: Jim Bunning. "I couldn't see the ball off him. He had these long arms and legs and he threw sort of sidearm and jumped in behind the ball."

Most Underrated: Roy Sievers.

Strongest Team: Yankees of the 1950's and early 1960's.

BUCK LEONARD

Leonard, called the Lou Gehrig of the Negro Leagues, entered professional baseball in 1933. He played for the Homstead Grays for 17 years—in Pittsburgh until 1938 and in Washington, D.C., in 1939 and after. He also spent five more years in the Mexican League after the Negro Leagues had given most of their better, younger players to the major leagues. Leonard batted .355 in his career and was elected to the Hall of Fame in 1972. Leonard chooses:

        1B—JOHNNY WASHINGTON
        2B—SAMMY HUGHES
        3B—RAY DANDRIDGE
        SS—WILLIE WELLS
        OF—FATS JENKINS
        OF—COOL PAPA BELL
        OF—BILL WRIGHT
         C—JOSH GIBSON
        RP—SATCHEL PAIGE
        LP—SLIM JONES

Deserve Cooperstown: Wells and Dandridge. "We're trying to get Dandridge in this year."

Strongest Team: 1935 Pittsburgh Crawfords. "They were the best team I have ever seen."

Comments: "Washington and Hughes played for the Baltimore Elite Giants, Dandridge and Wells were with the Newark Eagles, Jenkins was with the Black Yankees, Bell with the Crawfords, Wright with the Elite Giants, Gibson was with me on the Grays, Paige pitched for the Crawfords and later the Kansas City Monarchs, and Jones was with the Philadelphia Stars."

WHITEY LOCKMAN

Lockman, a .279 lefthand-hitting outfielder and first base-man for 15 years, was one of the key factors in the success of the Giants in the 1950's. He played left field for the Giants in 1945 and from 1947 to 1950. In 1951 he switched posi-tions with first baseman Monte Irvin; that switch plus the ad-dition of Willie Mays led to a pennant. Lockman lasted with the Giants into 1956, played for the Cardinals for the rest of that season, returned to the Giants for 1957, moved to San Francisco with them in 1958, split the 1959 season between the Orioles and the Reds, and ended his career for the latter team in 1960. His highest batting average was .301 in 1949 and he hit over 10 home runs six times. He later managed the Cubs from 1972 to 1974. Lockman's selections are:

> 1B—GIL HODGES
> 2B—JACKIE ROBINSON
> 3B—MIKE SCHMIDT
> SS—ERNIE BANKS
> OF—WILLIE MAYS
> OF—STAN MUSIAL
> OF—HANK AARON
> C—JOHNNY BENCH
> RP—EWELL BLACKWELL
> LP—SANDY KOUFAX

Toughest Pitcher: Curt Simmons.
Most Underrated: Bobby Thomson.
Strongest Teams: 1951 Giants, 1954 Indians.

MICKEY LOLICH

One of the most successful lefthanders in the history of the American League, Lolich compiled most of his 217–191 record in 13 seasons (1963–75) with the Tigers, closing out his career with the Mets (1976) and Padres (1978–79) in the National League. In 1971, he won 25 games with a 2.92 ERA, leading the league in wins, complete games (29), and strikeouts (308). In 1972 he came back to win another 22. Among the southpaw's other accomplishments was winning three games in the 1968 World Series against the Cardinals. He is currently in ninth place among all-time strikeout pitchers. Lolich chooses:

1B—ROD CAREW
2B—NELLIE FOX
3B—BROOKS ROBINSON
SS—OZZIE SMITH
OF—HANK AARON
OF—MICKEY MANTLE
OF—AL KALINE
C—JOHNNY BENCH
RP—GAYLORD PERRY
LP—STEVE CARLTON

Deserve Cooperstown: Fox, Perry, and Jim Palmer.
Toughest Batters: Robinson and Cesar Tovar.
Most Underrated: Mickey Stanley.
Strongest Team: 1972–74 Athletics.
Comments: ''The lineup above is of players I played with or played against. If I had to choose an all-star team of all time, I would still go with Robinson and Bench, but the rest of the team would be Lou Gehrig, Charlie Gehringer, Alan Trammell, Ted Williams, Joe DiMaggio, Willie Mays, Walter Johnson, and Warren Spahn.''

JIM LONBORG

Lonborg, a 6'5" righthander, was the mainstay of the pennant-winning 1967 Red Sox. That year he led the AL in wins with 22 and in strikeouts with 246, won the Cy Young Award, and won two and lost one in three World Series starts. Injuries plagued him after that season, but he played a total of 15 seasons with the Red Sox (1965–71), Brewers (1972), and Phillies (1973–79) and compiled a record of 157–137 with a 3.86 ERA. Lonborg picks:

1B—ROD CAREW
2B—JOE MORGAN
3B—BROOKS ROBINSON
SS—LUIS APARICIO
OF—CARL YASTRZEMSKI
OF—ROBERTO CLEMENTE
OF—MICKEY MANTLE
C—JOHNNY BENCH
RP—TOM SEAVER
LP—STEVE CARLTON

Deserve Cooperstown: Carew, Morgan, Bench, Seaver, and Carlton.
Toughest Batters: Tony Oliva and Dave Parker.
Most Underrated: Paul Blair.
Strongest Team: 1966 Orioles.

DALE LONG

Long holds one of baseball's most remarkable records. Between May 19 and May 28, 1956, the lefty first baseman played in eight games and hit a home run in each of those eight games. Long played 10 seasons in the major leagues with the Pirates (1951, 1955–57), Cardinals (1951), Cubs (1957–59), Giants (1960), Yankees (1960, 1962–63), and Senators (1961–62). A .267 lifetime hitter, he batted as high as .298 in 1957 and hit 20 or more homers in 1956, 1957, and 1958, with a high of 27, along with 91 RBI's, in 1956. He also tied for the NL lead with 13 triples in 1955. He appeared in two World Series, in 1960 and 1962, with the Yankees. Long's choices are:

> 1B—GIL HODGES or STAN MUSIAL
> 2B—BOBBY RICHARDSON
> 3B—BROOKS ROBINSON
> SS—TONY KUBEK
> OF—WILLIE MAYS
> OF—MICKEY MANTLE
> OF—TED WILLIAMS
> C—ROY CAMPANELLA
> RP—ROBIN ROBERTS
> LP—WHITEY FORD

Deserves Cooperstown: Ernie Lombardi.
Toughest Pitchers: Harvey Haddix and Ford.
Most Underrated: Roger Maris.
Strongest Teams: Dodgers of the 1950's, Yankees of the early 1960's.

ED LOPAT

Lopat was a clever lefthander who relied on breaking balls and offspeed pitches to baffle American League batters for 12 seasons, so much so that he earned the nickname "The Junkman." His lifetime record of 166–112 and 3.21 ERA was compiled with the White Sox (1944–47), Yankees (1948–55), and Orioles (1955). He won 21 games, his personal best, in 1951, and he led the AL in won-lost percentage (.800, 16–4) and ERA (2.42) in 1953. In five World Series (1949–53), he won four games and lost one. He managed the Athletics in 1963 and 1964 and was later KC's general manager. Lopat selects:

1B—WILLIE McCOVEY
2B—ROGERS HORNSBY
3B—EDDIE MATHEWS
SS—HONUS WAGNER
OF—BABE RUTH
OF—TED WILLIAMS
OF—JOE DiMAGGIO
C—BILL DICKEY
LP—WARREN SPAHN

Deserves Cooperstown: Ernie Lombardi.

Toughest Batters: Hoot Evers and Tom McBride. McBride played for the Red Sox and Senators from 1943 to 1948. He batted .275 over his six-year career.

Strongest Teams: "The strongest team I played against were the Dodgers of the late 1940's and early 1950's. The best I played with was the 1949 Yankee club."

AL LOPEZ

Lopez, enshrined in the Hall of Fame in 1977, was behind the plate in more major league games (1918) than any other catcher. He amassed this total over 19 seasons with the Dodgers (1928, 1930–35), Braves (1936–40), Pirates (1940–46), and Indians (1947). A lifetime .261 hitter, Lopez batted over .300 twice (.309 in 1930 and .301 in 1933). At the conclusion of his career he managed the Indians (1951–56) and White Sox (1957–65 and parts of 1968 and 1969). He was the only manager to finish ahead of the Yankees during the 1950's, winning pennants in 1954 (with the Indians) and 1959 (with the White Sox). Lopez, whose teams finished first or second every year from 1951 to 1959, chooses:

   1B—BILL TERRY
   2B—FRANKIE FRISCH or ROGERS HORNSBY
   3B—PIE TRAYNOR
   SS—GLENN WRIGHT
   OF—PAUL WANER or AL SIMMONS
   OF—TY COBB
   OF—BABE RUTH
    C—GABBY HARTNETT
   RP—DIZZY DEAN or DAZZY VANCE
   LP—CARL HUBBELL, LEFTY GROVE, or
       HERB PENNOCK

Toughest Pitchers: Bucky Walters, Hal Schumacher, and Ewell Blackwell. "Schumacher had this fast sinker, a heavy ball that bore into the batter."

Most Underrated: Wright and Babe Herman. "Herman was a decent first baseman and a decent outfielder. He had a bum rap with all that nonsense about being hit on the head or the shoulder by a fly ball. It made him look like a clown but he was a great hitter."

Comments: "Pennock was the most graceful pitcher I've ever seen. And Dickey and Cochrane are right behind Hartnett."

TURK LOWN

Although he finished his 11-year career (1951–62) with a mediocre 55–61 record, Lown will always be remembered as half of the bullpen partnership with Gerry Staley that brought the White Sox their last flag in 1959. The righthander reached Comiskey Park in 1958 after spending seven seasons with the crosstown Cubs and a few months with the Reds. While with the Cubs in 1957, he led the National League in appearances by a pitcher. In his banner 1959 season, he won nine against only two losses, while saving 15 other games and compiling a 2.89 ERA. Lown's choices:

1B—STAN MUSIAL
2B—NELLIE FOX
3B—BROOKS ROBINSON
SS—LUIS APARICIO
OF—HANK AARON
OF—WILLIE MAYS
OF—MICKEY MANTLE
C—ROY CAMPANELLA
RP—EARLY WYNN
LP—SANDY KOUFAX

Deserves Cooperstown: Fox.
Toughest Batter: Alvin Dark.
Most Underrated: Jim Landis.
Strongest Team: Dodgers of the 1950's.
Comments: ''The lineup above is players I played with or against in both leagues. I think an all-time all-star team, however, would have to be Lou Gehrig, Charlie Gehringer, Rogers Hornsby (let's put him at third), and Honus Wagner in the infield, Babe Ruth, Ty Cobb, and Joe DiMaggio in the outfield, Bill Dickey catching, Christy Mathewson the righthanded pitcher, and Warren Spahn the lefthanded pitcher.''

RED LUCAS

Lucas was, with a bow in the direction of Babe Ruth, the best hitting pitcher of the twentieth century. Lucas, a tricky right-hander, won 157 and lost 135 with the Giants (1923), Braves (1924), Reds (1926–33), and Pirates (1934–38). But he was also a good enough (lefthanded) hitter to bat .281 and be called upon to pinch hit 437 times in his career. Lucas selects:

> 1B—BILL TERRY
> 2B—ROGERS HORNSBY
> 3B—PIE TRAYNOR
> SS—GLENN WRIGHT
> OF—CHICK HAFEY
> OF—EDD ROUSH
> OF—PAUL WANER
> C—GABBY HARTNETT
> RP—DAZZY VANCE
> LP—CARL HUBBELL

Toughest Batter: Hornsby. ''He was the best hitter I ever saw no matter who was pitching.''

Most Underrated: Riggs Stephenson.

Strongest Team: 1929 Cubs.

Comments: ''As a hitter, I'd have to say the roughest pitchers I faced were Bill Hallahan, Dazzy Vance, and Burleigh Grimes. Particularly Hallahan. He was just wild enough to keep you loose up there.''

JERRY LYNCH

Lynch is best remembered as one of the premier pinch-hitters in the history of baseball. For years he held the record for pinch-hit home runs with 18 and collected 116 pinch-hits in his career, twice (1960 and 1961) leading the NL in pinch-hits with 19. But in 13 seasons with the Pirates (1954–56, 1963–66) and Reds (1957–63), he played a considerable number of games in the outfield and batted .277 with 115 homers (including those as a pinch-hitter). In his best season, 1958, the lefthanded hitter played 101 games in the outfield, batting .312 with 16 round-trippers. Lynch's picks are:

                 1B—GIL HODGES
                 2B—BILL MAZEROSKI
                 3B—EDDIE MATHEWS
                 SS—PEE WEE REESE
                 OF—HANK AARON
                 OF—TED WILLIAMS
                 OF—FRANK ROBINSON
                  C—JOHNNY BENCH
                 RP—BOB GIBSON
                 LP—WARREN SPAHN

Deserves Cooperstown: Mazeroski.
Toughest Pitcher: Art Fowler. Fowler pitched for the Reds, Dodgers, and Angels for nine seasons (1954–59, 1961–64). He won 54 and lost 51 and had a 4.03 ERA.
Most Underrated: Robinson and Mazeroski.
Strongest Teams: Braves, Reds, and Dodgers of the 1950's and 1960's.

TED LYONS

Lyons is one of the greatest pitchers to wear the uniform of the White Sox, for whom he pitched for 21 years (1923–42, 1946). A three-time 20-game winner, the righthanded Lyons won 260 and lost 230 and compiled a lifetime ERA of 3.67 with White Sox teams that were rarely in contention. He also managed the Sox from 1946 to 1948. He was elected to the Hall of Fame in 1955. Lyons chooses the following:

```
1B—GEORGE SISLER
2B—EDDIE COLLINS
3B—PIE TRAYNOR
SS—LUKE APPLING
OF—BABE RUTH
OF—TED WILLIAMS
OF—JOE DiMAGGIO
 C—GABBY HARTNETT
RP—WALTER JOHNSON
LP—LEFTY GROVE
```

Deserve Cooperstown: Wes Ferrell and Hal Newhouser.

Toughest Batters: Al Simmons and Bill Dickey. "But they gave everyone trouble. The other was Tom Oliver, the Boston outfielder. He punched the ball all over." In four seasons with the Red Sox (1930–33) Oliver batted .277.

Most Underrated: Bibb Falk and Jackie Hayes. "Hayes was one of the best in the business around second base until he went blind." Hayes was a second baseman with the Senators and White Sox (1927–40). He batted .265 in his career.

Comments: "Al Simmons probably deserves a place in that outfield. And, strictly for fielding, there was no one like Johnny Mostil. Charlie Gehringer deserves a place too. And Mickey Cochrane and Bill Dickey. And Ray Schalk for defense. Schalk once made a putout at every base."

FRANK MALZONE

Malzone, a third baseman with a deft glove and a solid bat, was one of the American League's stellar performers during his 11 years (1955–65) with the Red Sox. A lifetime .274 hitter, he had his best season in 1957 when he batted .292 with 15 home runs, 31 doubles, 82 runs scored, and 103 runs batted in. In 1962 he belted 21 home runs while hitting .283, scoring 74 runs, and driving home 95. Malzone was particularly adept at peppering Fenway Park's "Green Monster" in left field, as evidenced by the fact that he hit at least 30 doubles in four different seasons. He also won three consecutive Gold Gloves (1957–59). Malzone, who closed out his career with a gloomy season with the Angels, picks:

1B—BOOG POWELL
2B—BILL MAZEROSKI
3B—BROOKS ROBINSON
SS—LUIS APARICIO
OF—TED WILLIAMS
OF—MICKEY MANTLE
OF—WILLIE MAYS
C—YOGI BERRA
RP—JIM BUNNING
LP—SANDY KOUFAX

Deserve Cooperstown: Ken Keltner and Phil Rizzuto.
Toughest Pitcher: Bunning.
Most Underrated: Jackie Jensen.
Strongest Team: 1961 Yankees.
Comments: "In the outfield I'd also like to have Al Kaline, Roberto Clemente, and Stan Musial. I think Herb Score would have been the toughest lefthanded pitcher if his career hadn't been cut short by an injury."

JUAN MARICHAL

Righthander Marichal entered the Hall of Fame in 1983 after a 16-year (1960–75) career that saw him post a record of 243–142 and a 2.89 ERA. The ace of the Giants' staff for most of his big league life, he won 20 games six times, struck out at least 200 batters six times, and compiled 52 shutouts. Marichal's individual game accomplishments include retiring the first 19 batters he faced in his 1960 debut and hurling a no-hitter in 1963. Among his best seasons were 1963 (25–8, 2.41), 1966 (25–6, 2.23), 1968 (26–9, 2.43), and 1969 (league-leading 2.10 ERA). Oddly enough, he never won a Cy Young Award. Marichal, who closed his career with single seasons with the Red Sox and Dodgers, chooses:

1B—KEITH HERNANDEZ
2B—JULIAN JAVIER
3B—MIKE SCHMIDT
SS—MAURY WILLS
OF—MICKEY MANTLE
OF—WILLIE MAYS
OF—ROBERTO CLEMENTE
C—JOHNNY BENCH
RP—BOB GIBSON
LP—SANDY KOUFAX

Toughest Batters: Clemente, Pete Rose, and Hank Aaron.

Most Underrated: "Atlanta and Pittsburgh in the late 1960's and early 1970's. Aaron and Clemente were typical of the lack of recognition those teams suffered."

Strongest Team: 1975–76 Reds.

Comments: "I played with great first basemen like Willie McCovey and Orlando Cepeda, but as a pitcher I would want Hernandez behind me. The other active player who should have been on my team is Cal Ripken. But when it comes down to it, I'll just take the Big Red Machine. With them I would have won thirty games *minimum*. In fact, I told the Giants to trade me there on the condition that I wouldn't get paid until I'd won my thirty-first game. Then I'd soak them."

JON MATLACK

Southpaw Matlack had what amounted to two major league careers—glory years with the Mets (1971–77) when he, Tom Seaver, and Jerry Koosman gave New York the National League's most effective pitching triumvirate, and laborious seasons with the Rangers (1978–83) when he suffered from lack of batting support. Overall, the National League's 1972 Rookie of the Year actually ended up with a less than .500 record (125–126), though with a respectable ERA of 3.18. His finest seasons were 1972, when he won 15 with a 2.32 ERA, and 1976, when he was 17–10 with a 2.95 ERA. Matlack, who twice led the NL in shutouts, picks:

> 1B—PETE ROSE
> 2B—JOE MORGAN
> 3B—BUDDY BELL
> SS—DAVE CONCEPCION
> OF—DALE MURPHY
> OF—WILLIE MAYS
> OF—DAVE PARKER
> C—JERRY GROTE
> RP—TOM SEAVER
> LP—STEVE CARLTON

Toughest Batter: "There seemed to be a different one every season, but one who sticks out in my mind was John Boccabella. I think he's considered one of the worst hitters in baseball history, but I never thought so in 1973, when he was hitting me at will."

Most Underrated: Grote and Billy Williams.

Strongest Team: Reds of the 1970's.

LEE MAY

May, a righthand-hitting first baseman, clouted 354 home runs and batted .267 in 18 seasons with the Reds (1965–71), Astros (1972–74), Orioles (1975–80), and Royals (1981–82). His power marks included hitting at least 20 homers in 11 seasons, driving in at least 90 runs eight times, and leading the American League in runs batted in in 1976. His single most productive season was probably 1969 when he hit .278 with 38 home runs and 110 runs batted in. May chooses:

1B—EDDIE MURRAY
2B—BILL MAZEROSKI
3B—BROOKS ROBINSON
SS—LUIS APARICIO
OF—HANK AARON
OF—WILLIE MAYS
OF—ROBERTO CLEMENTE
C—JOHNNY BENCH
RP—BOB GIBSON
LP—SANDY KOUFAX

Toughest Pitcher: "It was either all of them or none of them. And I could usually tell the first time I went up to bat in a game. If I felt comfortable that first at bat, felt that I had all my mechanics down, I didn't care who was pitching. Same thing when I didn't have my mechanics. Then every pitcher was Tom Seaver."

Most Underrated: Vada Pinson. "Best center fielder I ever saw if you don't count Mays."

Strongest Team: Pirates of the late 1960's and early 1970's.

WILLIE MAYS

Mays, probably the most exciting player of his time, was elected to the Hall of Fame in 1979 after a career that has placed him ninth among all players in hits (3283), seventh in RBI's (1903), sixth in games played (2992), fifth in runs scored (2062), third in total bases (6066), third in home runs (660), and second in multiple-homer games (63). Over 22 seasons with the Giants in New York (1951–52, 1954–57) and San Francisco (1958–72) and the Mets (1972–73) he batted .302. He led the NL in batting once, runs scored twice, stolen bases four times, and home runs four times. He was named Rookie of the Year in 1951, won the NL MVP Award in 1954 and 1965, earned 12 consecutive Gold Gloves (1957–68), hit more than 50 homers twice, and drove in more than 100 runs ten times. Mays picks:

1B—STAN MUSIAL
2B—JACKIE ROBINSON
3B—EDDIE MATHEWS
SS—PEE WEE REESE
OF—HANK AARON
OF—WILLIE MAYS
OF—ROBERTO CLEMENTE
 C—ROY CAMPANELLA or JOHNNY BENCH
RP—BOB GIBSON, SAM JONES, JUAN MARICHAL,
    or DON DRYSDALE
LP—SANDY KOUFAX

Toughest Pitchers: Drysdale, Gibson, Koufax, Jones, Bob Rush, and Curt Simmons. "Drysdale and Gibson would just knock you down. I just couldn't pick up Rush's pitches. I later found out he had an eyesight problem so it's a wonder he could pitch at all."

Most Underrated: Aaron. "He got credit but never enough."

Strongest Team: "The 1951 Giants weren't the strongest team in the league that year but they were the best fighters. Maybe you don't always win with the strongest team."

BILL MAZEROSKI

Mazeroski was the dominant defensive second baseman in the National League for most of his 17 years (1956–72) with the Pittsburgh Pirates. A lifetime .260 hitter, he had exceptional power for a middle infielder, as attested to by the fact that he hit home runs in double figures six times. His single best year at the bat was probably 1962 when he hit .271 with 14 home runs, 24 doubles, and 81 runs batted in. Mazeroski, who will always be remembered for the ninth-inning home run in the seventh game of the 1960 World Series that gave the Pirates the championship over the Yankees, picks:

> 1B—BILL WHITE
> 2B—BOBBY RICHARDSON
> 3B—BROOKS ROBINSON
> SS—LUIS APARICIO
> OF—MICKEY MANTLE
> OF—WILLIE MAYS
> OF—HANK AARON
>   C—ROY CAMPANELLA
> RP—BOB GIBSON
> LP—SANDY KOUFAX

Toughest Pitchers: Gibson and Koufax.

Most Underrated: Roy Face. "A lot of people mention me when the question of underrated players comes up, but I'll never understand how a pitcher with a record like Face's has been so ignored. I guess it's a combination of having played for a relatively small city like Pittsburgh and having pitched a few years too soon, before relief pitchers really began getting recognition."

Strongest Team: Dodgers of the 1950's.

DICK McAULIFFE

McAuliffe was the glue of the Detroit infield for 14 of his 16 big league seasons (1960–75), first as a shortstop and then as a second baseman. Although he had a lifetime average of only .247, he was more than capable of hitting the long ball, as attested to by his 197 home runs. McAuliffe's best year was probably 1966, when he batted .274 with 23 homers—one of three seasons when he clobbered at least 20 round-trippers. He also drew more than 100 bases on balls twice and led the American League in runs scored in 1968. McAuliffe, who closed out his career with the Red Sox in 1974 and 1975, picks:

1B—GEORGE SCOTT
2B—BOBBY RICHARDSON
3B—BROOKS ROBINSON
SS—LUIS APARICIO
OF—MICKEY MANTLE
OF—TONY OLIVA
OF—CARL YASTRZEMSKI
C—ELSTON HOWARD
RP—BOB GIBSON
LP—WHITEY FORD

Toughest Pitchers: Harvey Haddix and Gary Peters.
Most Underrated: Bill Skowron. "Skowron may have been one of the few New York players relatively ignored by the press. He could field, hit, and hit with power. But I guess when you have teammates like Mickey Mantle, Roger Maris, Whitey Ford, and Yogi Berra, it's hard to get noticed."
Strongest Team: 1961 Yankees.

TIM McCARVER

McCarver batted a pesky .271 over a 21-year big league career (1959–80) that made him one of the few players in baseball history to appear in a boxscore in four different decades. With the Cardinals from 1959 to 1969, the lefthand-hitting catcher then moved on to the Phillies, Expos, Cardinals again, Red Sox, and Phillies a second time, along the way forming noted batteries with Bob Gibson and Steve Carlton. Offensively, McCarver had his best year in 1967 when he hit .295 with 26 doubles and 14 home runs. Other achievements included leading the league in triples in 1966 and batting .311 in three World Series. McCarver prefers:

> 1B—WILLIE STARGELL
> 2B—BILL MAZEROSKI
> 3B—MIKE SCHMIDT
> SS—OZZIE SMITH
> OF—HANK AARON
> OF—WILLIE MAYS
> OF—BILLY WILLIAMS
> C—JOHNNY BENCH
> RP—JUAN MARICHAL
> LP—SANDY KOUFAX

Deserve Cooperstown: Stargell, Mazeroski, Williams, and Willie McCovey.

Toughest Pitcher: Marichal.

Most Underrated: Julian Javier.

Strongest Teams: 1967 Cardinals, 1976 Reds.

Comments: "Marichal and Koufax are there, but you can add Gibson and Carlton. As a catcher, the toughest batter I had working on was Aaron."

158

MIKE McCORMICK

McCormick was a hard-throwing lefthander with good control, which he parlayed into a Cy Young Award in 1967 when he led the National League with 22 wins (against 10 losses) and a 2.85 ERA. He pitched for the Giants in New York (1956–57) and San Francisco (1958–62, 1967–70), as well as for the Orioles (1963–64), Senators (1965–66), Yankees (1970), and Royals (1971). His lifetime stats include 134 wins and 128 losses and a 3.73 ERA. He had the lowest ERA in the National League in 1960 (2.70), but injuries hampered him when the Giants won the pennant in 1962. McCormick picks:

```
1B—WILLIE McCOVEY
2B—BILL MAZEROSKI
3B—MIKE SCHMIDT
SS—MAURY WILLS
OF—HANK AARON
OF—WILLIE MAYS
OF—ROBERTO CLEMENTE
 C—JOHNNY BENCH or DEL CRANDALL
RP—JUAN MARICHAL
LP—SANDY KOUFAX or WARREN SPAHN
```

Toughest Batter: Clemente.
Most Underrated: Jim Ray Hart.
Strongest Team: 1962 Giants.

BARNEY McCOSKEY

McCoskey compiled a .312 lifetime batting average in 11 major league seasons with the Tigers (1939–42, 1946), Athletics (1946–48, 1950–51), Reds (1951), and Indians (1951–53). A lefty-swinging outfielder, he led the AL in triples (19) and tied for the lead in hits (200) in 1940 to bat .340 and help the Tigers to a pennant. McCoskey, who batted .304 in the 1940 World Series, chooses:

1B—HANK GREENBERG
2B—CHARLIE GEHRINGER
3B—KEN KELTNER
SS—LOU BOUDREAU
OF—TED WILLIAMS
OF—JOE DiMAGGIO
OF—STAN MUSIAL
C—BILL DICKEY
RP—BOB FELLER
LP—HAL NEWHOUSER

Deserves Cooperstown: Keltner.
Toughest Pitchers: Feller and Spud Chandler.
Most Underrated: Sam Chapman.
Strongest Team: 1940 Tigers.

WILLIE McCOVEY

McCovey, one of the greatest power hitters in the history of the National League, cracked 521 home runs in 22 seasons with the Giants (1959–73), Padres (1974–76), Athletics (1976), and Giants again (1977–80). A lifetime .270 hitter, the lefty-swinging first baseman led the league in homers three times, slugging average three times, runs batted in twice, and walks once. In seven different seasons he blasted at least 30 home runs. His single most productive season was 1969 when he was named the Most Valuable Player for batting .320 with 45 homers, 26 doubles, 121 walks, 126 runs batted in, and 101 runs scored. McCovey, whose 1959 debut earned him Rookie of the Year honors in the National League, likes:

        1B—WILLIE STARGELL
        2B—BILL MAZEROSKI
        3B—MIKE SCHMIDT
        SS—MAURY WILLS
        OF—HANK AARON
        OF—WILLIE MAYS
        OF—ROBERTO CLEMENTE
         C—JOHNNY BENCH
        RP—BOB GIBSON
        LP—SANDY KOUFAX

Deserves Cooperstown: Billy Williams.
Toughest Pitcher: Bob Veale. "It wasn't just because he was lefthanded. He could've been throwing with his right hand just for me and I still don't think I would've hit him."
Most Underrated: Aaron. "If he had been on the Yankees, everyone would have known about him long before he came near Babe Ruth's record."
Strongest Teams: Braves of the late 1950's, Pirates of the early 1960's.

LINDY McDANIEL

The tireless McDaniel stymied National and American League batters for 21 years (1955–75), winning 141 and losing 119 and retiring with the second highest number of relief wins (119) and eighth highest number of saves (172) in the history of the game. A member of the Cardinals from 1955 to 1962, he then moved on to the Cubs, Giants, Yankees, and Royals. His single finest season was probably 1960 for St. Louis, when he won 12, saved 26 others, and had an ERA of 2.09. On three different occasions he led the league in saves. McDaniel, who stands second to Hoyt Wilhelm in number of games by a pitcher, chooses:

1B—STAN MUSIAL
2B—RED SCHOENDIENST
3B—BROOKS ROBINSON
SS—LUIS APARICIO
OF—WILLIE MAYS
OF—FRANK ROBINSON
OF—MICKEY MANTLE
C—ROY CAMPANELLA
RP—BOB GIBSON
LP—WARREN SPAHN

Toughest Hitter: Frank Robinson.
Most Underrated: Hal Smith. "Hal Smith didn't hit with the power of a Campanella or a Bench, but he was the best defensive catcher I ever saw. When I was pitching to him on the Cardinals, I knew I didn't have to worry if the other team had a runner on third. I could still throw all the curves I wanted because, even if they bounced, Smith would get them. It was sad that his career was cut short by a bad heart."
Strongest Team: 1961 Yankees.

GIL McDOUGALD

McDougald spent his entire career (1951–60) with the Yankees. He was the American League Rookie of the Year in 1951. In his decade with the Yankees he played second base, third base, and shortstop regularly at one time or another. Twice he batted over .300 and eight times he hit more than 10 home runs. His lifetime average was .276. It was a line drive off his bat that smashed Herb Score, the Indians' young southpaw phenom, in the eye. McDougald played in eight World Series and, although he batted only .237 in the Fall Classic, he did hit seven homers, one of them a grand slam as a rookie. McDougald's selections are:

1B—LOU GEHRIG
2B—TONY LAZZERI
3B—EDDIE MATHEWS
SS—LUIS APARICIO
OF—JOE DiMAGGIO
OF—WILLIE MAYS
OF—HANK AARON
C—YOGI BERRA
RP—ALLIE REYNOLDS
LP—SANDY KOUFAX

Deserves Cooperstown: Reynolds.
Toughest Pitcher: Sal Maglie. "He never looked at the plate when he pitched. He looked right at you. And on every pitch he looked as if he was throwing the ball behind you. And then it would come across his body and over the plate."
Most Underrated: Jim Gilliam. "He did so many things well and didn't get credit. He was an excellent baserunner. He covered a lot of ground. And he was one of the better players in the clutch."
Strongest Team: 1951 Yankees.

TUG McGRAW

Southpaw reliever McGraw chalked up a record of 96–92 with 180 saves and a 3.14 ERA in 19 years with the Mets (1965–67, 1969–74) and Phillies (1975–84). The last major leaguer to have played under Casey Stengel, he was a major factor in both the Mets' pennant win in 1973 (25 saves) and in Philadelphia's 1980 world championship (5–4, 20 saves, 1.47 ERA). He also enjoyed a fine season in 1972, turning in an 8–6 record with 27 saves and an ERA of 1.80. McGraw picks:

1B—WILLIE STARGELL or KEITH HERNANDEZ
2B—JOE MORGAN or MANNY TRILLO
3B—MIKE SCHMIDT
SS—LARRY BOWA or BUD HARRELSON
OF—JOSE CRUZ
OF—WILLIE MAYS or GARRY MADDOX
OF—ROBERTO CLEMENTE
C—BOB BOONE or JERRY GROTE
RP—TOM SEAVER
LP—STEVE CARLTON or JERRY KOOSMAN

Toughest Batter: Tim Foli. "He never struck out. Since I was a relief pitcher who usually came into a game with men on base, a Foli who always made contact was the worst kind of batter to have up for me."

Most Underrated: "Any number of Mets from the 1969 and 1973 teams. Guys like Grote, Al Weis, Ron Taylor, and George Stone."

Strongest Teams: Reds of the 1970's, 1980 Phillies.

Comments: "I don't think a pitcher can choose a catcher he hasn't worked with. That's why I go with Boone and Grote. I can think of a lot of guys I'd want on my bench—starting with Derrell Thomas and Joel Youngblood as utility men, Greg Gross as a lefty pinch-hitter, and Manny Mota and Jose Morales as righty swingers."

DON McMAHON

Perhaps the most underrated relief pitcher since Hoyt Wilhelm made the bullpen respectable, McMahon compiled a lifetime mark of 90–68, with 153 saves and a 2.96 ERA, over 18 major league seasons (1957–74). After being chief fireman for pennant-winning Milwaukee clubs in the late 1950's, he went on to the Colt .45's (1962–63), Indians (1964–66), Red Sox (1966–67), White Sox (1967–68), Tigers (1968–69), and Giants (1969–74). His best years were 1959, when he led the National League in saves, and 1970, when he won nine games, saved 19 others, and had an ERA of 2.97. Only two of McMahon's decisions came as a starter, and both were losses for Houston in 1963. McMahon's picks:

1B—WILLIE McCOVEY
2B—RED SCHOENDIENST
3B—EDDIE MATHEWS
SS—OZZIE SMITH
OF—HANK AARON
OF—WILLIE MAYS
OF—ROBERTO CLEMENTE
C—DEL CRANDALL
RP—JUAN MARICHAL
LP—WARREN SPAHN

Deserve Cooperstown: Ernie Lombardi, McCovey, and Rollie Fingers.

Toughest Batter: Joe Torre. "Torre could always hit me pretty well, but he wasn't the only one. When I was first breaking in, I also had lots of trouble with Johnny Temple and Bob Skinner. Then there were McCovey and Orlando Cepeda. Near the end of my career, I guess I'd have to say Steve Garvey was the toughest."

Most Underrated: Schoendienst.

Strongest Team: Braves of the late 1950's.

ROY McMILLAN

McMillan, one of the finest fielding shortstops in baseball history, played for 16 years with the Reds (1951–60), Braves (1961–64), and Mets (1964–66). Although only a .243 hitter lifetime, he was capable of coming up with the big hit in clutch situations, as attested to by his 62 runs batted in for the Reds in 1956. He won Gold Gloves in 1957, 1958, and 1959. He has managed the Brewers (1972) and Mets (1975) on an interim basis. McMillan picks:

1B—GIL HODGES
2B—RED SCHOENDIENST
3B—EDDIE MATHEWS
SS—PEE WEE REESE
OF—WILLIE MAYS
OF—HANK AARON
OF—FRANK ROBINSON
C—ROY CAMPANELLA
RP—ROBIN ROBERTS
LP—WARREN SPAHN

Toughest Pitchers: Spahn and Bob Gibson.
Strongest Team: 1952–56 Dodgers.
Comments: "I don't think you can really talk about an underrated player because it's the media that's doing the rating in the first place and I'm not too interested in that. The same thing as far as who's in and who's not in the Hall of Fame. But I'll say one thing—that lineup I have there is really something. I don't even have room for Stan Musial!"

DOC MEDICH

Medich, a 6'5" righthander, pitched for 12 seasons, mostly in the American League. He came up with the Yankees (1972–75), was traded to the Pirates (1976), spent 1977 with three clubs (the A's, Mariners, and Mets), played for the Rangers (1978–82), and finished with the Brewers (1982). He won 19 games with the Yankees in 1974, tied for the league lead in shutouts with four in 1981, and ended his career—to become a doctor—with a record of 124–105 and an ERA of 3.78. Medich's picks are:

1B—CARL YASTRZEMSKI
2B—JOE MORGAN
3B—BUDDY BELL
SS—OZZIE SMITH
OF—ROBERTO CLEMENTE
OF—WILLIE MAYS
OF—HANK AARON
C—JOHNNY BENCH
RP—TOM SEAVER
LP—STEVE CARLTON

Toughest Batters: Rod Carew "for average," and Yastrzemski "for power".

Most Underrated: John Lowenstein.

Strongest Team: 1976 Reds.

BOB MILLER

This Miller is the answer to most trivia questions about baseball trades, having played for 10 different teams and switched uniforms 12 times during his 17-year career (1957–74). A product of the St. Louis farm system, the righthanded reliever's subsequent travels included two separate stints with the Mets, Cubs, and Padres, as well as three seasons when he played for three different teams. In addition, he pitched for the Dodgers, Twins, Indians, White Sox, Pirates, and Tigers. While his lifetime record was an undistinguished 69–81 (52 saves, 3.37 ERA), Miller had solid years for the Dodgers between 1963 and 1966, turning in ERAs of 2.89, 2.62, 2.97, and 2.77. He also led the NL in appearances by a pitcher in 1964. Miller's choices:

> 1B—STAN MUSIAL
> 2B—BILL MAZEROSKI
> 3B—EDDIE MATHEWS
> SS—DAVE CONCEPCION
> OF—MICKEY MANTLE
> OF—WILLIE MAYS
> OF—ROBERTO CLEMENTE
> C—JOHNNY BENCH
> RP—JUAN MARICHAL
> LP—SANDY KOUFAX

Deserve Cooperstown: Mazeroski, Concepcion, and Bench.

Toughest Batters: Felipe Alou and Willie McCovey.

Most Underrated: Mazeroski.

Strongest Team: "Of all the teams I played with—and everybody knows there were a lot of them—the 1971 Pirates were the best. In fact, they were also the best team I ever saw."

Comments: "I'd also like to say that, if I had a designated hitter, it would be Hank Aaron."

MINNIE MINOSO

Outfielder Minoso batted a lusty .298 over 17 years with the Indians (1949–51), White Sox (1951–57), Indians again (1958–59), White Sox again (1960–61), Cardinals (1962), Senators (1963), White Sox yet again (1964), and the White Sox twice more for stunt appearances for Bill Veeck (1976 and 1980). A .300 batter seven times and a 100–RBI man four times, he led the American League in hits in 1960, in doubles in 1957, in triples in 1951, 1954, and 1957, and in stolen bases in 1951, 1952, and 1953. His single best season was probably 1954 when he batted .320 with 19 homers, 18 triples, 29 doubles, 116 runs batted in, and 119 runs scored. Minoso picks:

```
1B—BILL SKOWRON
2B—NELLIE FOX
3B—BROOKS ROBINSON
SS—PHIL RIZZUTO
OF—TED WILLIAMS
OF—MICKEY MANTLE
OF—HANK AARON
 C—YOGI BERRA
RP—BOB LEMON
LP—WHITEY FORD
```

Deserves Cooperstown: Fox.
Toughest Pitchers: Hoyt Wilhelm and Ed Lopat.
Most Underrated: Pee Wee Reese. "It took them too long to put him in the Hall of Fame."
Strongest Team: Yankees of the 1950's.
Comments: "The difference between .250 and .300 hitters is work. When I got two hits the first two at bats, I wouldn't be satisfied unless I had at least three for the game. The .250 hitters let down during a game, so they end up letting down through a season and then through a career."

DALE MITCHELL

Mitchell, a lefthanded outfielder, played almost his entire career with the Indians (1946–56), although he moved over to the Dodgers at the tail end of 1956, just in time to become part of one of the most famous vignettes in baseball history: Mitchell striking out on a called third strike, the final out in Don Larsen's World Series perfect game. Mitchell batted .312 over his career, with a high of .336 in 1948. The following year he led the American League in both hits (203) and triples (23). He also appeared in the 1948 and 1954 World Series with Cleveland. Mitchell selects:

```
1B—MICKEY VERNON
2B—JOE GORDON
3B—KEN KELTNER or GEORGE KELL
SS—PHIL RIZZUTO or LOU BOUDREAU
OF—JOE DiMAGGIO
OF—TED WILLIAMS
OF—MICKEY MANTLE
 C—ROY CAMPANELLA
RP—BOB LEMON
LP—WHITEY FORD
```

Deserves Cooperstown: Allie Reynolds.
Most Underrated: Jim Hegan. "If there is any better defensive catcher in the history of the game, he must have been something."
Strongest Team: 1949–53 Yankees.
Comments: "Lemon used to say that the only way to pitch to Williams was low and inside. Not that he couldn't hit the low, inside pitch but at least he would pull it. The pitcher's mound is too damn close to risk his hitting it anywhere else."

JOHNNY MIZE

Mize, elected to the Hall of Fame in 1981, was one of the great power hitters of the late 1930's and 1940's. The big lefty-swinging first baseman played for the Cardinals (1936–41), Giants (1942, 1946–49), and Yankees (1949–53). He batted .312, including a league-leading .349 in 1939 and a career high .364 in 1937. He stroked 359 homers, including league-leading totals in 1939 (28), 1940 (43), 1947 (51), and 1948 (40). He also led the NL in RBI's three times, and in slugging four times. He hit three home runs in a game six times, a major league record. He played in five World Series for the Yankees (1949–53), and hit three homers in the 1952 classic. Mize picks:

> 1B—LOU GEHRIG
> 2B—CHARLIE GEHRINGER
> 3B—STAN HACK
> SS—PHIL RIZZUTO
> OF—WILLIE MAYS
> OF—JOE DiMAGGIO
> OF—TED WILLIAMS
> C—ERNIE LOMBARDI
> RP—DIZZY DEAN
> LP—WARREN SPAHN

Deserves Cooperstown: Rizzuto.
Toughest Pitcher: Russ Bauers. ''He was a big, tall right-hander with a big, tall curve that started up near your eyes and when it reached you, down it came.'' Bauers won 31 and lost 30 in eight big league seasons with the Pirates, Cubs, and Browns. In 1937 he won 13 and lost six with a 2.88 ERA.
Most Underrated: Hack.
Strongest Team: 1949–53 Yankees.
Comments: ''I'll pick Gehrig over Stan Musial and Jimmie Foxx, Rizzuto over Pee Wee Reese, Lombardi over Gabby Hartnett and Bill Dickey, and Dean over Bob Feller—but I wouldn't mind having any of them either.''

JO-JO MOORE

Moore was the offensive catalyst and center field anchor for the Giants for 12 years (1930–41). A lifetime .298 hitter, he batted over .300 five times and scored more than 100 runs three times. He was generally regarded as one of the best defensive outfielders of the 1930's. Moore picks:

1B—BILL TERRY
2B—CHARLIE GEHRINGER
3B—PIE TRAYNOR
SS—TRAVIS JACKSON
OF—PAUL WANER
OF—JOE DiMAGGIO
OF—MEL OTT
C—BILL DICKEY
RP—BOB FELLER
LP—LEFTY GOMEZ

Toughest Pitcher: Feller.
Most Underrated: Carl Hubbell. "It's the best politicians, not the best players, who are most likely to get in the Hall of Fame. That's not to say all of those in there don't deserve to be there. Hubbell, for instance, was even greater than his statistics show, and he certainly belongs in Cooperstown."
Strongest Team: 1936–37 Yankees.

TERRY MOORE

Moore was a spectacular defensive center fielder for 11 seasons (1935–42, 1946–48) with the Cardinals. He batted .280 in his career, with a season high of .304 in 1940. Twice (1939 and 1940) he hit 17 home runs. He appeared in two World Series (1942 and 1946) with the Cardinals. Playing with Stan Musial and Enos Slaughter on either side of him, he was part—and often a forgotten part—of one of the greatest outfields in history. Moore chooses:

    1B—LOU GEHRIG
    2B—CHARLIE GEHRINGER
    3B—PIE TRAYNOR
    SS—ARKY VAUGHAN
    OF—BABE RUTH
    OF—JOE DiMAGGIO
    OF—PAUL WANER
     C—BILL DICKEY
    RP—DIZZY DEAN
    LP—CARL HUBBELL

Deserves Cooperstown: Riggs Stephenson. "The caliber of players voted into the Hall of Fame should be able to hit, throw, field, run, and have a great desire for the game—not just a home run hitter with just one or two of these abilities."

Toughest Pitcher: Hubbell.

Most Underrated: Stan Hack.

Strongest Teams: 1942 Cardinals, 1942 Yankees.

JOE MORGAN

Few players achieved a reputation for being a winner as firmly as did Morgan during his 22 years with the Astros (1963–71), Reds (1972–79), Astros again (1980), Giants (1981–82), Phillies (1983), and Athletics (1984). A perennial force for contending or pennant-winning teams, the left-hand-hitting second baseman closed out his career with a National League career mark in walks (1799), 689 stolen bases, a .271 batting average, and a record-breaking (for a second baseman) 268 home runs. In both 1975 and 1976 he was named NL MVP—in 1975 for batting .327 with 17 home runs, 27 doubles, 94 runs batted in, 107 runs, 132 walks, and 67 stolen bases; in 1976 for hitting .320 with 27 homers, 30 doubles, 111 runs batted in, 113 runs, 114 walks, and 60 stolen bases. Morgan chooses:

> 1B—WILLIE McCOVEY or TONY PEREZ
> 2B—BILL MAZEROSKI
> 3B—MIKE SCHMIDT
> SS—DAVE CONCEPCION
> OF—WILLIE STARGELL
> OF—WILLIE MAYS
> OF—HANK AARON
> C—JOHNNY BENCH
> RP—JUAN MARICHAL or BOB GIBSON
> LP—SANDY KOUFAX

Toughest Pitcher: Jon Matlack.
Most Underrated: Perez. "He wasn't noticed as much as me, Bench, and Rose. I suppose it was only because we could talk better. And I really think that when you're talking about underrated players, you're basically talking about players who haven't established an entertaining relationship with the media."
Strongest Team: 1976 Reds.

WALLY MOSES

Moses, a lefthand-hitting outfielder, averaged .291 in 17 seasons (1935–51) with the Athletics, White Sox, Red Sox, and Athletics again. His batting feats include hitting over .300 the first seven years of his career, leading the American League in triples in 1943, and topping the league in doubles in 1945. His best year was 1937, when he hit .320 with 25 home runs, 48 doubles, 13 triples, and 113 runs scored. Moses picks:

>   1B—LOU GEHRIG
>   2B—CHARLIE GEHRINGER
>   3B—KEN KELTNER
>   SS—LUKE APPLING
>   OF—TED WILLIAMS
>   OF—JOE DiMAGGIO
>   OF—AL SIMMONS
>   C—BILL DICKEY
>   RP—JOHNNY ALLEN
>   LP—LEFTY GROVE

Toughest Pitcher: Allen. "Trying to hit him was like trying to hit a brick."

Strongest Team: Yankees of the late 1930's, Yankees 1961.

Comments: "I once went into Connie Mack's office and noticed that, of all the hundreds of players he'd managed over the years, the only one he had a photograph of was Al Simmons. When I asked him why that was, he looked up at me and said, 'Mister Moses, when the winning run is on second base in the ninth inning and Al Simmons is at bat, the game is over.' "

DON MOSSI

Mossi had a productive career as both a reliever and a starter with the Indians (1954–58), Tigers (1959–63), White Sox (1964), and Athletics (1965). As a starter, his best years were 1959 (17–9, 3.36) and 1961 (15–7, 2.96); primarily out of the bullpen he was 6–1 with a 1.94 ERA with the pennant-winning 1954 Indians. His overall record was 101–80 (27–24 in relief). He appeared in three of the four games in the 1954 World Series and gave up only three hits and no runs. Mossi selects:

1B—BILL SKOWRON
2B—NELLIE FOX
3B—BROOKS ROBINSON
SS—LUIS APARICIO
OF—TED WILLIAMS
OF—AL KALINE
OF—MICKEY MANTLE
C—YOGI BERRA
RP—BOB LEMON
LP—WHITEY FORD

Toughest Batters: Williams and Kaline.
Most Underrated: Jim Hegan. ''Pitching to him was like pitching to a mattress. That's how soft his hands were.''
Strongest Team: Yankees of the 1950's. ''I enjoyed pitching against the Yankees more than any other team. When you beat them you had done something.''

MANNY MOTA

The player with the most pinch hits (150) in the history of the game, Mota batted .304 over a 20-year career with the Giants (1962), Pirates (1963–68), Expos (1969), and Dodgers (1969–82). Despite his greater fame for being able to come off the bench and deliver in key situations, the right-hand-hitting outfielder was no slouch as a regular either; in fact, in the only four seasons in which he played at least 100 games in the field, he hit .332, .321, .321, and .305. Mota picks:

                1B—WILLIE McCOVEY
                2B—JULIAN JAVIER
                3B—RON SANTO
                SS—RUBEN AMARO
                OF—WILLIE MAYS
                OF—FELIPE ALOU
                OF—BILLY WILLIAMS
                 C—JOHN ROSEBORO
                RP—BOB GIBSON
                LP—JIM BREWER

Deserve Cooperstown: Alou, Williams, and Brewer.
Toughest Pitcher: Sandy Koufax.
Most Underrated: Williams.
Strongest Team: 1976–81 Dodgers.

DON MUELLER

Mueller, the quintessential banjo hitter of the 1950's, compiled a .296 average over a 12-year career with the Giants (1948–57) and White Sox (1958–59). A lefthanded batter with little power, the outfielder used his spraying ability to lead the National League in hits in 1954 and to turn in such season batting marks as .342 (1954) and .333 (1953). Mueller was also extremely difficult to strike out, whiffing a mere 146 times in 4364 major league at bats. In 1956 he fanned only seven times in 453 at bats. Mueller's picks:

> 1B—STAN MUSIAL
> 2B—RED SCHOENDIENST
> 3B—EDDIE MATHEWS
> SS—MARTY MARION
> OF—MONTE IRVIN
> OF—WILLIE MAYS
> OF—ROBERTO CLEMENTE
> C—ROY CAMPANELLA
> RP—SAL MAGLIE
> LP—HARVEY HADDIX

Deserve Cooperstown: Nellie Fox and Ken Boyer.
Toughest Pitcher: Haddix.
Most Underrated: Alvin Dark.
Strongest Team: 1954 Giants. "We not only beat the Dodgers for the pennant, but we swept Cleveland four straight in the World Series. You can't do it any quicker than that."

HUGH MULCAHY

Mulcahy, a broad-shouldered righthander, won only 45 and lost 89 in his eight years with the Phillies (1935–40, 1945–46) and part of one season with the Pirates (1947). His .336 won-lost percentage is the lowest by a pitcher with 100 or more decisions. But he labored for dismal Philadelphia teams that finished seventh or last seven times during his tenure. He lost 20 games in 1938 and 22 in 1940, leading the league both years. He was the first major league player to enter the armed forces during World War II. Mulcahy chooses:

```
1B—JOHNNY MIZE
2B—BILLY HERMAN
3B—FREDDIE LINDSTROM
SS—LEO DUROCHER, MARTY MARION, or
       BILLY JURGES
OF—ENOS SLAUGHTER
OF—MEL OTT
OF—JOE MEDWICK
 C—GABBY HARTNETT or ERNIE LOMBARDI
RP—DIZZY DEAN
LP—CARL HUBBELL
```

Toughest Batter: Mize. "I was a lowball pitcher and he was a lowball hitter. Especially early on I couldn't get him out. Later in my career I had a little more luck with him."

Strongest Team: Cardinals.

Comments: "I have to mention Dolf Camilli for his glove work and Bill Terry for his glove work and his bat. And don't forget Bucky Walters and Paul Derringer, two great right-handers."

VAN LINGLE MUNGO

Mungo was the ace of the Dodgers pitching staff in the early 1930's. The big righthander pitched for Brooklyn from 1931 until 1941, then moved to the Giants for 1942 and 1943 and returned to the Giants in 1945 when he won 14 and lost seven. Lifetime he was 120–115 and won 68 games in four years (1933–36) with a team that finished sixth twice, fifth once, and seventh once. Mungo's picks are:

1B—LOU GEHRIG
2B—ROGERS HORNSBY
3B—PIE TRAYNOR
SS—HONUS WAGNER
OF—JOE DiMAGGIO
OF—BABE RUTH
OF—TED WILLIAMS
C—AL LOPEZ
RP—DIZZY DEAN
LP—CARL HUBBELL

Toughest Batter: Paul Waner. "He could hit anyone."
Strongest Team: Cardinals of the 1930's. "I pitched against all the good ones but the Cardinals were the best."

BOBBY MURCER

Murcer batted a hard .277 over 17 seasons with the Yankees
(1965–74), Giants (1975–76), Cubs (1977–79), and Yankees again (1979–83). Although he never quite lived up to media hoopla that he would succeed Joe DiMaggio and Mickey
Mantle as a Hall of Fame center fielder from the Bronx, he
retired with 252 home runs and a neat collection of record-
tying or record-breaking slugging feats. His best years were
1971 (.331, 25 home runs, 25 doubles, 91 walks, 94 runs
batted in, 94 runs scored) and 1972 (.292, 33 home runs, 30
doubles, 96 runs batted in, 102 runs scored, AL leadership
in both runs scored and total bases). Murcer selects:

        1B—DON MATTINGLY
        2B—JOE MORGAN
        3B—BROOKS ROBINSON
        SS—LUIS APARICIO
        OF—MICKEY MANTLE
        OF—WILLIE MAYS
        OF—CARL YASTRZEMSKI
         C—THURMAN MUNSON
        RP—CATFISH HUNTER
        LP—WHITEY FORD

Deserves Cooperstown: Phil Rizzuto.
Toughest Pitchers: Mickey Lolich and Jim Kaat.
Strongest Teams: 1970 Orioles, 1980 Yankees.
Comments: ''It may seem premature to be picking Mat-
tingly, but I don't think he's in anybody's shadow at first base
when it comes to defense or just being in the game from the
first pitch. And I don't think he can be accused of being a
shabby hitter, either.''

RAY NARLESKI

Narleski was half of the Indians' spectacular bullpen duet (with Don Mossi) in his rookie year, 1954. The fastballing righthander pitched, mostly out of the bullpen, for the Indians through the 1958 season and spent one final year with the Tigers. He appeared in a league-leading 60 games in 1955. He won 43 and lost 33 and held opponents to 3.60 earned runs per nine innings. He appeared in two games in the 1954 World Series and gave up only one earned run in four innings. Narleski's selections are:

> 1B—MICKEY VERNON
> 2B—PETE RUNNELS or NELLIE FOX
> 3B—AL ROSEN
> SS—LUIS APARICIO
> OF—TED WILLIAMS
> OF—MICKEY MANTLE
> OF—AL KALINE
> C—JIM HEGAN
> RP—EARLY WYNN
> LP—WHITEY FORD

Deserves Cooperstown: Fox.

Toughest Batter: Runnels. "I couldn't go to any spot with him because he had no definite pattern to his swing. I'd pitch him away and he'd go to the opposite field. Then I'd pitch him low and inside and he'd still go to the opposite field with a kind of golfing swing."

Most Underrated: Hegan. "With all the hitting on that team you need someone to handle the pitchers and Hegan was the best at that."

Strongest Team: 1954 Indians. "Every ballplayer on that team pulled. Everyone did a job."

DON NEWCOMBE

Newcombe, the pitching anchor for the Boys of Summer teams in Brooklyn, compiled a record of 149–90 over a 10-year career that saw him on the Dodgers between 1949 and 1958, the Reds between 1958 and 1960, and the Indians for the final months of 1960. A three-time 20-game winner, he led the National League in winning percentage twice (1955 and 1956) and led in strikeouts in 1951. In addition to his pitching talents, Newcombe was a fine hitter and frequent pinch-hitter for the Dodgers. In 1955 he clouted seven homers to establish a league mark for pitchers. Newcombe's picks:

> 1B—STAN MUSIAL
> 2B—JACKIE ROBINSON
> 3B—EDDIE MATHEWS
> SS—PEE WEE REESE
> OF—HANK AARON
> OF—WILLIE MAYS
> OF—ROBERTO CLEMENTE
> C—ROY CAMPANELLA
> RP—ROBIN ROBERTS
> LP—SANDY KOUFAX

Deserve Cooperstown: Jim Gilliam, Red Schoendienst, and Don Newcombe.

Toughest Batters: Musial, Mays, and Aaron.

Most Underrated: Gilliam.

Strongest Teams: "The strongest teams I ever played with or against were the Dodger teams of 1955 and 1956. The 1955 team won the only World Championship ever won by Brooklyn and the 1956 team went to the World Series as well."

HAL NEWHOUSER

Newhouser (207–150, 3.06 ERA) was the premier lefthander in the American League in the late forties. He pitched from 1939 until 1955, with the Tigers for all but the last two years, which he spent with the Indians. Between 1944 and 1948 he led the league in wins four times (with a high of 29 in 1944), in won-lost percentage once, in ERA twice, in strikeouts twice, and in shutouts once. His records in 1944 (29–9, 2.22 ERA, 187 strikeouts, six shutouts); 1945 (25–9, 1.81 ERA, 212 strikeouts, eight shutouts); and 1946 (26–9, 1.94 ERA, 275 strikeouts, six shutouts) were truly exceptional. He won the MVP Award in the first two of those years. Newhouser chooses:

1B—HANK GREENBERG or STAN MUSIAL
2B—CHARLIE GEHRINGER, JOE GORDON, or BOBBY DOERR
3B—GEORGE KELL or AL ROSEN
SS—LOU BOUDREAU, PHIL RIZZUTO, LUIS APARICIO, or MARTY MARION
OF—AL KALINE
OF—TED WILLIAMS
OF—WILLIE MAYS
C—PAUL RICHARDS or BILL DICKEY
RP—BOB FELLER or ROBIN ROBERTS
LP—LEFTY GOMEZ, SANDY KOUFAX, WHITEY FORD, or HAL NEWHOUSER

Deserve Cooperstown: Rizzuto, Marion, and Newhouser. "You're talking to one. I am the only pitcher to win the Most Valuable Player Award two years in a row and the only American League pitcher to win it twice."

Toughest Batter: Joe DiMaggio.

Most Underrated: Richards. "I only wish Richards could've hit .300."

BILL NICHOLSON

Nicholson, whose hefty cuts earned him the nickname of "Swish" among players and fans alike, clouted 235 home runs over a 16-year career that began briefly with the Athletics in 1936, flowered with the Cubs between 1939 and 1948, and ended with the Phillies from 1949 to 1953. A lifetime .268 hitter, he was one of the few genuine sluggers in the big leagues during World War II, leading the National League in both home runs and runs batted in in 1943 (29, 128) and 1944 (33, 122). In 1944 he also scored 116 runs, making him about the league's most productive player. Nicholson's choices:

> 1B—JOHNNY MIZE
> 2B—BILLY HERMAN
> 3B—EDDIE MATHEWS
> SS—MARTY MARION
> OF—STAN MUSIAL
> OF—WILLIE MAYS
> OF—MEL OTT
> C—ROY CAMPANELLA
> RP—ROBIN ROBERTS
> LP—WARREN SPAHN

Toughest Pitcher: Max Lanier.
Most Underrated: Andy Pafko.
Strongest Team: 1951 Giants. "The Dodgers and Cardinals were certainly difficult to beat in the 1940's and 1950's, but the Giants in 1951 were in a class by themselves. As soon as they called up Mays, they began to put together the miracle that ended with Bobby Thomson's homer. I think they were unbeatable for most of the season."

GARY NOLAN

Nolan won 110 games and lost 70 in a 10-year career with the Reds (1967–73, 1975–77) and Angels (1977). The right-hander was 14–8 (2.58) in his rookie year and went on to help the Reds to four pennants in 1970 (18–7, 3.26), 1972 (15–5, 1.99), 1975 (15–9, 3.16), and 1976 (15–9, 3.46). He led the NL in won-lost percentage in 1972 (.750), had a 1.35 ERA in four NL Championship Series, and won one and lost two in four World Series. Nolan, whose career was plagued by injuries, selects:

1B—PETE ROSE
2B—BILL MAZEROSKI
3B—BROOKS ROBINSON
SS—LUIS APARICIO
OF—HANK AARON
OF—WILLIE MAYS
OF—ROBERTO CLEMENTE
C—JOHNNY BENCH
RP—BOB GIBSON
LP—SANDY KOUFAX

Deserve Cooperstown: Rose and Bench.
Toughest Batter: Billy Williams.
Most Underrated: Jim Gilliam.
Strongest Teams: 1975 Reds, 1967 Pirates.

JOE NUXHALL

Nuxhall, the youngest player ever to appear in a major league game, made his debut with the Cincinnati Reds on June 10, 1944—at the age of 15 years, 10 months, and 11 days. His next game was eight years later, also with the Reds, with whom he spent most of his career (1944, 1952–60, 1962–66). He also pitched for the Athletics (1961) and the Angels (1962). His lifetime record was 135–117 with a 3.90 ERA. His best year was 1955, when he won 17, including a league-leading five shutouts, and lost 12, with a 3.47 ERA. Nuxhall selects:

    1B—TED KLUSZEWSKI
    2B—JACKIE ROBINSON
    3B—KEN BOYER
    SS—ERNIE BANKS
    OF—WILLIE MAYS
    OF—HANK AARON
    OF—GUS BELL
     C—SMOKEY BURGESS
    RP—BOB GIBSON
    LP—SANDY KOUFAX or WARREN SPAHN

Deserve Cooperstown: Ernie Lombardi and Nellie Fox.
Toughest Batter: Boyer.
Most Underrated: Bell.
Strongest Teams: Dodgers of the 1950's, 1956 Reds.

BILLY O'DELL

Southpaw O'Dell demonstrated over his 13 years (1954–67) of big league service that he could finish what he had started. Used as a starter by his first two teams in Baltimore and San Francisco, he was particularly effective in the Giants' pennant year of 1962 when he won 19 and struck out 195. As the relief ace for the Braves in 1965, he won 10 games, saved 18 others, and had an ERA of 2.18. After a short tour with Pittsburgh in 1966–67, he retired with a record of 105–100, and a 3.29 ERA. O'Dell selects:

```
1B—WILLIE McCOVEY
2B—BOBBY RICHARDSON
3B—BROOKS ROBINSON
SS—LUIS APARICIO
OF—WILLIE MAYS
OF—MICKEY MANTLE
OF—ROBERTO CLEMENTE
 C—DEL CRANDALL
RP—DON DRYSDALE
LP—WHITEY FORD
```

Toughest Batter: Hank Aaron. "I guess there's nothing too strange about Hank Aaron usually getting a good piece of the ball off me. Frank Howard and Sherm Lollar were others who used to give me a lot of trouble. But the guy I never understood was Bobby Wine. He couldn't hit anyone else in the league, but he could always hit me. Who knows why?" Wine batted .215 in 12 major league seasons with the Phillies and Expos.

Most Underrated: Harvey Kuenn.
Strongest Team: Yankees of the 1950's.

JOE OESCHGER

Oeschger entered the ranks of baseball's immortals on May 1, 1920 when he started and completed a 26-inning game against the Dodgers, whose pitcher, Leon Cadore, also pitched the entire game. The final score was 1-1 when the game was called on account of darkness. Oeschger, pitching for the Braves, gave up only nine hits and walked four. The righthander began pitching for the Phillies in 1914 and stayed with the Phils until early 1919, moved to the Giants for a few games, ended the season with the Braves, for whom he pitched through 1923, returned to the Giants and Phillies in 1924, and ended his career with the Dodgers in 1925. He won 20 games in 1921, had his best ERA in 1917 (2.75), and won 83 and lost 116 with a 3.81 ERA in his career. Oeschger chooses:

       1B—HAL CHASE
       2B—EDDIE COLLINS
       3B—PIE TRAYNOR
       SS—RABBIT MARANVILLE
       OF—ZACK WHEAT
       OF—EDD ROUSH
       OF—WILLIE MAYS
        C—JOHNNY BENCH
       RP—GROVER CLEVELAND ALEXANDER

Strongest Team: New York Giants.
Comments: "Over these many years since 1914–25, it is quite difficult to choose a specific player who would excel overall."

BOB O'FARRELL

O'Farrell became part of baseball legend in the last game of the 1926 World Series when he threw out Babe Ruth in an attempted steal—the out that gave St. Louis the championship over the Yankees. The throw was in fact only one of several peaks in the catcher's 21-year career (1915–35) with the Cubs, Cardinals, Giants, and Reds. A lifetime .273 hitter, O'Farrell batted over .300 five times in his career, including his amazing 1923 season for Chicago when he averaged .319 with 25 doubles, 12 homers, 84 runs batted in, 73 runs scored, 67 walks, and even 10 stolen bases! Even better was 1926, when he was not only voted the league's Most Valuable Player for leading the Cardinals into the World Series, but was also given the managership of the team for the following season. He was also manager of the Reds in 1934. O'Farrell's picks are:

      1B—LOU GEHRIG
      2B—FRANKIE FRISCH
      3B—ROGERS HORNSBY
      SS—TOMMY THEVENOW
      OF—BABE RUTH
      OF—TED WILLIAMS
      OF—STAN MUSIAL
       C—JIMMIE WILSON
      RP—GROVER CLEVELAND ALEXANDER
      LP—HIPPO VAUGHN

Toughest Pitcher: Vaughn.
Most Underrated: Thevenow. A shortstop with five NL teams between 1924 and 1928, Thevenow hit .247.
Strongest Team: 1926 Cardinals.
Comments: ''I want both Frisch and Hornsby, so that's why I'm putting Hornsby at third. Frisch was a better defensive second baseman.''

TONY OLIVA

One of the finest hitters of his era, the lefthand-swinging
Oliva batted .304 in 15 seasons with the Twins between 1962
and 1976. His accomplishments included winning the American League batting title in 1964, 1965, and 1971, leading in
slugging average in 1971, in hits in five different seasons,
and in doubles four times. His single best year was probably
1964, when he batted .323 with 32 home runs, 43 doubles,
94 runs batted in, and 109 runs scored. Oliva prefers:

                1B—HARMON KILLEBREW
                2B—BOBBY RICHARDSON
                3B—BROOKS ROBINSON
                SS—ZOILO VERSALLES
                OF—AL KALINE
                OF—MICKEY MANTLE
                OF—FRANK ROBINSON
                 C—EARL BATTEY
                RP—BOB GIBSON
                LP—SANDY KOUFAX

Deserve Cooperstown: Nellie Fox and Minnie Minoso.
Toughest Pitchers: Sam McDowell and Hoyt Wilhelm.
"McDowell and Wilhelm were tough for opposite reasons.
With McDowell, who was big and lefthanded and wild, you
never knew what was coming, so you could never get com-
fortable at the plate. He was the direct opposite of Wilhelm,
who threw knuckleballs almost every pitch but who was still
hard to hit."
Most Underrated: Cesar Tovar.
Strongest Team: 1965 Twins.

CLAUDE OSTEEN

Southpaw Osteen compiled a deceptive 196–195 (3.30 ERA) record over an 18-year (1957–75) major league career. After spending his first seven seasons with the mediocre Reds and the expansion Senators, he came into his own as the third starter behind Sandy Koufax and Don Drysdale on the Dodgers, winning 20 games in both 1969 and 1972. In addition to his 20 victories in 1969, he hurled seven shutouts and compiled a 2.66 ERA. Osteen, who also pitched for the Astros, Cardinals, and White Sox, prefers:

```
1B—WILLIE McCOVEY
2B—BOBBY RICHARDSON
3B—EDDIE MATHEWS
SS—ROY McMILLAN
OF—HANK AARON
OF—WILLIE MAYS
OF—ROBERTO CLEMENTE
 C—JOHNNY BENCH
RP—DON DRYSDALE
LP—SANDY KOUFAX
```

Deserves Cooperstown: Billy Williams.
Toughest Batter: "All the singles hitters, especially Ron Hunt and Julian Javier. Among power hitters the worst for me was Orlando Cepeda."
Most Underrated: Jim Lefebvre.
Strongest Team: Yankees of the 1960's.
Comments: "Some of my alternatives would be Bill Mazeroski and Ryne Sandberg at second, Brooks Robinson at third, Jerry Grote and John Roseboro as catchers, and Tom Seaver with Drysdale as a righthanded starter."

MARV OWEN

Some 50 years after the fact, third baseman Owen remains most famous for the hard tag on the Cardinals, Joe Medwick in the seventh game of the 1934 World Series that set off a chain of events barely short of a full-fledged riot in Detroit. In fact, however, he was a fine glove man and a dangerous hitter, batting .275 over nine years with the Tigers (1931, 1933–37), White Sox (1938–39), and Red Sox (1940). His best seasons were with Detroit in 1934 (.317, 96 runs batted in) and 1936 (.295, 105 runs batted in). Owens chooses:

> 1B—LOU GEHRIG
> 2B—CHARLIE GEHRINGER
> 3B—OSSIE BLUEGE
> SS—LUKE APPLING
> OF—AL SIMMONS
> OF—JOE DiMAGGIO
> OF—TED WILLIAMS
> C—MICKEY COCHRANE
> RP—RED RUFFING
> LP—LEFTY GROVE

Deserve Cooperstown: Ernie Lombardi and Glenn Wright.
Toughest Pitcher: Grove.
Most Underrated: Billy Rogell. "I played alongside Rogell, so I know about all the little things he did that never showed up in box scores."
Strongest Teams: 1934–35 Tigers, Yankees of the 1930's.
Comments: "If I had a designated hitter on my team, it would have to be either Jimmie Foxx or Hank Greenberg."

ANDY PAFKO

Pafko was an offensive mainstay of the National League for 17 years (1943–59), even though frequently overshadowed by teammates like Hank Sauer, Duke Snider, Gil Hodges, and Hank Aaron. With the Cubs from 1943 to 1951, Dodgers for 1951 and 1952, and Braves from 1953 to 1959, he batted .285 and hit 213 home runs. An outfielder sometimes called on to play third base, Pafko had 30-homer and 100-RBI seasons twice, with his best year probably 1948, when he clouted 26 home runs, drove home 101 runs, and batted .312. Pafko's picks:

> 1B—STAN MUSIAL
> 2B—JACKIE ROBINSON
> 3B—EDDIE MATHEWS
> SS—MARTY MARION
> OF—HANK AARON
> OF—WILLIE MAYS
> OF—DUKE SNIDER
> C—ROY CAMPANELLA
> RP—ROBIN ROBERTS
> LP—WARREN SPAHN

Toughest Pitcher: Ewell Blackwell.
Most Underrated: Enos Slaughter.
Strongest Team: 1952 Dodgers. "I guess the 1952 Dodgers were as close to a dream team as I ever saw. We sure hit a lot. I had nineteen home runs and wasn't even close to being high on the team. But it wasn't just a strong team, it was a good team in the sense of everyone knowing what his job was and going out and doing it. The manager, Chuck Dressen, had a lot to do with that."

MILT PAPPAS

Pappas, a big, durable righthander, won more games (209) than any other pitcher who never won 20 games in a season. (His high was 17 in both 1971 and 1972.) He won 110 games in the American League, all with the Orioles between 1957 and 1965, and 99 in the National League with the Reds (1966–68), Braves (1968–70) and Cubs (1970–73). Thus, he barely missed becoming only the third pitcher to win 100 or more games in both leagues. His lifetime ERA was 3.40, with a low of 2.60 in 1965. And he pitched a no-hitter against the Padres in 1972. Pappas picks:

> 1B—ERNIE BANKS
> 2B—PETE ROSE
> 3B—BROOKS ROBINSON
> SS—LUIS APARICIO
> OF—ROBERTO CLEMENTE
> OF—TED WILLIAMS
> OF—HANK AARON
> C—JOHNNY BENCH
> RP—BOB GIBSON
> LP—SANDY KOUFAX

Deserve Cooperstown: Milt Pappas and Nellie Fox.
Toughest Batter: Williams.
Most Underrated: Gaylord Perry.
Strongest Team: 1960 Yankees.

MEL PARNELL

Parnell, the southpaw who defied the odds by becoming a big winner in front of Fenway Park's close left field wall, won 123 and lost 75 in 10 seasons (1947–56) with the Red Sox. A two-time 20-game winner, he was particularly impressive in 1949, when he led the American League in wins (25), ERA (2.77), and complete games (27). He was no slouch in 1953, either, when his 21–8 record included four shutouts of the pennant-winning Yankees. Parnell, who hurled a no-hitter only two months before retiring in 1956, likes:

1B—MICKEY VERNON
2B—BOBBY DOERR
3B—FRANK MALZONE
SS—PHIL RIZZUTO
OF—TED WILLIAMS
OF—JOE DiMAGGIO
OF—DOM DiMAGGIO
C—SAMMY WHITE
RP—ELLIS KINDER
LP—BOBBY SHANTZ

Deserves Cooperstown: Rizzuto.
Toughest Batter: Luke Appling. "He was the easiest guy in the game to get two strikes on, but, somehow, you never got that third one past him."
Most Underrated: Doerr and Vern Stephens.
Strongest Team: Yankees of the late 1940's and 1950's.
White caught for the Red Sox from 1951 to 1959 and played two additional seasons in the NL. His lifetime average was .262. Kinder pitched for four teams from 1946 to 1957 and compiled a record of 102 and 71 with a 3.43 ERA.

CAMILO PASCUAL

Widely acknowledged as the best curveball pitcher of his era in the American League, Pascual managed a record of 174–170 despite laboring for many years with the lowly Senators. His marks for the Washington-Minnesota franchise (1954–66) include winning 20 games twice, leading the AL in strikeouts three times, in shutouts three times, and in complete games three times. The righthander's finest season was probably 1963, when he was 21–9 with an ERA of 2.46. Pascual, who also pitched for the second Washington Senators franchise from 1967 to 1969, and briefly for the Reds, Dodgers, and Indians, selects:

>   1B—VIC POWER
>   2B—NELLIE FOX
>   3B—BROOKS ROBINSON
>   SS—LUIS APARICIO
>   OF—TONY OLIVA
>   OF—MICKEY MANTLE
>   OF—AL KALINE
>   C—EARL BATTEY
>   RP—JUAN MARICHAL
>   LP—HERB SCORE

Deserves Cooperstown: Fox.

Toughest Batters: Mantle "always", and Robinson "especially in the clutch".

Most Underrated: Aparicio. "It took too long to vote him into the Hall of Fame. He was not just a great fielder and runner, he was the spirit that made both the White Sox and Orioles winners."

Strongest Team: 1961 Yankees.

Comments: "Four others I should mention. Willie Mays was the greatest player I ever *watched*, if not played against. The same for Sandy Koufax as a pitcher. And Bobby Richardson and Cesar Tovar were like Aparicio."

CLAUDE PASSEAU

Passeau was a late bloomer on the mound, starting his career as a Pirate (1935) and a Phillie (1936–39), but enjoying most of his success as a Cub (1939–47). Holder of an overall record of 162–150, he had his best seasons in 1940 (20–13, 2.50 ERA) and 1945 (17–9, 2.46 ERA, five shutouts). The right-hander led the National League in games started in 1937 and in strikeouts in 1939. Passeau chooses:

> 1B—DOLF CAMILLI
> 2B—BILLY HERMAN
> 3B—PEPPER MARTIN
> SS—MARTY MARION
> OF—STAN MUSIAL
> OF—TERRY MOORE
> OF—DUKE SNIDER
> C—GABBY HARTNETT
> RP—DIZZY DEAN
> LP—CARL HUBBELL

Toughest Batter: Musial.
Most Underrated: Marion.
Strongest Team: Cardinals of the 1930's.
Comments: "I know he doesn't have the numbers of someone like a Hartnett or a Johnny Bench, but I don't think credit is ever given to players like Clyde McCullough. He was about the most aggressive man I ever saw on a field. He kept everybody awake. And, speaking as a pitcher, I always appreciated that."

McCullough caught for the Cubs and Pirates for 15 years (1940–43, 1946–56) and batted .252.

FREDDY PATEK

Patek was a slick fielding shortstop with the Pirates (1968–70), Royals (1971–79), and Angels (1980–81). A lifetime .242 hitter, he led the AL with 11 triples in 1971 and with 53 stolen bases in 1977. He also led (or tied for the lead) in double plays by a shortstop for four consecutive seasons (1971–74). In four AL Championship Series (1970, 1976–78) he batted .288 and drove in 11 runs. Patek selects:

```
1B—EDDIE MURRAY
2B—COOKIE ROJAS or FRANK WHITE
3B—GEORGE BRETT
SS—ROBIN YOUNT
OF—WILLIE STARGELL or HANK AARON
OF—WILLIE MAYS
OF—ROBERTO CLEMENTE
 C—THURMAN MUNSON
RP—CATFISH HUNTER
LP—SANDY KOUFAX
```

Toughest Pitcher: Nolan Ryan. "He threw hard and had a good breaking ball and he was just wild enough to be intimidating."

Most Underrated: Rojas. "Playing in the Midwest he had very little national exposure."

Strongest Teams: 1977 Royals, 1971–75 Athletics. "For one year the Royals were as good as any team I've ever seen, but over a period of time I would have to say the Athletics. They had power, defense, and pitching. They were well rounded and they dominated the league."

JOHNNY PESKY

Pesky, who played everywhere in the infield except first base, was primarily a shortstop—and probably the best lefthanded-hitting shortstop baseball has ever seen. His .307 lifetime average with the Red Sox (1942, 1946–52), Tigers (1952–54), and Senators (1954) included six .300-plus seasons, with a career-high .335 in 1946. He led the AL in hits—with 205, 208, and 207—in his first three seasons. He is perhaps best known for allegedly holding the ball too long while Enos Slaughter scored from first base with the winning run in the 1946 World Series. He later managed the Red Sox in 1963, most of 1964, and part of 1980. Pesky picks:

1B—BILL WHITE
2B—BOBBY DOERR
3B—GEORGE KELL
SS—PEE WEE REESE
OF—TED WILLIAMS
OF—JOE DiMAGGIO
OF—MICKEY MANTLE
C—JOHNNY BENCH
RP—BOB FELLER
LP—HAL NEWHOUSER

Deserve Cooperstown: White, Doerr, and Newhouser.
Toughest Pitchers: Feller, Bob Lemon, and Newhouser.
Most Underrated: Phil Rizzuto.
Strongest Team: Yankees.

GARY PETERS

Peters, a hard-throwing southpaw, had a career record of 124–103 and a lifetime ERA of 3.25 with the White Sox (1959–69) and Red Sox (1970–72). He led the AL in wins with 20 in 1964 and in ERA in 1963 (2.33) and 1966 (1.98). He struck out more than 200 batters twice, in 1964 (205) and 1967 (215). He was American League Rookie of the Year in 1963. Peters's selections are:

             1B—HARMON KILLEBREW
             2B—BOBBY RICHARDSON
             3B—BROOKS ROBINSON
             SS—LUIS APARICIO
             OF—TED WILLIAMS
             OF—JOE DiMAGGIO
             OF—CARL YASTRZEMSKI
              C—JOHNNY BENCH
             RP—TOM SEAVER
             LP—WHITEY FORD

Toughest Batters: Killebrew and Richardson.
Most Underrated: Jim Landis.
Strongest Team: 1964 Yankees.

BABE PHELPS

Phelps, whose .367 in 1936 was the highest batting average ever recorded for a catcher in a single season, played in the majors for 11 years (1931, 1933–42). Originally a member of the Senators, he enjoyed his most productive years in the National League, for the Cubs (1933–34), Dodgers (1935–41), and Pirates (1942). He retired with a lifetime batting mark of .310, but with not enough plate appearances to qualify as a genuine rival to Bill Dickey or Ernie Lombardi. The Phelps all-stars are:

1B—BILL TERRY
2B—BILLY HERMAN
3B—COOKIE LAVAGETTO
SS—PEE WEE REESE
OF—STAN MUSIAL
OF—MEL OTT
OF—DIXIE WALKER
C—GABBY HARTNETT
RP—DIZZY DEAN
LP—CARL HUBBELL

Deserves Cooperstown: Nellie Fox.
Toughest Pitchers: Dean and Hubbell.
Most Underrated: Leo Durocher.
Strongest Team: Giants managed by Bill Terry.
Comments: "I don't think enough credit is given to managers in baseball. For myself, I'd have to pick Durocher and Casey Stengel as the best. Stengel didn't suddenly become a genius with the Yankees in the 1950's. He just never had good teams before then."

DAVE PHILLEY

The switch-hitting Philley managed to maintain a .270 average in 18 big league seasons for the White Sox (1941, 1946–51), Athletics (1951–53), Indians (1954–55), Orioles (1955–56), White Sox again (1956–57), Tigers (1957), Phillies (1958–60), Giants (1960), Orioles again (1960–61), and Red Sox (1962). The outfielder's best year was 1953, when he hit .303 with 30 doubles and scored 80 runs for the Athletics. Forced to become a pinch-hitter toward the end of his career, Philley turned out to be one of the best in the history of the game—leading the National League in hits off the bench in 1958 and the American League in the same category in 1961. He also set a major league record by getting nine consecutive pinch-hits for the Phillies in his last eight 1958 plate appearances and in his first 1959 at bat. Philley prefers:

     1B—ORLANDO CEPEDA
     2B—BOBBY DOERR
     3B—BROOKS ROBINSON
     SS—PHIL RIZZUTO
     OF—JOE DiMAGGIO
     OF—TED WILLIAMS
     OF—MICKEY MANTLE
      C—YOGI BERRA
     RP—BOB FELLER
     LP—BOBBY SHANTZ

Toughest Pitcher: Jesse Flores. Flores' lifetime record was 44–59 (3.18 ERA) with three teams in seven seasons (1942–47, 1950).

Most Underrated: Pete Suder.

Strongest Team: 1954 Indians.

Comments: ''For me the key to pinch-hitting was walking up to the plate with the thought that it was the pitcher, not me, who was under the gun. After all, it was him, not me, who put that tying run on third and that winning run on second. Now that might not have been the whole truth, but it was what I needed to dig in with confidence.''

BILLY PIERCE

Pierce was one of the premier southpaw pitchers of the 1950's. After two brief stints with the Tigers (1945 and 1948), he became the ace of the White Sox staff (1949–61) before being traded to the San Francisco Giants (1962–64). He led the American League in strikeouts in 1953 and in complete games three times (1956, 1957, and 1958), and tied for the league lead in wins in 1957 with 20. (He also won 20 in 1956). He went 16–6 in his first year with the Giants to help San Francisco to the NL pennant. He pitched in both the 1959 and 1962 World Series, won one and lost one and had an ERA of 1.89. His lifetime marks include a 211–169 record a 3.26 ERA. Pierce's selections are:

1B—WILLIE McCOVEY
2B—NELLIE FOX
3B—EDDIE MATHEWS
SS—LUIS APARICIO
OF—WILLIE MAYS
OF—TED WILLIAMS
OF—MICKEY MANTLE
C—YOGI BERRA
RP—BOB FELLER
LP—WHITEY FORD

Deserve Cooperstown: Fox and Billy Williams.
Toughest Batter: Ted Williams.
Most Underrated: Al Kaline "for many years."
Strongest Team: Yankees of the 1950's and early 1960's.
Comments: It is very hard to pick one team. Great players like Hank Aaron, Ernie Banks, Lou Boudreau, Roberto Clemente, Frank Howard, George Kell, and Sandy Koufax should be on any all-star team of the 1950's and 1960's. And, of course, Stan Musial and Joe DiMaggio were two of the very best, but I did not play a lot against either."

JIMMY PIERSALL

Few players attracted as much controversy as the agitating (and agitated) Piersall during his 17 years with the Red Sox (1950–58), Indians (1959–61), Senators (1962–63), Mets (1963), and Angels (1963–67). One of the game's better defensive center fielders in the early part of his career, he won two Gold Gloves, but he was also a solid hitter, winding up with an overall average of .272. His best year at the plate was 1956, when he led the American League in doubles with 40, belted 14 home runs, batted in 87 runs, scored 91, and hit .293. Piersall, who celebrated his 100th career home run by circling the bases backward, picks:

> 1B—VIC POWER
> 2B—RYNE SANDBERG
> 3B—BROOKS ROBINSON
> SS—LUIS APARICIO
> OF—ROBERTO CLEMENTE
> OF—WILLIE MAYS
> OF—TED WILLIAMS
> C—JOHNNY BENCH
> RP—BOB LEMON
> LP—WHITEY FORD

Deserves Cooperstown: Billy Pierce.
Toughest Pitcher: Hoyt Wilhelm.
Strongest Team: Yankees of the 1950's.
Comments: "Al Kaline, Paul Blair, and Carl Yastrzemski also belong in the outfield. And Yogi Berra goes right behind Bench."

VADA PINSON

Pinson, one of the most dangerous offensive players in the National League for many years and an equally speedy outfielder, batted .286 in 18 seasons (1958–75). Most of his career highlights came as a member of the Reds (1958–68), for whom he led the league in hits in 1961 and 1963, in doubles in 1959 and 1960, in triples in 1963 and 1967, and in runs scored in 1959. Overall, Pinson hit at least 20 home runs seven times, scored 100 runs four times, had over 200 hits four times, and drove in more than 100 runs twice. His .343 batting average in 1961 was one of the main factors in Cincinnati's pennant win. He was also an expert base stealer. Pinson, who went on to play for the Cardinals, Indians, Angels, and Royals after the Reds, selects:

1B—BILL WHITE
2B—JOE MORGAN
3B—GRAIG NETTLES
SS—LUIS APARICIO
OF—FRANK ROBINSON
OF—ROBERTO CLEMENTE
OF—HANK AARON
C—JOHNNY BENCH
RP—JUAN MARICHAL
LP—SANDY KOUFAX

Toughest Pitchers: Marichal and Bob Gibson.
Most Underrated: Curt Flood. ''Flood had the misfortune of being a center fielder in the National League at the same time that Willie Mays was. Plus, he didn't hit as many homers as Willie did. But for a day-in, day-out player who could hit, run, and catch the ball, I think he's one who never got the credit he deserved.''
Strongest Team: 1961–62 Yankees.

GEORGE PIPGRAS

Pipgras was a wild young righthanded fastball pitcher when he came to the New York Yankees in 1923. He was up and down between the Yankees and the minor leagues in 1923 and 1924, spent all of 1925 and 1926 in the bushes, and came to the Yankees to stay in 1927. He lasted with the New Yorkers until early in the 1933 season when he went to Boston, where he pitched well until he broke his arm throwing a pitch. He hung on with the Red Sox until 1935 and later (1939–45) umpired in the American League. (He once threw 17 players out of a White Sox-Browns game.) His lifetime record was 102–73, and in 1928 he led the AL in wins with 24. He pitched in three World Series games—one each in 1927, 1928, and 1932—and won them all. Pipgras selects:

```
1B—LOU GEHRIG
2B—CHARLIE GEHRINGER
3B—JOE SEWELL
SS—LUKE APPLING
OF—BABE RUTH
OF—EARLE COMBS
OF—JIMMIE FOXX
 C—BILL DICKEY
RP—WALTER JOHNSON
LP—LEFTY GOMEZ
```

Toughest Batter: Bibb Falk.
Jimmie Foxx played only 21 games in the outfield, but his .325 lifetime average and 534 career home runs make it easy to understand why someone would be willing to play him out of position.

JOHNNY PODRES

Podres, the southpaw who brought Brooklyn its only world championship with two World Series wins in 1955, had a 148–116 record in 15 big league seasons between 1953 and 1969. Although he never won 20 games and was overshadowed for much of his career by Sandy Koufax and Don Drysdale, he was thought by many to be the Dodgers' most reliable hurler in pressure games. His best years were 1957, when he led the league in ERA and shutouts, and 1961, when he led in winning percentage (.783) with a mark of 18–5. In World Series competition the lefthander retired with a record of 4–1 (2.11 ERA). Podres, who closed out his career with brief stints with the Tigers and Padres, picks:

1B—GIL HODGES
2B—BILL MAZEROSKI
3B—KEN BOYER
SS—PEE WEE REESE
OF—DUKE SNIDER
OF—WILLIE MAYS
OF—ROBERTO CLEMENTE
C—ROY CAMPANELLA
RP—DON DRYSDALE
LP—SANDY KOUFAX

Toughest Batter: Clemente. "It always seemed like he let me get two strikes on him. Then, just when I'm beginning to think I can finish him off, boom, another line drive over the infield."

Most Underrated: Carl Furillo. "Furillo may not have been the fastest guy in the National League, but he could hit, throw, and field with anyone, especially when the chips were down."

Strongest Team: 1955 Dodgers.

NELSON POTTER

Potter won 92 games and lost 97 in a 12-year major league career that included stops with the Cardinals (1936), Athletics (1938–41, 1948), Red Sox (1941), Browns (1943–48), and Braves (1948–49). His best year was 1944, when he won 19 and lost only seven with a 2.83 ERA to help pitch the St. Louis Browns to their only pennant. He appeared in two World Series, 1944 with the Browns and 1948 with the Braves. Potter picks:

1B—JIMMIE FOXX
2B—JOE GORDON
3B—RED ROLFE
SS—JOE CRONIN
OF—JOE DiMAGGIO
OF—TED WILLIAMS
OF—STAN MUSIAL
C—BILL DICKEY
RP—DIZZY DEAN
LP—WARREN SPAHN

Toughest Batter: "That has to be Hal Trosky of the Indians. He was a great breaking ball hitter and I was a breaking ball pitcher. I just couldn't get him out until later when I came up with a slider."

Strongest Team: 1941 Red Sox. "No question about it. The Red Sox the year Williams hit .406. And besides Williams we had hitters like Foxx, Bobby Doerr, Cronin, and Dom DiMaggio."

Comments: "I have to go with Foxx because I only saw Lou Gehrig at the end of his career."

BOOG POWELL

Powell, the lefthanded power on the great Baltimore teams in the 1960's and early 1970's, amassed 339 home runs in his 17 years with the Orioles (1961–74), Indians (1975–76), and Dodgers (1977). A lifetime .266 batter, the hulking first baseman led the American League in slugging percentage in 1964 and topped the 30-homer mark four times. His best seasons were 1969, when he batted .304 with 37 homers and 121 runs batted in, and 1970, when he was named the league's MVP for hitting .297 with 35 home runs, 104 walks, and 114 runs batted in. Powell selects:

> 1B—EDDIE MURRAY
> 2B—DAVE JOHNSON
> 3B—BROOKS ROBINSON
> SS—MARK BELANGER
> OF—FRANK ROBINSON
> OF—PAUL BLAIR
> OF—ROBERTO CLEMENTE
> C—JOHNNY BENCH
> RP—JIM PALMER
> LP—JIM KAAT

Toughest Pitcher: Kaat.
Most Underrated: Blair. "He was absolutely the greatest, as good in center field as Robinson was at third."
Strongest Team: 1970 Orioles.

VIC POWER

Power was a colorful, fancy fielding first baseman with the Athletics (first in Philadelphia in 1954 and then in Kansas City from 1955 to 1958), Indians (1958–61), Twins (1962–64), Angels (1964), Phillies (1964), and Angels again (1965). His lifetime .284 average included season marks of .319 (1955), .309 (1956), and .312 (1958). He hit 10 or more homers eight times with a high of 19 in 1955, stroked 20 or more doubles eight times with a high of 37 in 1958, and won seven consecutive Gold Gloves from 1958 to 1964. Power picks:

> 1B—MICKEY VERNON
> 2B—NELLIE FOX
> 3B—BROOKS ROBINSON
> SS—LUIS APARICIO
> OF—TED WILLIAMS
> OF—MICKEY MANTLE
> OF—AL KALINE
> C—YOGI BERRA
> RP—EARLY WYNN
> LP—WHITEY FORD

Deserves Cooperstown: Vic Power. "I'm waiting for someone to mention my name but the writers didn't like my style of play. I won seven Gold Gloves but I also introduced the one-handed catch and they called me a showboat. But I'm not a showboat. The guy who invented this game couldn't figure out a way to make us wear two gloves. The first baseman uses one hand when an infielder throws the ball to him. I told my manager, Jimmy Dykes, I was going to use the one-handed catch because it pleased the fans and he said, 'Never argue with success.' "

Toughest Pitcher: Wynn. "He was too smart and had too many pitches. And he remembered how he got you out."

Most Underrated: Rocky Colavito and Harmon Killebrew.

DICK RADATZ

Radatz, who was called "The Monster," was a ferocious looking six-foot-six-inch righthanded relief pitcher for the Red Sox (1962–66), Indians (1966–67), Cubs (1967), Tigers (1969), and Expos (1969). He recorded more than 20 saves in each of his first four seasons, leading the AL with 24 in 1962 and 29 in 1964. (He had 25 in 1963 and 22 in 1965.) In each of the first three of those seasons he also led the AL in wins by a relief pitcher with 9, 15, and 16. His ERA's for those three years, in which he was virtually unhittable, were 2.24, 1.97, and 2.29. Radatz, whose lifetime statistics include a 52–43 record, a 3.13 ERA, and 122 saves, picks:

1B—NORM CASH
2B—BOBBY RICHARDSON
3B—BROOKS ROBINSON
SS—LUIS APARICIO
OF—MICKEY MANTLE
OF—WILLIE MAYS
OF—BILLY WILLIAMS
C—JOHNNY BENCH
RP—JUAN MARICHAL
LP—SANDY KOUFAX

Toughest Batter: Tony Kubek. "He was a good contact hitter, primarily against fastball pitchers."

Most Underrated: Tony Oliva, Roger Maris, Cash, and Williams.

Strongest Team: Yankees of the early 1960's. "I say that even though I had good luck against them."

PEDRO RAMOS

Ramos was a hard-throwing journeyman righthander for 15 big league seasons. His career—with the Senators-Twins (1955–61), Indians (1962–64), Yankees (1964–66), Phillies (1967), Pirates (1969), Reds (1969), and the reincarnated Senators (1970)—ended with a 117–160 record and a 4.08 earned run average. He led the AL in losses four times, with dismal Washington and Minnesota clubs, and surrendered Mickey Mantle's 1956 blast that struck the right field facade at Yankee Stadium, just a few feet shy of clearing the roof. Ramos picks:

1B—MICKEY VERNON
2B—BOBBY RICHARDSON
3B—BROOKS ROBINSON
SS—LUIS APARICIO
OF—TED WILLIAMS
OF—JOE DiMAGGIO
OF—ROBERTO CLEMENTE
C—YOGI BERRA
RP—TOM SEAVER
LP—SANDY KOUFAX

Deserve Cooperstown: Camilo Pascual, Tony Oliva, and Larry Doby.
Toughest Batter: Williams.
Most Underrated: Al Kaline.
Strongest Team: Yankees of the late 1950's and early 1960's.

VIC RASCHI

Raschi, "The Springfield Rifle," won 132 and lost only 66 in ten seasons with the Yankees (1946–53), Cardinals (1954–55), and Athletics (1955). In three consecutive years (1949–51) he won 21 games, leading the AL in won-lost percentage (.724) in 1950 and in strikeouts (164) in 1951. His lifetime ERA was 3.72. Raschi, whose record in six World Series was 5–3 with a 2.24 ERA, selects:

        1B—JOHNNY MIZE
        2B—GERRY COLEMAN
        3B—GIL McDOUGALD
        SS—PHIL RIZZUTO
        OF—GENE WOODLING or HANK BAUER
        OF—JOE DiMAGGIO
        OF—STAN MUSIAL
         C—YOGI BERRA
        RP—ALLIE REYNOLDS
        LP—HARVEY HADDIX

Toughest Batters: George Kell and Hoot Evers. "Especially Kell. He hit everything I threw up there."

Most Underrated: Woodling and Bauer.

Strongest Team: 1949–53 Yankees.

PEE WEE REESE

The field captain and heart of the Boys of Summer teams in Brooklyn, Reese gained entry to the Hall of Fame in 1984 on the basis of a 16-year (1940–42, 1946–58) career with the Dodgers during which he batted .269. A deft shortstop in the field, he was also no slouch at the bat or on the bases, at one time or another leading the National League in walks, stolen bases, and runs scored. His most productive years at the plate were probably 1949, when he batted .279 with 16 home runs and 132 runs scored, and 1951, when, hitting out of the number two spot in the lineup, he managed to drive home 84 runs. Reese prefers:

> 1B—GIL HODGES
> 2B—JACKIE ROBINSON
> 3B—BILLY COX
> SS—DAVE CONCEPCION
> OF—DUKE SNIDER
> OF—WILLIE MAYS
> OF—JOE DiMAGGIO
> C—ROY CAMPANELLA
> RP—EWELL BLACKWELL
> LP—WARREN SPAHN

Toughest Pitcher: Blackwell.

Most Underrated: Carl Furillo.

Strongest Team: "The 1950's Dodgers were the strongest team of any era."

Comments: "Spahn, of course, stopped pitching against the Dodgers because we were so powerful from the right side of the plate that we killed him every time out. But I don't think that should detract from the fact that he was the most successful southpaw pitcher in the history of the National League. As for the single greatest player I ever saw, I would have to say it was DiMaggio. He did it all, and he did it so gracefully!"

ALLIE REYNOLDS

Reynolds, "The Big Chief," started with the Indians (1942–46) and came to the Yankees (1947–54) in a controversial trade for second baseman Joe Gordon. He led the AL in winning percentage (.704) in 1947 and ERA (2.06) in 1952, the only season in which he won 20 games (20–8), six of them shutouts, to lead the league in that category as well. But perhaps his most remarkable season was 1951, in which he pitched two no-hitters, won 17 while losing eight, pitched a league-leading seven shutouts—and was the ace reliever on the staff. His lifetime record was 182–107. And in six World Series he won seven and lost only two. Reynolds picks:

1B—MICKEY VERNON
2B—JOE GORDON
3B—KEN KELTNER
SS—LOU BOUDREAU
OF—JOE DiMAGGIO
OF—MICKEY MANTLE
OF—GENE WOODLING
C—BILL DICKEY
RP—BOB FELLER
LP—WHITEY FORD

Toughest Batters: Eddie Mayo and Skeeter Webb. "Webb hit .210 off everyone else and .400 off me. I was young and I was throwing everything in his area. I hadn't yet learned how to be articulate with the ball." Mayo was a .252 hitter as an infielder with four teams in nine years (1936–38, 1943–48).

Most Underrated: Woodling. "He did nothing exceptional but he did everything every day."

Strongest Team: Yankees of the 1950's "for their great desire, fight, and spirit."

Comments: "I'll tell you who wasn't tough for me—Ted Williams. I just walked him. I was paid to win ballgames, not to confront him. I'm not dumb."

DUSTY RHODES

Rhodes was the batting star for the Giants in the 1954 World Series, collecting four hits, including two home runs and seven RBI's in six games. The rest of his career—seven years with the Giants, 1952–57 in New York and 1959 in San Francisco–was a mere shadow of that Series. He batted .253 and hit 54 homers, pinch-hitting as often as he played in the outfield. His best season was 1954, when he hit .341 (.333 as a pinch-batter) and hit 15 homers in only 164 at bats. Rhodes picks:

> 1B—GIL HODGES
> 2B—JACKIE ROBINSON
> 3B—BROOKS ROBINSON
> SS—HONUS WAGNER
> OF—JOE DiMAGGIO
> OF—WILLIE MAYS
> OF—BABE RUTH
> C—WALKER COOPER
> RP—MARV GRISSOM or ROY FACE
> LP—CURT SIMMONS

Deserves Cooperstown: Ernie Lombardi.
Toughest Pitcher: Simmons.
Most Underrated: Don Mueller.
Strongest Team: Dodgers of the early 1950's.
Comments: ''Years ago a major league club had no more than two star pitchers. Today they have five and two or three top relief pitchers. Baseball today is ten times faster than yesteryear.''

BOBBY RICHARDSON

Richardson, who spent his entire career (1955–66) with the Yankees, was one of the outstanding defensive second basemen of all time. A career .266 hitter, Richardson led the AL in at bats in three consecutive seasons (1962–64) and in hits (209) in 1962. He rarely struck out and batted career highs of .302 in 1962 and .301 in 1959. He also won five consecutive Gold Gloves (1961–65). In seven World Series (1957–58, 1961–64) he batted .305, including marks of .367 in 1960, .391 in 1961, and .406 in 1964. He was named Series MVP in 1960. He also holds several World Series records. Richardson picks:

1B—BILL SKOWRON
2B—DICK GREEN
3B—BROOKS ROBINSON
SS—PHIL RIZZUTO
OF—MICKEY MANTLE
OF—ROGER MARIS
OF—AL KALINE
C—YOGI BERRA
RP—BOB TURLEY
LP—WHITEY FORD

Toughest Pitcher: Sandy Koufax. "In the first game of the 1963 World Series Koufax struck out fifteen. He struck me out three times and he struck Tony Kubek out three times. Mantle, who batted behind us, just shook his head all afternoon. That day he was the toughest pitcher I ever saw."

Most Underrated: Tony Kubek. "He was consistent. He made all the plays. He was a clutch hitter. And he was a team leader. But we just had too many stars."

Comments: "I want Skowron's bat more than anything else. Green was the finest infielder I have ever seen and his hitting was sufficient. Clete Boyer is a close second to Robinson. In fact, in every department except hitting he may have been superior. I would want Ford to pitch in any money game."

BROOKS ROBINSON

Robinson, probably the greatest defensive third baseman in baseball history, was elected to the Hall of Fame in 1983 after 23 years (1955–77) with the Orioles during which he batted .267 with 268 home runs. Although mainly known for his brilliance afield (he won a Gold Glove for 16 consecutive years), he was also a potent bat, as attested to by the MVP trophy he won in 1964 for hitting .317 with 28 home runs, 35 doubles, and a league-leading 118 runs batted in. In six different seasons he hit at least 20 round-trippers. Robinson, who retired in the top ten for both most career games and career at bats, likes:

1B—EDDIE MURRAY
2B—NELLIE FOX
3B—GEORGE BRETT
SS—CAL RIPKEN
OF—FRANK ROBINSON
OF—MICKEY MANTLE
OF—AL KALINE
C—THURMAN MUNSON
RP—JIM PALMER
LP—WHITEY FORD

Toughest Pitchers: Frank Lary and Earl Wilson. "Fast balls in and sliders from righthanders were not my favorite thing when I was hitting." Wilson won 121 and lost 109 (3.69 ERA) in 11 seasons (1959–60, 1962–70) with the Red Sox, Tigers, and Padres.

Most Underrated: Paul Blair.

Strongest Team: 1961 Yankees.

BILLY ROGELL

Rogell, a switch-hitter, was one of the great shortstops to play the game. He spent his 14 seasons with only three clubs—the Red Sox (1925, 1927–28), Tigers (1930–39), and Cubs (1940). His best years came in Detroit, where he hit .295 in 1933 and .296 (with 114 runs scored and 100 RBI's) in 1934. He also batted .283 in two World Series (1934 and 1935). Rogell's selections are:

1B—GEORGE SISLER
2B—CHARLIE GEHRINGER
3B—PIE TRAYNOR
SS—TRAVIS JACKSON
OF—TY COBB
OF—TRIS SPEAKER
OF—BABE RUTH
C—MICKEY COCHRANE
RP—WALTER JOHNSON
LP—LEFTY GROVE

Deserves Cooperstown: Lefty O'Doul.
Toughest Pitcher: Bob Feller.
Most Underrated: Pete Fox. Fox batted .298 between 1933 and 1945 with the Tigers and Red Sox. He batted .321 in 1935 and .331 in 1937.
Strongest Team: 1927 Yankees.
Comments: "There are too many big league clubs today. The talent is stretched too far."

JOHN ROSEBORO

Although only a career .249 hitter, catcher Roseboro was the spine of the Los Angeles teams that featured Sandy Koufax and Don Drysdale on the mound. A 14-year (1957–70) major league veteran, he played for the Dodgers in their final season in Brooklyn, then moved in as Roy Campanella's successor when the team moved west. In 1968 he moved over to Minnesota and, the following year, keyed the Twins to a divisional championship. He retired after a brief stint with the Washington Senators in 1970. Roseboro picks:

> 1B—WILLIE McCOVEY
> 2B—CHARLIE NEAL
> 3B—EDDIE MATHEWS
> SS—MAURY WILLS
> OF—HANK AARON
> OF—WILLIE MAYS
> OF—MICKEY MANTLE
> C—JOHNNY BENCH
> RP—JUAN MARICHAL
> LP—SANDY KOUFAX

Toughest Batter: Roberto Clemente.

Most Underrated: Norm Larker. "I don't care what anybody says—he was not just a good hitter, he was an excellent hitter who could play first and always hustled like hell. If I were starting a baseball club, I'd start with Norm Larker." First baseman Larker hit .275 in six years (1958-63) with the Dodgers and three other NL teams.

Strongest Teams: Reds and Giants of the early 1960's.

Comments: "I know I'll be accused of being prejudiced for taking former teammates like Neal and Wills, but that's what I think."

AL ROSEN

Rosen, a righthand-hitting third baseman, batted .285 over a 10-year (1947–56) career with Indians that came to an end because of injuries. In his seven full seasons with Cleveland, however, he established himself as one of the American League's most dangerous power hitters, driving in 100 runs five times, leading the circuit in home runs and RBI's twice and in slugging percentage and runs scored once. His most productive season was 1953, when he was named American League MVP for his 43 home runs, 145 runs batted in, 115 runs scored, and .336 batting average. Rosen, now president of the San Francisco Giants, likes:

                1B—MICKEY VERNON
                2B—NELLIE FOX
                3B—GEORGE KELL
                SS—PHIL RIZZUTO
                OF—TED WILLIAMS
                OF—JOE DiMAGGIO
                OF—MICKEY MANTLE
                 C—YOGI BERRA
                RP—BOB LEMON
                LP—BOBBY SHANTZ

Deserves Cooperstown: Rizzuto.

Toughest Pitcher: Allie Reynolds. "He was so tough for me that, somewhat perversely I suppose, I looked forward to hitting against him."

Most Underrated: Jim Hegan and Gene Woodling. "Nobody before or after could call a game like Hegan. Woodling was just one of many Yankees who never seemed to get headlines but who always did their jobs when called upon."

Strongest Team: 1954 Indians. "We must have had *some* ability to win all those games."

JOE RUDI

Rudi, described by many of his contemporaries as one of the best clutch hitters of his time, batted .264 over 16 years with the Athletics (1967–76), Angels (1977–80), Red Sox (1981), and Athletics again (1982). As one of the vital elements in Oakland's pennant wins in the early seventies, the righthand-hitting outfielder contributed a .305 average, 19 home runs, 94 runs scored, and the American League leadership in hits and triples in 1972, then came back two years later to bat .293 with 22 homers, 99 runs batted in, and the AL lead in doubles and total bases. Rudi, who collected 12 grand slams during his career, opts for:

> 1B—GENE TENACE
> 2B—DICK GREEN
> 3B—SAL BANDO
> SS—BERT CAMPANERIS
> OF—GEORGE HENDRICK
> OF—BILLY NORTH
> OF—REGGIE JACKSON
> C—RAY FOSSE
> RP—CATFISH HUNTER
> LP—VIDA BLUE

Toughest Pitcher: Jim Palmer.
Strongest Team: "Guess. Why would I pick anyone else except those Oakland teams that won everything? One thing that rarely gets mentioned about those teams is that we had three relief pitchers—Rollie Fingers, Darold Knowles, and Paul Lindblad—who would have been the bullpen ace of any other team. Instead, we had all three of them."

RED RUFFING

Righthander Ruffing entered the Hall of Fame in 1967 after putting together a 273–225 record over 22 seasons with the Red Sox (1924–30), Yankees (1930–42, 1945–47), and White Sox (1947). The most astonishing thing about his career was that, while with Boston, his mark of 39–96 ranked him about the worst in baseball history; once traded to the Bronx, however, he won 231 against only 124 losses. A four-time 20-game winner with New York, Ruffing led the AL in strikeouts in 1932, in wins and winning percentage in 1938, and in shutouts in both 1938 and 1939. Between 1936 and 1939 he showed remarkable consistency, turning in records of 20–12, 20–7, 21–7, and 21–7. Ruffing, who also compiled a 7–2 mark in World Series games, selects:

1B—LOU GEHRIG
2B—CHARLIE GEHRINGER
3B—RED ROLFE
SS—PHIL RIZZUTO
OF—AL SIMMONS
OF—JOE DiMAGGIO
OF—BABE RUTH
C—BILL DICKEY
RP—WALTER JOHNSON
LP—LEFTY GROVE

Strongest Teams: Yankees and Athletics of the 1930's. "If it wasn't us, it was them."

PETE RUNNELS

Runnels, a two-time American League batting champion (.320 in 1960 and .326 in 1962), played three positions as a regular. Over his 14-year career he appeared in 644 games at first base, 642 at second base, and 463 at shortstop. A left-handed contact hitter, he batted .291 lifetime with the Senators (1951–57), Red Sox (1958–62), and Colt .45's (1963–64). He also managed the Red Sox for part of the 1966 season. Runnels's choices are:

    1B—MICKEY VERNON
    2B—NELLIE FOX
    3B—BROOKS ROBINSON
    SS—PHIL RIZZUTO
    OF—TED WILLIAMS
    OF—MICKEY MANTLE
    OF—AL KALINE
     C—JIM HEGAN
    RP—EARLY WYNN
    LP—WHITEY FORD

Deserves Cooperstown: Fox.
Toughest Pitcher: Dick Donovan.
Most Underrated: Eddie Yost.
Strongest Team: 1954 Indians. "Cleveland had great starting pitchers and the best bullpen that year. The Yankees were the best over my entire career. And, of course, my selections come strictly from the American League, where I played most of the time."

BOB RUSH

Few pitchers worked as strenuously and with so little reward as Rush did for the lowly Cubs in the 1950's. A 13-year major leaguer with the Cubs (1948–57), Braves (1958–60), and White Sox (1960), the big righthander had an overall record of 127–152, which included eight seasons when he hurled at least 200 innings for the Wrigley franchise, eight years when he managed to win in double figures, and a 1952 campaign when he won 17 and sported a 2.70 ERA. Rush, who also was the winning pitcher in the 1952 All-Star Game, picks:

> 1B—STAN MUSIAL
> 2B—JACKIE ROBINSON
> 3B—EDDIE MATHEWS
> SS—PEE WEE REESE
> OF—WILLIE MAYS
> OF—HANK AARON
> OF—DUKE SNIDER
> C—ROY CAMPANELLA
> RP—ROBIN ROBERTS
> LP—WARREN SPAHN

Toughest Batter: Musial.

Most Underrated: Aaron. "It seemed to take an awful long time for people to recognize what a great player Aaron was. Part of the problem was, of course, that he didn't play in New York or California. But I also think a lot of people seemed to look at him as a one-dimensional player—home run or nothing—and he was anything but that."

Strongest Team: Dodgers of the 1950's.

RON SANTO

Santo, who ranks fourth in home runs among all third baseman, behind Eddie Mathews, Mike Schmidt, and Graig Nettles, was at the core of the great Cubs offense from 1960 ·
1973. (He also played for the White Sox in 1974.) His 342
homers—including 20 or more 11 times—qualify him as a
major slugger. He also batted over .300 four times, drove in
over 100 runs four times, led the NL in walks four times, and
led the league in triples with 13 in 1964. His season highs
were a .313 average (1964), 33 homers (1965), and 123 RBI's
(1969). Santo's choices are:

>   1B—BILL WHITE or ERNIE BANKS
>   2B—GLENN BECKERT
>   3B—EDDIE MATHEWS or KEN BOYER
>   SS—DON KESSINGER
>   OF—ROBERTO CLEMENTE
>   OF—WILLIE MAYS
>   OF—HANK AARON
>   C—JOHNNY BENCH
>   RP—DON DRYSDALE or BOB GIBSON
>   LP—SANDY KOUFAX

Toughest Pitcher: "No one really. To be able to hit is a
gift and when the physical gift and the indefinable mental
component come together on a given day, you can hit anyone. When they don't, you can't."

Most Underrated: Beckert and Boyer. "The stats showed
Boyer to be a much better player than he was perceived as
being."

Comments: "No one could go into the hole as well as Kessinger. No one could throw as well as Bench, catch as well,
or hit as well. Mays was the ultimate player. On a given day
no one could beat Koufax."

HANK SAUER

One of the National League's most feared sluggers in the years immediately after World War II, Sauer batted .266 and whacked 288 home runs over 15 seasons (1941–42, 1945, 1948–59). Originally with the Reds, he spent most of his productive years as a member of the Cubs between 1949 and 1955, later going on to play with the Cardinals and Giants. Among the righthanded-hitting outfielder's accomplishments: five straight years (1948–52) of hitting at least 30 homers, clubbing 41 round-trippers in 1954, batting in more than 100 runs three different seasons, and winning the National League's Most Valuable Player award in 1952 on the strength of leading the circuit in both homers and runs batted in. Sauer picks:

```
1B—LOU GEHRIG
2B—JACKIE ROBINSON
3B—BROOKS ROBINSON
SS—PEE WEE REESE
OF—STAN MUSIAL
OF—JOE DiMAGGIO
OF—ROBERTO CLEMENTE
 C—ERNIE LOMBARDI
RP—EWELL BLACKWELL
LP—SANDY KOUFAX
```

Deserves Cooperstown: Lombardi.

Toughest Pitcher: Blackwell. "I don't see how any right-handed hitter from that period can say anybody but Blackwell. I played with him as well as against him and I even cringed for the hitters when they were the enemy."

Most Underrated: Marty Marion. "I think it's about time that people recognized what a great clutch hitter and fielder he was. He'd always have what we called 'quiet numbers,' but they were always there."

Strongest Team: Dodgers of the 1950's.

GEORGE SELKIRK

Selkirk, a lefthanded hitter, was Babe Ruth's replacement in right field when the Yankees shipped the Babe to the Boston Braves in 1935. Known as "Twinkletoes," Selkirk spent his entire career with the Yankees (1934–42), sometimes playing regularly in either left or right field and sometimes serving as the fourth outfielder behind such luminaries as Joe DiMaggio, Tommy Henrich, and Charlie Keller. He got in enough playing time, however, to bat .290 and hit 108 homers, including a high of 21 in 1939 and five additional seasons with 10 or more. He appeared in six World Series, starring in the 1936 classic with a .333 average and two homers. Selkirk was a scout, minor league manager, farm director, and general manager (for the Senators from 1962 until 1969). Selkirk selects:

1B—LOU GEHRIG
2B—CHARLIE GEHRINGER
3B—PIE TRAYNOR
SS—BILLY ROGELL
OF—JOE DiMAGGIO
OF—TY COBB
OF—BABE RUTH
C—BILL DICKEY
RP—BOB FELLER
LP—LEFTY GROVE

Deserves Cooperstown: Nellie Fox.
Toughest Pitcher: Grove. "He was so terribly fast. He had no curve but he didn't need one. On a good day he would just power the ball by you, and if you can't see it you can't hit it."

Most Underrated: DiMaggio. "No matter how much everyone says about him it will never be enough. He was the greatest winning ballplayer of my time."

Strongest Team: 1937 Yankees.

JOE SEWELL

Sewell, a Hall of Fame shortstop and third baseman since 1977, was called up to take over at shortstop for the Indians when Ray Chapman was killed in 1920. He stayed with Cleveland through 1930, shifting to third base in 1929, and spent his last three years at third base for the Yankees. He batted .312 lifetime with a season high of .353 in 1923. He struck out only 114 times in 7132 at bats. Twice he struck out only three times in a season, and in three other seasons he struck out only four times. Sewell chooses:

> 1B—LOU GEHRIG
> 2B—CHARLIE GEHRINGER
> 3B—PIE TRAYNOR
> SS—HONUS WAGNER
> OF—BABE RUTH
> OF—TRIS SPEAKER
> OF—TY COBB
> C—BILL DICKEY
> RP—WALTER JOHNSON
> LP—LEFTY GROVE

Deserve Cooperstown: Riggs Stephenson, Luke Sewell, Ernie Lombardi, and Joe Wood. "Stephenson was one of the best outfielders the Cubs ever had, played left field on several pennant winners, and had a .336 average. My brother Luke was a good, smart catcher with the best arm around."

Toughest Pitcher: Dutch Leonard. "He was a spitball pitcher with a good curve. And he was mean; he'd throw right at you."

Most Underrated: Sammy West. "He was a .300 hitter and one of the best outfielders. You couldn't get a base hit to centerfield with him out there. And you don't hear a thing about him anymore."

Strongest Team: 1932 Yankees. "I'll take the 1932 Yankee team over the 1927 Yankees. Check the averages for that year."

RIP SEWELL

Sewell, a righthanded hurler who specialized in the blooper pitch, played briefly with the Tigers in 1932 but spent the bulk of his career with the Pirates (1938–49). His lifetime record was 143–97, all with the Pirates, and his career ERA was 3.48. In both 1943 and 1944 he won 21 games, tying for the NL lead in the former year. Sewell, who is perhaps best remembered for giving up a three-run homer to Ted Williams on a blooper in the 1946 All-Star Game, picks:

> 1B—JOHNNY MIZE
> 2B—BILLY HERMAN
> 3B—GRAIG NETTLES
> SS—ARKY VAUGHAN
> OF—RALPH KINER
> OF—STAN MUSIAL
> OF—PAUL WANER
> C—AL LOPEZ
> RP—MORT COOPER
> LP—CARL HUBBELL

Deserves Cooperstown: "I would hesitate to say. A few are there that don't belong and a few who are not there do belong."

Toughest Batter: Musial.

Strongest Team: Cardinals.

BOBBY SHANTZ

Lefthander Shantz pitched for 16 years (1949–64), most of them with less than mediocre clubs, but still managed to retire with a record of 119–99 (3.38 ERA). A member of the Athletics from 1949 to 1956, he then moved on to the Yankees, Pirates, Colt .45's, Cardinals, Cubs, and Phillies. His most impressive year was certainly for the A's in 1952 when he was named MVP in the American League for a record of 24–7 (2.48 ERA). With the Yankees in 1957 he led the league in ERA (2.45). Shantz is one of only two players ever to be drafted by two expansion teams, having been selected by both the Houston Colt .45's and the short-lived second version of the Washington Senators. Shantz, who was also awarded eight consecutive Gold Gloves (1957-64) for his defensive abilities, prefers:

> 1B—GIL HODGES
> 2B—BILL MAZEROSKI
> 3B—KEN BOYER
> SS—LUIS APARICIO
> OF—HANK AARON
> OF—MICKEY MANTLE
> OF—WILLIE MAYS
> C—YOGI BERRA
> RP—BOB LEMON
> LP—WHITEY FORD

Deserves Cooperstown: Nellie Fox.
Toughest Batter: Ted Williams.
Most Underrated: Roberto Clemente.
Strongest Team: Yankees of the 1950's.

LARRY SHERRY

Sherry, a righthanded relief specialist for 11 seasons, made four appearances in the 1959 World Series, winning two games and saving another while giving up only one run in $12\frac{2}{3}$ innings for an 0.71 ERA. Sherry's lifetime record was 53–44 with a 3.67 ERA. He also had 82 saves with the Dodgers (1958–63), Tigers (1964–67), Astros (1967), and Angels (1968). His best seasons were 1960 (14–10, 7 saves), 1961 (4–4, 15 saves), and 1966 (8–5, 20 saves). Sherry's selections are:

```
1B—BILL WHITE
2B—BILL MAZEROSKI
3B—KEN BOYER
SS—ROY McMILLAN
OF—HANK AARON
OF—WILLIE MAYS
OF—ROBERTO CLEMENTE
 C—JOHN ROSEBORO
RP—DON DRYSDALE
LP—SANDY KOUFAX
```

Toughest Batter: Aaron.
Most Underrated: Jim Gilliam.
Strongest Team: 1958–63 Braves.

CHRIS SHORT

Short, a hard throwing lefthander, pitched most of his career (1959–72) for Phillies teams that were mediocre or worse. His lifetime record was only 135–132, but he had a 3.43 ERA and won 20 games in 1966 and 19 in 1968. In five seasons he had an ERA under 3.00, with a low of 2.20 in 1964, and twice he struck out more than 200 batters. Short, who ended his career with the Brewers in 1973, chooses:

                1B—DICK ALLEN
                2B—PETE ROSE
                3B—KEN BOYER
                SS—MAURY WILLS
                OF—JIM WYNN
                OF—WILLIE MAYS
                OF—ROBERTO CLEMENTE
                 C—JOHNNY BENCH
                RP—BOB GIBSON
                LP—SANDY KOUFAX

Deserve Cooperstown: Richie Ashburn and Jim Bunning.
Toughest Batter: Rose.
Most Underrated: Billy Williams.
Strongest Team: 1966 Dodgers.

ROY SIEVERS

Sievers, a righthanded slugging first baseman and outfielder, spent his best seasons with two of the worst teams ever assembled. In 11 seasons with the Browns (1949–53) and Senators (1954–59) he saw the cellar six times, seventh place four times, and sixth place once. He also played for the White Sox (1960–61), Phillies (1962–64), and the second version of the Senators (1964–65). He batted .267 and hit 318 homers (including 20 or more every year from 1954 to 1962) in his career. He was Rookie of the Year in 1949 on the basis of a .306 average, 16 homers, and 91 RBI's. In 1957 he led the AL in homers with 42 and RBI's with 114 while batting .301. Sievers selects:

> 1B—MICKEY VERNON
> 2B—BOBBY DOERR
> 3B—BROOKS ROBINSON
> SS—LUIS APARICIO
> OF—TED WILLIAMS
> OF—JOE DiMAGGIO
> OF—MICKEY MANTLE
> C—YOGI BERRA
> RP—BOB FELLER or ALLIE REYNOLDS
> LP—WHITEY FORD or HAL NEWHOUSER

Deserves Cooperstown: Enos Slaughter.
Toughest Pitcher: Reynolds.
Strongest Team: Yankees of the 1950's.

CURT SIMMONS

Simmons came up to the Phillies on the last day of the 1947 season as an 18-year-old lefthanded fastball pitcher. In 1950 he helped pitch the Phillies to a pennant with a 17–8 record and a 3.40 ERA, but he was drafted late in the season and spent the dramatic pennant clinching, the World Series, and all of the 1951 season in the army. He returned in 1952 to win 14 and lose eight with a 2.82 ERA and to tie for the league lead in shutouts with six. He remained with the Phils until 1960, when, his career threatened by a lawn mower accident in which he lost a toe, he was sent to the Cardinals. He stayed in St. Louis until early 1966—going 18–9 with a 3.43 ERA for the pennant-winning 1964 Cards—and finished up with the Cubs (1966–67) and the Angels (1967). His lifetime record was 193–183 with a 3.54 ERA. Simmons selects:

    1B—STAN MUSIAL
    2B—GRANNY HAMNER or JACKIE ROBINSON
    3B—EDDIE MATHEWS
    SS—PEE WEE REESE
    OF—DEL ENNIS
    OF—RICHIE ASHBURN or WILLIE MAYS
    OF—HANK AARON
     C—ROY CAMPANELLA
    RP—DON DRYSDALE
    LP—WARREN SPAHN or SANDY KOUFAX

Toughest Batter: Hank Sauer.

KEN SINGLETON

The switch-hitting Singleton batted .282 over a 15-year career with the Mets (1970–71), Expos (1972–74), and Orioles (1975–84). Although he had shown signs of power skills in the National League, it was not until he joined Baltimore that he became one of the game's finest offensive players. His best season was probably 1979 when he led the Orioles to a pennant with 35 home runs, 29 doubles, 111 runs batted in, and a .295 average. Singleton, who clouted 246 home runs during his career, likes:

```
1B—EDDIE MURRAY
2B—BOBBY GRICH
3B—GEORGE BRETT
SS—ROBIN YOUNT
OF—JIM RICE
OF—PAUL BLAIR
OF—DWIGHT EVANS
 C—CARLTON FISK
RP—JIM PALMER
LP—RON GUIDRY
```

Deserves Cooperstown: Billy Williams.
Toughest Pitcher: Jack Morris. "He was always the toughest for me, at least while he was throwing hard sliders. Ironically, though, when he picked up the split-fingered fastball from Roger Craig, the pitch that's been credited with turning the Tiger staff into winners, that's when I started to hit him a little. I always preferred those split-fingered pitches to the hard sliders."
Most Underrated: Murray. "Absolutely the best player in major league baseball."
Strongest Teams: 1982 Brewers, 1983 Orioles.

DICK SISLER

Sisler hit one of baseball's most dramatic home runs when his tenth-inning three-run blast on the last day of the 1950 season gave Philadelphia a pennant-winning victory over Brooklyn. A lifetime .276 hitter over eight major league seasons, the lefthand-swinging first baseman came up with the Cardinals in 1946, moved over to the Phillies in 1948, then closed out his career with the Reds (1952) and Cardinals again (1952–53). Despite his memorable blast off Don Newcombe in 1950, Sisler in fact clouted only 55 home runs during his career and never more than 13 in a season. Sisler, who managed the Reds in 1964 and 1965, picks:

> 1B—GEORGE SISLER
> 2B—ROGERS HORNSBY
> 3B—PIE TRAYNOR
> SS—HONUS WAGNER
> OF—TED WILLIAMS
> OF—JOE DiMAGGIO
> OF—BABE RUTH
> C—MICKEY COCHRANE
> RP—WALTER JOHNSON
> LP—STEVE CARLTON

Toughest Pitcher: Curt Simmons.
Most Underrated: Enos Slaughter.
Comments: "Of course I pick my dad for first base even though I can remember seeing him play only three times near the end of his career. The first time he tried to steal home and was thrown out. The second time he got a triple. The third time he got an infield hit off a pitcher named Syl Johnson, who didn't like what he considered a cheap hit. One word led to another until the umpires finally had to hold my dad back from going over to the mound after Johnson."

ENOS SLAUGHTER

Slaughter, elected to the Hall of Fame in 1985 after a long and controversial wait, starred as a lefthand-hitting outfielder for the Cardinals between 1938 and 1953. The lifetime .300 hitter then moved on to the American League, where he bounced back and forth between the Yankees and Athletics until 1959, when he returned to the National League to close out his 19-year career as a pinch-hitter with the Braves. A St. Louis representative to the NL All-Star team on 10 occasions, Slaughter led the league in doubles in 1939, in hits and triples in 1942, and in runs batted in in 1946. He also scored 100 runs in three different seasons. Slaughter, whose career was synonymous with the famous run from first base that gave the Cardinals the 1946 World Championship over the Red Sox, picks:

> 1B—STAN MUSIAL
> 2B—JACKIE ROBINSON
> 3B—BROOKS ROBINSON
> SS—PEE WEE REESE
> OF—JOE MEDWICK
> OF—TERRY MOORE
> OF—MEL OTT
> C—ROY CAMPANELLA
> RP—EWELL BLACKWELL
> LP—WHITEY FORD

Toughest Pitcher: Carl Erskine.
Most Underrated: Moore.
Strongest Teams: Cardinals of the 1940's, Dodgers of the 1950's.
Comments: "I also have to mention Dolf Camilli, Marty Marion, Walker Cooper, and Pete Reiser. I always thought Reiser was a much better outfielder for the Dodgers than either Duke Snider or Carl Furillo. He never gave an inch. I guess that's what ended up being his undoing. Damn shame, those injuries of his."

AL SMITH

Smith, an outfielder-third baseman with the Indians (1953–57, 1964), White Sox (1958–62), Orioles (1963) and Red Sox (1964), batted .272 and hit 164 homers. He batted as high as .315 in 1960 and .306 in 1955 and hit 10 or more home runs in every season except his first and last. (His season highs were 28 in 1961 and 22 in 1955.) He also led the AL in runs scored in 1955. He appeared in both the 1954 and 1959 World Series. Smith's choices are:

1B—STAN MUSIAL
2B—JOE GORDON
3B—BROOKS ROBINSON
SS—LUIS APARICIO
OF—TED WILLIAMS
OF—WILLIE MAYS
OF—HANK AARON
C—ROY CAMPANELLA
RP—EARLY WYNN
LP—WARREN SPAHN

Toughest Pitcher: Allie Reynolds.
Most Underrated: Bobby Avila.
Strongest Team: 1954 Indians.
Comments: "The team I've picked comes from both the National and American Leagues, although I played only in the AL."

DUKE SNIDER

Snider, a Hall of Famer since 1980, was the lefthanded power on the great Brooklyn Dodger teams of the 1950's. A lifetime .295 hitter, the center fielder swatted 407 homers in 18 seasons with the Dodgers (1947–62), Mets (1963), and Giants (1964). He batted over .300 seven times (with a high of .341 in 1954), hit 40 or more homers his last five seasons in Brooklyn (including a league-leading 43 in 1956), and had six 100-plus RBI seasons (and led the NL with 136 in 1955).

    1B—GIL HODGES or STAN MUSIAL
    2B—JACKIE ROBINSON
    3B—EDDIE MATHEWS
    SS—PEE WEE REESE
    OF—ROBERTO CLEMENTE or TED WILLIAMS
    OF—JOE DiMAGGIO
    OF—MICKEY MANTLE or WILLIE MAYS
     C—BILL DICKEY, ROY CAMPANELLA, or
          YOGI BERRA
    RP—JUAN MARICHAL
    LP—SANDY KOUFAX

Toughest Pitcher: Bill Henry. "He was a lefty who threw all fastballs and even though I could usually hit the fastball, the harder he threw the more I popped up."

Most Underrated: Carl Furillo. "Carl would do a great job—he led the league in hitting in 1953—but he'd do it without notice. He just wasn't all that colorful."

Strongest Team: 1952 Dodgers. "Just compare the Boys of Summer to the Big Red Machine. As great as the Reds were, only two of them would make the starting lineup if you combined the two teams—and Johnny Bench would have to play third and Pete Rose would have to play left."

Comments: "I'll take DiMaggio over any other outfielder. Marichal had all the pitches. And Koufax, well, it was as if he were throwing imaginary baseballs."

WARREN SPAHN

Spahn, the most successful southpaw in baseball history, gained entry to the Hall of Fame in 1973 on the basis of a lifetime record of 363–245 (3.09 ERA). With the exception of a final season split between the Mets and Giants, he spent all 21 years of his major league career in a Braves uniform. Among his accomplishments were winning 20 games 13 times, leading the league in wins eight times, in earned run average three times, in strikeouts four times, and in complete games nine times. Although he won the Cy Young Award only once, in 1957 for a record of 21–11 (2.69 ERA), in both 1953 and 1963 he turned in records of 23-7, with a 2.10 ERA in the former year and a 2.60 ERA in the latter. Spahn, who also pitched two no-hitters, chooses:

1B—GIL HODGES, STAN MUSIAL, or JOE ADCOCK
2B—BILL MAZEROSKI
3B—BILLY COX, BROOKS ROBINSON, or
    EDDIE MATHEWS
SS—JOHNNY LOGAN or PEE WEE REESE
OF—HANK AARON, BILLY BRUTON, or
    WILLIE MAYS
OF—BOBBY THOMSON or BILL VIRDON
OF—MICKEY MANTLE
 C—DEL CRANDALL or JOHNNY BENCH
RP—LEW BURDETTE, BOB BUHL, or BOB GIBSON
LP—SANDY KOUFAX

Most Underrated: "The Milwaukee teams in general.
Toughest Batter: "Everybody who got up to the plate represented one-twenty-seventh of the problem."
Comments: "The problem with comparisons like this is that you're ultimately being asked to compare apples and oranges. Crandall, for instance, was a great lowball catcher on a lowball pitching team, but Bench had a better arm and better bat. Hodges and Cox for defense, Musial and Mathews for offense. I think comparisons like this are often misleading."

GERRY STALEY

The righthander Staley's 15 major league seasons (1947–61) were more or less divided into a first part as one of the National League's top starters and a second part as one of the American League's most effective relievers. Holder of a 134-111 lifetime record, he came into the NL with the Cardinals in 1947, going on to win 19 games in 1951, 17 in 1952, and 18 in 1953. After brief stints with the Reds and Yankees, he switched to the bullpen following a 1956 trade to the White Sox, becoming a key man in Chicago's 1959 pennant victory with eight wins and 14 saves and topping himself the following year with 13 wins and 10 saves. Staley, who closed out his career with the Athletics and Tigers, picks:

1B—BABE YOUNG
2B—RED SCHOENDIENST
3B—EDDIE MATHEWS
SS—MARTY MARION
OF—ENOS SLAUGHTER
OF—STAN MUSIAL
OF—DUKE SNIDER
C—GIL HODGES
RP—ROBIN ROBERTS
LP—WARREN SPAHN

Deserves Cooperstown: Schoendienst.
Toughest Batters: Musial and Ted Williams.
Most Underrated: Marion.
Strongest Team: Dodgers of the 1950's.
Comments: "I don't think picking Hodges as the catcher is odd at all. The man was absolutely great when he came up and did the catching for the Dodgers. Later, of course, he moved over to first and was replaced by Roy Campanella, but, great as Campy and a couple of others were, they weren't any better defensively than Hodges."

Young batted .273 in eight seasons (1936, 1939-42, 1946-48) with the Giants and two other NL teams. He hit 79 home runs in his career, 25 of them in 1941.

WILLIE STARGELL

The powerful Stargell rewrote most of the statistical history of the Pittsburgh franchise and a good deal of that of the National League when his 21 years (1962–82) with the Pirates produced 475 homers, 1540 runs batted in, and 953 extra-base hits. A lifetime .282 hitter, the lefty-swinging outfielder-first baseman led the NL in homers in both 1971 and 1973 and was named the circuit's MVP (in a tie with Keith Hernandez) in 1979. His most potent years at the plate were undoubtedly 1971 (.295, 48 home runs, 125 runs batted in, 104 runs scored) and 1973 (.299, 44 home runs, 119 runs batted in, 106 runs scored). Stargell picks:

  1B—WILLIE McCOVEY
  2B—BILL MAZEROSKI or JOE MORGAN
  3B—BILL MADLOCK or MIKE SCHMIDT
  SS—DAVE CONCEPCION
  OF—HANK AARON or FRANK ROBINSON
  OF—WILLIE MAYS or DALE MURPHY
  OF—ROBERTO CLEMENTE or DAVE PARKER
   C—JOHNNY BENCH
  RP—JUAN MARICHAL
  LP—SANDY KOUFAX or STEVE CARLTON

Toughest Pitchers: Marichal, Fergie Jenkins, Don Sutton, Phil Niekro, and Joe Niekro. "I guess one game I'll never forget was one in which Marichal struck me out three times on three different pitches thrown three entirely different ways."

Most Underrated: Madlock, George Hendrick, and Ron Cey.

Strongest Teams: "You'd have to say the Big Red Machine teams in Cincinnati, but, as twenty-five-man units, I think a lot of people overlook the Giants and Reds in the late 1960's and early 1970's."

JOHN STEARNS

Serious arm and hand injuries cut short catcher Stearns's promising career in 1984 after 11 years with the Phillies (1974) and the Mets (1975–84). A lifetime .260 hitter with a particular penchant for doubles, he could also run for a backstop, evidenced by his record-breaking 25 steals in 1978. In the same year, he clouted 15 home runs and drove home 73 runs while batting .264. Stearns, the Met representative to several all-star games, picks:

1B—KEITH HERNANDEZ
2B—JOE MORGAN
3B—MIKE SCHMIDT
SS—OZZIE SMITH
OF—DAVE WINFIELD
OF—DALE MURPHY
OF—ANDRE DAWSON
C—JOHNNY BENCH
RP—TOM SEAVER
LP—STEVE CARLTON

Toughest Pitchers: Gene Garber and Kent Tekulve. "Both of them dropped down on you after all that motion, so it was hard to pick up the ball."

Most Underrated: "The guys I suppose you would call the .260 infielders. Players like Phil Garner, who always do the little things to help a team. He's a very unselfish player. I think Johnny Ray is also underrated, although he's better than a .260 hitter."

Strongest Team: 1975–76 Reds.

RIGGS STEPHENSON

Stephenson has the highest lifetime batting average (.336) of any player who is not in the Hall of Fame. He came to the Indians as an infielder from the University of Alabama. He stayed with the Indians, mostly as a utility player, until 1926, when he went to the Cubs, where with Hack Wilson and Kiki Cuyler he formed one of the greatest outfields of all time. His best season was 1929, when he hit .362, clubbed 17 homers, and drove in 110 runs. "Steve" stayed with the Cubs through 1934 and batted .316 and .444 in his two World Series (1929 and 1932). Stephenson selects:

```
1B—LOU GEHRIG
2B—ROGERS HORNSBY
3B—PIE TRAYNOR
SS—JOE SEWELL
OF—TRIS SPEAKER
OF—TY COBB
OF—BABE RUTH
 C—GABBY HARTNETT
RP—WALTER JOHNSON
LP—LEFTY GROVE
```

Toughest Pitcher: Dazzy Vance. "He pitched off a high mound and he was a big man, so the ball came down at you instead of straight toward you. And his fastball would rise, too. He also had a sharp overhand curve, what we called a drop. Then he'd cut his shirt around the right arm so you couldn't pick up the ball."

Strongest Teams: 1929 Athletics, 1932 Yankees.

STEVE STONE

Righthander Stone compiled a record of 107–93 in 11 years with the Giants (1971–72), White Sox (1973, 1977–78), Cubs (1974–76), and Orioles (1979–81). Burdened with mediocre teams for most of his career, he had no mound peer in 1980 when, as the ace of the Baltimore staff, he turned in a mark of 25–7, leading the American League in wins and percentage and walking off with the Cy Young trophy for his efforts. Stone, whose career was cut short by injuries, chooses:

> 1B—DICK ALLEN
> 2B—RYNE SANDBERG
> 3B—BROOKS ROBINSON
> SS—OZZIE SMITH
> OF—HANK AARON
> OF—WILLIE MAYS
> OF—ROBERTO CLEMENTE
> C—JOHNNY BENCH
> RP—TOM SEAVER
> LP—SANDY KOUFAX

Toughest Batter: Cecil Cooper. "I think he hit five homers off me in 1979 and 1980."

Most Underrated: "The more television gets into the game, the harder it becomes for anyone to be underrated. Everything is under a microscope, from the smallest running tactic to the grand-slam home run, and everything gets noticed by everybody right away. I just don't believe anyone who has ever played on the Game of the Week can be described as underrated."

Strongest Team: Reds of the 1970's.

MEL STOTTLEMYRE

The ace of the Yankees during the team's long winter at the bottom of the American League, righthander Stottlemyre won 164 against 139 losses with an exceptional 2.97 ERA in his 11 years (1964–74) in pinstripes. A three-time 20-game winner, he also averaged fewer than three runs a game yielded in six different seasons and led the AL in complete games twice. His single best year was probably 1965 when he turned in a record of 20–9 (2.63 ERA). Stottlemyre, whose career was cut short by a torn rotator cuff, likes:

1B—KEITH HERNANDEZ
2B—BOBBY RICHARDSON
3B—BROOKS ROBINSON
SS—OZZIE SMITH
OF—CARL YASTRZEMSKI
OF—MICKEY MANTLE
OF—FRANK ROBINSON
C—ELSTON HOWARD
RP—BOB GIBSON
LP—WHITEY FORD

Toughest Batter: Tony Oliva. "No question about it. The man had no weaknesses."

Most Underrated: Oliva. "The fact is that, just because he played for a relatively small city like Minneapolis, nobody really understood how great he was."

Strongest Team: Orioles of the mid- and late 1960's.

Comments: "Elston Howard did the little things for a pitcher that don't always show up in the box score but that usually make the difference between winning and losing. Of today's players, I'd say Gary Carter is the same way. Ford, I'd say, was the smartest pitcher I ever saw, although Carlton's not bad, either. Ask me the same questions in a couple of years and I might pick Dwight Gooden over Gibson."

GUS SUHR

Suhr, a lefthand-hitting first baseman, fit in well on the slugging Pirate teams of the 1930's. He was a fixture at first in Forbes Field for almost 10 years (1930–39), establishing a National League consecutive game record of 822 at first base (since broken by Steve Garvey). A lifetime .279 hitter, he batted as high as .312 (1936), hit 10 or more homers five times, and drove in more than 100 runs three times. He finished his career with parts of two seasons (1939–40) with the Phillies. Suhr's selections are:

> 1B—BILL TERRY
> 2B—ROGERS HORNSBY
> 3B—PIE TRAYNOR
> SS—ARKY VAUGHAN
> OF—JOE MEDWICK
> OF—FREDDIE LINDSTROM
> OF—PAUL WANER
> C—GABBY HARTNETT
> RP—PAUL DERRINGER
> LP—CARL HUBBELL

Toughest Pitchers: Ed Brandt and Bill Hallahan. ''Brandt was a sidearm lefty, and being lefthanded, I had a lot of trouble with him. And Hallahan was just wild and fast.'' Brandt had a record of 121-146 with a 3.86 ERA in eleven seasons (1928–38) with the Braves and two other NL seasons.

Most Underrated: Vaughan.

Strongest Team: Giants of the 1930's.

Comments: ''Billy Herman was a better fielder than Hornsby but Hornsby was the hitter. And right behind Hartnett would be Ernie Lombardi.''

RON SWOBODA

Swoboda, who will always be remembered for his startling defense in the 1969 World Series, batted .242 in nine major league seasons (1965–73). Breaking in with the Mets in 1965, he seemed on his way to becoming the expansion franchise's first home-grown power hitter when he clouted 19 home runs in his rookie season, but in fact he never reached that mark again. For consistency, his best year at the plate was the .281 mark he turned in for New York in 1967. Swoboda, who also played for the Expos and Yankees before retiring, chooses:

                1B—WILLIE McCOVEY
                2B—BILL MAZEROSKI
                3B—BROOKS ROBINSON
                SS—BUD HARRELSON
                OF—HANK AARON
                OF—WILLIE MAYS
                OF—ROBERTO CLEMENTE
                 C—JOHNNY BENCH
                RP—BOB GIBSON
                LP—SANDY KOUFAX

Toughest Pitcher: Gibson. "I just can't believe that anyone who ever had to face him *wouldn't* say Gibson. Anyone who picks somebody else just wasn't paying attention to what was coming toward them."

Strongest Team: Reds of the 1970's.

GENE TENACE

Tenace, a righthand-hitting catcher, batted .241 over 16 years with the Athletics (1969–76), Padres (1977–80), Cardinals (1981–82), and Pirates (1983). He demonstrated his power by blasting 20 home runs or more in five different seasons, but was even more known for his patience at the plate, drawing 100 walks in six years and leading the American League in that category in 1974 and the National League in 1977. His finest offensive season was undoubtedly 1975, when he hit 29 homers, drew 106 walks, knocked in 87 runs, and scored 83 times. Tenace, who established a World Series record in 1972 by homering in his first two at bats and tied a record in 1973 by walking 11 times in a seven-game series, likes:

1B—WILLIE STARGELL
2B—DICK GREEN
3B—SAL BANDO
SS—OZZIE SMITH
OF—JOE RUDI
OF—DAVE WINFIELD
OF—REGGIE JACKSON
C—TONY PENA
RP—CATFISH HUNTER
LP—VIDA BLUE

Deserve Cooperstown: Jackson, Hunter, and Rollie Fingers.

Toughest Pitchers: Nolan Ryan and J.R. Richard.

Most Underrated: Rudi. ''And I just say him as one of several on the Oakland teams from the early 1970's. We won three straight World Series, but you'd never know it. Everyone knows about the Yankees in the 1950's and 1960's, and they even talk about the Big Red Machine. Well, we were better than those Cincinnati teams. Look at the record.''

Strongest Team: Athletics of the 1970's.

RALPH TERRY

Terry pitched for 12 years in the major leagues, won 107 games, lost 99, and completed his career with a 3.62 ERA. He worked for the Yankees (1956–57, 1959–64), Athletics (1957–58, 1966), Indians (1965), and Mets (1966–67). The 6'3" righthander led the American League in wins (23) in 1962 and was the winner in the seventh game of the World Series that year. Terry's choices are:

1B—JOE COLLINS or VIC POWER
2B—BOBBY RICHARDSON
3B—CLETE BOYER
SS—LUIS APARICIO
OF—MICKEY MANTLE
OF—WILLIE MAYS
OF—HANK AARON
 C—YOGI BERRA or ELSTON HOWARD
RP—ALLIE REYNOLDS
LP—SANDY KOUFAX

Toughest Batter: Ted Williams. "It was great to walk him."

Most Underrated: Roy Sievers.

Strongest Team: 1961 Yankees.

Comments: "My greatest moment was, of course, the seventh game of the 1962 Series. Ralph Houk came out to ask me how my control was and whether we should pitch to Willie McCovey. There were runners on second and third and I figured if I walked McCovey there would be no room to maneuver. Besides, Orlando Cepeda, who was up next, had had three hits the day before. We decided to pitch to McCovey but not give him anything good. Anyway, McCovey hit that line drive to Bobby Richardson and that was that."

FRANK THOMAS

Frank Thomas batted .266 and walloped 286 home runs over a 16-year (1951–66) career that initially saw him trying to fill Ralph Kiner's shoes as Pittsburgh's one-man offense (and only gate attraction) in the early 1950's. From 1959 to 1966 he traveled from one end of the National League to the other, stopping off with the Reds, Cubs, Braves, Mets (in their inaugural season), Phillies, and Astros. His best years were in 1953 (30 homers, 102 RBI's) and 1958 (35 homers, 109 RBI's) for the Pirates, and in 1962 for the Mets (34 homers, 94 RBI's). Thomas picks:

1B—GIL HODGES
2B—BILL MAZEROSKI
3B—EDDIE MATHEWS
SS—ROY McMILLAN
OF—DUKE SNIDER
OF—WILLIE MAYS
OF—HANK AARON
C—ROY CAMPANELLA
RP—ROBIN ROBERTS
LP—WARREN SPAHN

Toughest Pitchers: Don Drysdale and Bob Gibson.
Most Underrated: "Myself. I never got the recognition I should have gotten."
Strongest Team: "The 1961 Milwaukee Braves were the toughest team I was ever on, even though they didn't win the pennant that year."
Comments: "I admit there are some American Leaguers who might break into my lineup, but the fact is that I never actually played against them and prefer sticking to those I saw personally."

BOBBY THOMSON

Although he will always be best remembered for his story-book homer against the Dodgers in the 1951 playoffs, Thomson had a number of highs in his 15-year career with the Giants (1946–53, 1957), Braves (1954–57), Cubs (1958–59), Red Sox (1960), and Orioles (1960). Among his accomplishments were hitting at least 20 home runs eight times, driving in 100 runs four times, and leading the National League in triples in 1952. It was in the glory year of 1951, however, that the outfielder-third baseman found he could do no wrong: 32 home runs, 27 doubles, 73 walks, 89 runs scored, and 101 runs batted in. Thomson, who was also a fine defensive outfielder, picks:

1B—STAN MUSIAL
2B—JACKIE ROBINSON
3B—EDDIE MATHEWS
SS—ALVIN DARK
OF—TED WILLIAMS
OF—JOE DiMAGGIO
OF—WILLIE MAYS
C—WES WESTRUM
RP—ALLIE REYNOLDS
LP—HERB SCORE

Toughest Pitcher: Ewell Blackwell.
Most Underrated: Don Mueller. ''Mueller never got much respect because he was mainly a singles hitter. Even Leo Durocher, when he was managing the Giants, didn't seem to like him much because he had a big rear end and didn't run very well. But I always thought Mueller was a great clutch hitter, and games are won on singles and doubles as much as on homers.''
Strongest Team: Dodgers of the 1950's.

EARL TORGESON

Earl Torgeson, a lefthanded first baseman for 15 years, came up with the Braves (1947–52), and also played for the Phillies (1953–55), Tigers (1955–57), White Sox (1957–61), and Yankees (1961). A lifetime .265 hitter with 149 home runs, Torgeson's best year was 1950 when he batted .290 with 23 homers, 30 doubles, 119 walks, 120 runs, and 87 RBI's. Torgeson selects the following:

     1B—GIL HODGES
     2B—JACKIE ROBINSON
     3B—BROOKS ROBINSON
     SS—LUIS APARICIO
     OF—HANK AARON
     OF—MICKEY MANTLE
     OF—WILLIE MAYS
      C—ROY CAMPANELLA
     RP—FRANK LARY
     LP—HERB SCORE

Toughest Pitcher: Al Brazle. "I still have nightmares about him. I played against him in the Pacific Coast League and in the National League and I couldn't see his pitch. He was sort of a sinkerball pitcher. I think when I finally got a hit off him they released him."

Most Underrated: Terry Moore. "He was a stabilizing influence but he was hidden on that Cardinal team."

Strongest Team: Dodgers of the 1950's. "I always felt like I was walking into a bull ring at Ebbets Field. You'd leave after a four-game series mentally and physically exhausted."

Comments: "I picked this team as if my life were on the line in the game they would play. Of course, if my life were on the line I would want to play, but I have to go with Hodges for power and defense. Other possibilities are Clete Boyer at third, Pee Wee Reese at short, Yogi Berra, Del Crandall, or Jim Hegan behind the plate, and Robin Roberts on the mound."

JOE TORRE

Torre, a power-hitting catcher who closed out his career alternating between first and third base, slugged 252 home runs and batted .297 in 18 years with the Braves (1960–68), Cardinals (1969–74), and Mets (1975–77). Although his finest season was undoubtedly 1971, when he was named the National League's Most Valuable Player for leading the league in batting, hits, total bases, and runs batted in, he also shone in 1966 (.315, 36 homers, 101 runs batted in). Torre, who has managed the Mets and Braves, prefers:

1B—WILLIE McCOVEY
2B—BILL MAZEROSKI
3B—MIKE SCHMIDT
SS—OZZIE SMITH
OF—HANK AARON
OF—WILLIE MAYS
OF—ROBERTO CLEMENTE
C—JOHNNY BENCH
RP—BOB GIBSON
LP—SANDY KOUFAX

Toughest Pitcher: Gibson. "There was Gibby and then there was everyone else."
Strongest Team: 1976 Reds.

CECIL TRAVIS

Usually overlooked in discussions of the game's best all-around shortstops, Travis belted an impressive .314 in 12 seasons with the Senators between 1933 and 1941 and 1945 and 1947. In 1941, his last season before being called into military service, he led the American League in hits while batting .359 with 19 triples, 39 doubles, 101 runs driven in, and 106 runs scored. Other good offensive years were 1937 when he batted .344 and 1938 when he averaged .335. Travis, who was also a fine fielder, chooses:

1B—LOU GEHRIG
2B—CHARLIE GEHRINGER
3B—OSSIE BLUEGE
SS—JOE CRONIN
OF—TED WILLIAMS
OF—JOE DiMAGGIO
OF—EARL AVERILL
C—BILL DICKEY
RP—BOB FELLER
LP—LEFTY GROVE

Toughest Pitchers: Feller, Grove, Lefty Gomez, and Mel Harder.

Most Underrated: Bluege. "He was the best fielder I ever saw at third, including Brooks Robinson, and he could hit the ball, too. I guess he just didn't hit the long ball enough to get the recognition he deserved."

Strongest Team: Yankees of the 1930's.

VIRGIL TRUCKS

Trucks pitched in the American League for 17 seasons with the Tigers (1941–43, 1945–52, 1956), Browns (1953), White Sox (1953–55), Athletics (1957–58), and Yankees (1958). He won 20 games in 1953, led the league in strikeouts (153) and shutouts (six) in 1949, and finished with a career record of 177–135 and a 3.39 ERA. He had only two losing seasons in his career, 1947 (10–12) and 1952, when he won only five games while losing 19—but two of those five victories were no-hitters! Trucks selects:

1B—LOU GEHRIG
2B—CHARLIE GEHRINGER
3B—PIE TRAYNOR
SS—LUKE APPLING
OF—BABE RUTH
OF—JOE DiMAGGIO
OF—TED WILLIAMS
C—MICKEY COCHRANE
RP—TED LYONS
LP—CARL HUBBELL

Deserve Cooperstown: "Ben Chapman and me. I believe Chapman had a lot better major league average than a lot of people in the Hall of Fame. I also know my credentials are better than several others in there."

Toughest Batter: Williams.

Most Underrated: Jim Rivera, Frank Crosetti, and Roy Cullenbine. Outfielder-first baseman Cullenbine played for six teams from 1938 to 1947. He batted .276 with 110 home runs.

Strongest Teams: "The strongest team I played against was the New York Yankees in the 1940's. The best I played for was the 1953 Chicago White Sox."

BOB TURLEY

The big righthanded Turley, who developed the no-windup delivery, won the Cy Young Award in 1958 on the basis of a 21–7 season, leading the league in wins, winning percentage (.750), and complete games (19). His career spans a dozen years with the Browns (1951, 1953), Orioles (1954), Yankees (1955–62), Angels (1963), and Red Sox (1963). He earned the name "Bullet Bob" because of his overpowering fastball. In five World Series, he won four and lost three and was the hero of the 1958 Series, winning the fifth and seventh games and coming in to get the last out in relief in the sixth game. Turley selects:

  1B—MICKEY VERNON
  2B—BOBBY RICHARDSON or NELLIE FOX
  3B—BROOKS ROBINSON
  SS—LUIS APARICIO
  OF—MICKEY MANTLE
  OF—ROBERTO CLEMENTE
  OF—HANK AARON
   C—YOGI BERRA
  RP—BOB FELLER
  LP—WHITEY FORD

Toughest Batter: Fox. "He was a close personal friend but on the field he'd get on base against me any way he could. He'd hit two home runs a year and one would be off me."

Most Underrated: Roger Maris. "He's remembered for the 61 home runs but he was also a great fielder and had a great arm. And he always played in Mantle's shadow."

Strongest Team: 1961 Yankees. "The most impressive thing about the Yankees of the late fifties and early sixties was the caliber of play in September. Sometimes it seemed they played .800 ball in September."

ELMER VALO

Valo batted over .300 seven times in a 20-year (1940-43, 1946-61) career in the American and National leagues. A lifetime .282 hitter with a reputation for being particularly tough in the clutch, the lefthand-batting outfielder played for the Athletics until 1956, after which he moved on to the Phillies, Dodgers, Indians, Yankees, Senators-Twins, and the Phillies again. Valo has become a favorite of trivia addicts because he is the only native of Czechoslovakia to play in the majors and also because he is the only player to have moved with three franchises (with the A's from Philadelphia to Kansas City, with the Dodgers from Brooklyn to Los Angeles, and with the Senators from Washington to Minnesota). Valo picks:

> 1B—GIL HODGES
> 2B—BOBBY DOERR
> 3B—RED ROLFE
> SS—EDDIE JOOST
> OF—JOE DiMAGGIO
> OF—TED WILLIAMS
> OF—MICKEY MANTLE
> C—BILL DICKEY
> RP—BOB FELLER
> LP—MICKEY McDERMOTT

Deserve Cooperstown: Doerr "among others".
Toughest Pitcher: McDermott.
Most Underrated: Pete Suder. "Suder was a teammate on the A's who never got much recognition because our teams weren't particularly good. But he was the kind of key infielder—always batted near .270, always made the double play—who would take down millions today."
Strongest Team: Yankees of the 1940's and 1950's.

DAZZY VANCE

Vance, a Hall of Famer since 1955, was probably the finest pitcher in the history of the Brooklyn Dodgers. From the time he came up with the Pirates in 1915 until his retirement in 1935, he compiled a record of 197–140, with an ERA of 3.24 and a strikeout total of 2045. Although he also hurled for the Yankees, Cardinals, and Reds, in addition to the Pirates, all but seven of his wins were registered in a Brooklyn uniform. A three-time 20-game winner, he also led the National League in ERA three times, in complete games twice, and in strike-outs for seven consecutive years (1922-28). Vance's picks:

        1B—GEORGE SISLER
        2B—ROGERS HORNSBY
        3B—PIE TRAYNOR
        SS—HONUS WAGNER
        OF—TY COBB
        OF—JOE DiMAGGIO
        OF—BABE RUTH
         C—BILL DICKEY
        RP—WALTER JOHNSON
        LP—LEFTY GROVE

The interesting thing about Vance's choices is that they include only three National Leaguers, one of whom (Wagner) was retired before the righthander ever took to the mound. Of the 16 years he spent in the majors, Vance spent about 15 of them in the senior circuit.

JOHNNY VANDER MEER

Vander Meer, who will forever be identified with the back-to-back no-hitters he threw against Boston and Brooklyn on June 11 and June 15, 1938, had an otherwise spotted 13-year career (1937–43, 1946–51). With the Reds from 1937 to 1949, Cubs in 1950, and Indians in 1951, he came in with a lifetime mark two games under .500 (119–121), led the National League in walks twice, and never won 20 games in a single season. On the other hand, he did have years when he won 18 (1942), 17 (1948), and 16 (1941) games, did lead the National League in strikeouts in 1941, 1942, and 1943, and, of course, did have those no-hitters. Vander Meer's picks:

1B—BILL TERRY
2B—ROGERS HORNSBY
3B—PIE TRAYNOR
SS—JOE CRONIN
OF—PAUL WANER
OF—JOE DiMAGGIO
OF—BABE RUTH
C—ERNIE LOMBARDI
RP—EWELL BLACKWELL
LP—CARL HUBBELL

Deserves Cooperstown: Lombardi. "I'll never really understand why Lombardi isn't in the Hall of Fame. He's the only catcher ever to lead the league in hitting twice, he seldom struck out, he could throw as well as anyone. I guess it's because he couldn't run and because he played for a good team only twice in his career. But I still believe he's a Hall of Famer if there ever was one."

Toughest Batter: Walker Cooper.
Most Underrated: Lombardi.

BOB VEALE

Southpaw Veale had a record of 120–95 (3.08 ERA) in 13 years (1962–74) with the Pirates and Red Sox. The first pitcher in the history of the Pittsburgh franchise to chalk up 200 strikeouts, he achieved the feat three times and also retired with a sterling mark of having allowed a home run only every 21.2 innings. His best years were 1964 (18–12, 2.74 ERA, league-leading 250 strikeouts) and 1965 (17–12, 2.84, 276 strikeouts). Veale likes:

1B—WILLIE McCOVEY
2B—BILL MAZEROSKI
3B—DON HOAK
SS—GENE ALLEY
OF—TOMMY DAVIS
OF—WILLIE MAYS
OF—ROBERTO CLEMENTE
C—JOHNNY BENCH
RP—BOB GIBSON
LP—SANDY KOUFAX

Deserves Cooperstown: Billy Williams.
Toughest Batter: Orlando Cepeda.
Most Underrated: Clemente and Williams.
Strongest Team: Cardinals of the late 1960's.
Comments: ''Hoak was never thought of as one of the great players, but he was a fighter and knew everything about National League hitters there was to know. He made the Pittsburgh infield as good as it was because he knew how to line up in the field against every batter who got into the batter's box.''

MICKEY VERNON

Vernon was a lefty first baseman who was a wizard with a bat and a glove in four decades. He batted .286 in his career, including batting championship averages of .353 in 1946 and .337 in 1953. He also led the AL in doubles three times (with a career high of 51 in 1946). While not considered a power hitter, he did hit 20 homers in 1954 and 18 in 1949. His season high for RBI's was 115 in 1953. In addition, he holds several American League fielding records for first basemen: most games, putouts, assists, and chances accepted in a career; and most assists in a season (155 in 1949). And he holds the major league record for most double plays in a career. Most of his efforts were for the lowly Senators (1939–48, 1950–55), although he also saw service with the Indians (1949–50, 1958), Red Sox (1956–57), Braves (1959), and Pirates (1960). Vernon picks:

1B—JIMMIE FOXX
2B—CHARLIE GEHRINGER
3B—BROOKS ROBINSON
SS—LUKE APPLING
OF—TED WILLIAMS
OF—JOE DiMAGGIO
OF—MICKEY MANTLE
C—BILL DICKEY
RP—BOB FELLER
LP—LEFTY GROVE

Deserves Cooperstown: Bobby Doerr.
Toughest Pitcher: Feller.
Most Underrated: Cecil Travis.
Strongest Team: 1949–53 Yankees.
Comments: "I picked all American Leaguers. I played spring training games and All-Star Games against National League greats and would have included them. But there is only room for one name at each position."

BILL VIRDON

Virdon, a lefthanded swinging center fielder and leadoff man, played for the Cardinals (1955–56) and Pirates (1956–65, 1968). He was the National League Rookie of the Year in 1955. He got off to a poor start in 1956, batting .211 in 24 games for the Cards, before being traded to the Pirates and batting .334 in his last 133 games for an overall season average of .319, his highest. He played in the 1960 World Series and hit the shot that took a bad hop and struck Tony Kubek in the throat, eventually leading to Pittsburgh's victory. Subsequently he managed the Pirates (1972–73), Yankees (1974–75), Astros (1975–82), and Expos (1983–84). Virdon's choices are:

1B—KEITH HERNANDEZ
2B—BILL MAZEROSKI
3B—EDDIE MATHEWS
SS—OZZIE SMITH
OF—ROBERTO CLEMENTE
OF—WILLIE MAYS
OF—STAN MUSIAL
C—ROY CAMPANELLA
RP—JUAN MARICHAL
LP—SANDY KOUFAX

Toughest Pitcher: Koufax.
Most Underrated: Curt Flood.
Strongest Team: 1955 Dodgers.

DICK WAKEFIELD

Wakefield, baseball's first bonus baby, batted .293 in nine war-interrupted years between 1941 and 1952. The lefthand-hitting outfielder's best years were with the Tigers, especially in 1943, when he led the American League in hits and doubles, scored 91 runs, and averaged .316. The following season he batted .355 for Detroit. Wakefield, who closed out his injury-filled career with brief stints with the Yankees and Giants, picks:

    1B—MICKEY VERNON
    2B—JOE GORDON
    3B—GEORGE KELL
    SS—PHIL RIZZUTO
    OF—TED WILLIAMS
    OF—JOE DiMAGGIO
    OF—STAN MUSIAL
     C—BILL DICKEY
    RP—ALLIE REYNOLDS or JOHNNY NIGGELING
    LP—THORNTON LEE

Toughest Pitcher: Lee. "He threw a very heavy ball and had great control."

Most Underrated: Pete Suder and Walt Judnich.

Strongest Team: 1946 Tigers.

Johnny Niggeling, cited by Wakefield as a righthand pitching preference, had an extremely modest 64–69 record in nine years with the Braves, Reds, Browns, Senators, and Braves again. While in the American League, however, he turned in such ERA marks as 2.66, 2.59, and 2.32 for mediocre clubs.

Judnich hit .281 with 90 homers in seven seasons (1940–42, 1946–49) with the Browns and two other teams. In his rookie season the lefty outfielder batted .303 with 24 homers and 89 RBI's.

HARRY WALKER

"The Hat" was one of the National League's most consistent hitters in his 11 years of service with the Cardinals (1940–47), Phillies (1947–48), Cubs (1949), Reds (1949), and Cardinals again (1950–51, 1955). A lifetime .296 hitter, he captured the batting championship with a .363 average in 1947 despite being traded in midseason to Philadelphia from St. Louis. The lefthand-hitting outfielder also led the league that year in triples (16) and threw in 29 doubles to offset his reputation as a singles hitter. As player-manager of the Cardinals in 1955, he still had enough to get five hits in 14 at bats. Walker, who also managed the Pirates (1965–67) and Astros (1968–72) and who remains one of the game's most celebrated batting instructors, chooses:

> 1B—LOU GEHRIG
> 2B—CHARLIE GEHRINGER
> 3B—EDDIE MATHEWS
> SS—ERNIE BANKS
> OF—STAN MUSIAL
> OF—HANK AARON
> OF—BABE RUTH
> C—BILL DICKEY
> RP—ROBIN ROBERTS
> LP—WARREN SPAHN

Deserves Cooperstown: Dixie Walker. "The main trouble with baseball today is that everything has become diluted by numbers. A few years ago I would have never said my brother Dixie belonged in the Hall of Fame, but with the people being let in now, why not? He was as good as some of them. Same thing with the number of teams. Make sixteen teams out of the twenty-six around today, and they'd be stronger than the sixteen of the 1950's. But twenty-six? Too weak."

Toughest Pitcher: Al Brazle.

Strongest Team: 1942 Cardinals.

BUCKY WALTERS

Walters began his career as a third baseman with the Braves (1931–32) and Red Sox (1933–34) and always remained a decent hitter (.243 lifetime). Traded to the Phillies in mid-1934, he became a pitcher for the Phils (1935–38), Reds (1938–48), and Braves (1950), winning 198 and losing 160 in his career. He led the National League in both wins (27 and 22) and ERA (2.29 and 2.48) in Cincinnati's pennant-winning seasons of 1939 and 1940. He was the NL's Most Valuable Player in 1939. And he managed the Reds for part of 1948 and all of 1949. Walters's choices:

> 1B—BILL TERRY, FRANK McCORMICK,
>   or STAN MUSIAL
> 2B—BILLY HERMAN
> 3B—PIE TRAYNOR
> SS—ARKY VAUGHAN
> OF—PAUL WANER
> OF—JOE MEDWICK
> OF—CHUCK KLEIN
>   C—ERNIE LOMBARDI
> RP—DIZZY DEAN
> LP—LEFTY GROVE

Toughest Batter: Rip Collins.

Most Underrated: Collins and Billy Myers. "Myers had a great arm and was a great playmaker." Shortstop Myers was a .257 hitter with the Reds and Cubs from 1935 to 1941.

Comments: "I can't put one of the first basemen over the others. Lombardi had a great arm and was a great hitter. They played him deep because he was so slow, but I'd like to see him hit on Astroturf where they couldn't do that. Dean was the best righthander before he got hurt.

"The thing I remember most was pitching in old Baker Bowl. You always seemed to have three on and a lefthander up in that place."

BILL WAMBSGANSS

Wamby was a scrappy second baseman with the Indians (1914–23), Red Sox (1924–25), and Athletics (1926). He had a .259 lifetime batting average and a season high of .295 in 1918. Wambsganss is the only player ever to make an unassisted triple play in a World Series game, a feat he performed in the fifth game in 1920. Wambsganss selects:

> 1B—GEORGE SISLER
> 2B—LARRY LAJOIE
> 3B—FRANK BAKER
> SS—JOE SEWELL
> OF—TY COBB
> OF—TRIS SPEAKER
> OF—BABE RUTH
> C—RAY SCHALK
> RP—WALTER JOHNSON
> LP—BABE RUTH

Deserve Cooperstown: Joe Wood and Ken Keltner.

Toughest Pitchers: Johnson and Ruth. "Johnson was all rhythm. He had this easy motion, between overhand and sidearm, and you'd never expect him to be so fast, but sometimes you couldn't see the ball."

Most Underrated: Larry Gardner. "He was colorless, but he was excellent in the clutch."

Strongest Teams: 1920 Indians, 1920 Dodgers.

Comments: "We were leading 7–1 in that fifth game of the Series because Elmer Smith hit a home run with the bases loaded and Jim Bagby hit one with two on. Pete Kilduff and Otto Miller both singled in the fifth. I played Clarence Mitchell, the pitcher, deep because he was a good hitter. He hit a line drive to my right. I took a couple of steps to my right and jumped, then continued to second base for the second out. I could see Miller approach second base out of the corner of my eye and I just walked over and touched him. Miller told me the next day that he thought Tris Speaker, who played a shallow center field, had tossed the ball in to force him out."

BILL WERBER

Werber was a scrappy, outspoken, swift third baseman. A graduate of Duke University, he came up with the Yankees in 1930 as a shortstop, played two years in the minors, and was converted to the hot corner when he came to Boston in 1933. He also played for the Athletics (1937–38), went to the Reds in time to play in two World Series (1939–41), and finished with the Giants (1942). His lifetime average was .271 and he led the AL in stolen bases three times. Werber's choices are:

> 1B—LOU GEHRIG
> 2B—CHARLIE GEHRINGER
> 3B—BILL WERBER
> SS—LUKE APPLING
> OF—EARLE COMBS
> OF—DOC CRAMER
> OF—SAMMY WEST
> C—BILL DICKEY
> RP—PAUL DERRINGER
> LP—LEFTY GROVE

Deserve Cooperstown: Ernie Lombardi and Wes Ferrell.
Toughest Pitchers: Herb Pennock and Mel Harder. "Pennock would dish you up a lot of junk. He had three pitches, each one slower than the others, and you'd stand there and swing three or four times before the ball reached the plate. I got four doubles off Harder once in Fenway and I don't think I ever got another hit off him."
Most Underrated: Cramer.
Comments: "Sam Rice probably belongs in the outfield too. And as for myself, well, no one could run faster. There wasn't anyone better in the clutch. And no one could cover more ground."

BILL WHITE

White batted .286 and stroked 202 home runs in 13 big league seasons with the Giants in New York (1956) and San Francisco (1958), Cardinals (1959–65, 1969), and Phillies (1966–68). The lefthanded first baseman hit 20 or more homers in seven different seasons, six of them consecutive (1961–66), drove in more than 100 runs in four seasons, and batted better than .300 four times. His season high batting average was .324 in 1962. White, who played in the 1964 World Series for the Cardinals, picks:

> 1B—*
> 2B—BILL MAZEROSKI
> 3B—KEN BOYER
> SS—ROY McMILLAN
> OF—FRANK ROBINSON
> OF—WILLIE MAYS
> OF—HANK AARON
> C—ROY CAMPANELLA
> RP—BOB GIBSON
> LP—SANDY KOUFAX

Most Underrated: Eddie Murray.
Comments: * "I'll leave first base blank because I'm prejudiced."

ROY WHITE

White, a switch-hitter, played his entire career with the Yankees (1965–79), compiling a .271 batting average and 160 home runs as a left fielder and designated hitter. He could hit for average (.290 in 1969, .296 in 1970, .292 in 1971, .290 in 1975) or for power (22 homers and 94 RBI's in 1970, 19 homers and 84 RBI's in 1971), and he could run (232 stolen bases). His sixth-inning homer in the fourth game of the 1978 championship series produced the game-winning and pennant-winning runs. After his years with the Yankees he played in Japan for a few seasons. White selects:

    1B—BOOG POWELL
    2B—ROD CAREW
    3B—BROOKS ROBINSON
    SS—LUIS APARICIO
    OF—CARL YASTRZEMSKI
    OF—TONY OLIVA
    OF—MICKEY MANTLE
     C—THURMAN MUNSON
    RP—JIM PALMER
    LP—MIKE CUELLAR

Deserves Cooperstown: Phil Rizzuto.
Toughest Pitcher: Cuellar.
Most Underrated: Oliva.
Strongest Team: 1970 Orioles.

PINKY WHITNEY

Whitney was a .295-hitting National League third baseman from 1928 to 1939. He played for the Phillies twice (1928–33, 1936–39) and in between worked for the Braves. His two best seasons were 1930, when he batted .342, and 1937, when he hit .341. Whitney's selections are:

1B—BILL TERRY
2B—FRANKIE FRISCH
3B—PIE TRAYNOR
SS—DICK BARTELL
OF—TRIS SPEAKER
OF—TY COBB
OF—CHUCK KLEIN
C—JIMMIE WILSON
RP—BURLEIGH GRIMES
LP—CARL HUBBELL

Deserves Cooperstown: Pinky Whitney.
Toughest Pitcher: Hubbell. "That screwball was murder. And he knew how to pitch."
Most Underrated: Kiddo Davis. "He was a center fielder with the Phils and the Giants and he could run, throw, and hit. Plus he was a very good fielder." Davis batted .282 in eight seasons. His high was .309 with the 1932 Phillies.
Strongest Team: 1934 Cardinals.
Comments: "On a par with Bartell was Arky Vaughan. He was a fine shortstop and he could hit."

BILLY WILLIAMS

Few power hitters have gone as unnoticed as Williams did while batting .290 over an 18-year career with the Cubs (1959–74) and Athletics (1975–76). With most of the attention on Chicago teammate Ernie Banks, the lefthand-hitting outfielder went about winning Rookie of the Year honors in 1961, leading the league in hits and runs in 1970, leading the league in batting and slugging averages in 1972, clouting at least 20 homers in 14 seasons, amassing 426 round-trippers in his career, and retiring with the then-record of having played in 1,117 consecutive National League games. His most productive seasons were undoubtedly 1970 (.322, 42 home runs, 34 doubles, 129 runs batted in, 137 runs scored) and 1972 (.333 batting average, .606 slugging average, 37 home runs, 34 doubles, and 122 runs batted in). Williams prefers:

> 1B—WILLIE McCOVEY
> 2B—BILL MAZEROSKI
> 3B—BROOKS ROBINSON
> SS—ERNIE BANKS
> OF—HANK AARON
> OF—WILLIE MAYS
> OF—ROBERTO CLEMENTE
> C—JOHNNY BENCH
> RP—DON DRYSDALE
> LP—SANDY KOUFAX

Deserves Cooperstown: Nellie Fox.
Toughest Pitcher: Ray Sadecki. "It was really very simple. He knew he could get me out and I knew he could get me out. So he always got me out."
Most Underrated: Vada Pinson.
Strongest Team: Reds of the early 1970's.

WHITEY WITT

As a 21-year-old rookie shortstop with the Philadelphia Athletics in 1916, Witt played alongside 41-year-old second baseman Nap Lajoie in his final season. After two seasons as a shortstop, Connie Mack used Witt as an outfielder-second baseman for two more seasons, then exclusively as an outfielder in 1921. Traded to the Yankees in 1922, Witt batted leadoff and played centerfield between Bob Meusel and Babe Ruth (1922–25) before moving to the Dodgers for one final season (1926). A lifetime .287 hitter, the lefty-swinging hitter appeared in the 1922 and 1923 World Series. Knocked unconscious by a bottle thrown by a fan in the first game of a late season doubleheader against the Browns in 1922, Witt returned the following day with a bandaged head to drive in the game-winning—and pennant-winning—run. Witt's choices:

> 1B—GEORGE SISLER
> 2B—LARRY LAJOIE
> 3B—PIE TRAYNOR
> SS—HONUS WAGNER
> OF—TRIS SPEAKER
> OF—BABE RUTH
> OF—JOE DiMAGGIO
> C—BILL DICKEY
> RP—WALTER JOHNSON
> LP—LEFTY GROVE

Deserves Cooperstown: Whitey Witt. "Babe Ruth said I was the greatest bunter who ever lived."

Toughest Pitcher: Dutch Leonard. "He loved to hit you in the head or, if he was feeling kindly, in the ribs."

Most Underrated: Harry Hooper.

Strongest Team: 1923 Yankees.

JOE WOOD

Wood had two big league careers. As a pitcher with the Red Sox from 1908 to 1915 he won 116 games. In 1912 he won 34 games and lost only five to lead the AL in wins, won-lost percentage (.872), and shutouts (10). The following season he hurt his arm, however, and pitched irregularly for the next few years. (He was good enough to win 15 and lose five in 1915 and top all AL pitchers in winning percentage, .750, and ERA, 1.49.) After sitting out 1916 he joined the Indians as an outfielder until 1922. His lifetime batting average was .283. Wood selects:

1B—GEORGE SISLER, HAL CHASE, or
    STUFFY McINNIS
2B—EDDIE COLLINS or LARRY LAJOIE
3B—LARRY GARDNER, BOBBY WALLACE, or
    FRANK BAKER
SS—HONUS WAGNER, EVERETT SCOTT, or
    DONIE BUSH
OF—HARRY HOOPER, SAM CRAWFORD, JOE
    JACKSON, or HARRY HEILMANN
OF—TRIS SPEAKER or TY COBB
OF—DUFFY LEWIS, BOBBY VEACH, DAVY JONES,
    or CHARLIE JAMIESON
 C—WALLY SCHANG, IRA THOMAS, RAY SCHALK,
    or JEFF SWEENEY
RP—WALTER JOHNSON, STAN COVELESKI, ED
    WALSH, or CY YOUNG
LP—EDDIE PLANK or HERB PENNOCK

Toughest Batter: Crawford.
Most Underrated: Gardner.
Strongest Team: Athletics.
Comments: "I've always maintained that if there were a higher classification than the major leagues, Ty Cobb would be in it all by himself. Cobb was a step ahead of everyone."

GENE WOODLING

Woodling, called "Old Dependable" in his years with the Yankees, was one of the relatively unpublicized heroes of the great Yankee teams of the early 1950's. He came up with Cleveland in 1943 and returned to the Indians in 1946. He was a reserve outfielder with the Pirates in 1947, and was Minor League Player of the Year in 1948. His Yankee tenure lasted from 1949 to 1954. He was traded to Baltimore in 1955, went to Cleveland in mid-season, stayed with the Indians through 1957, worked for the Orioles again in 1958–60, moved to the Senators in 1961–62, and finished with the Mets in 1962. A lifetime .284 hitter with 147 homers, his best year was 1957 (.321, 19 homers, 78 RBI's—all career highs). He also batted .318 in five World Series. Woodling selects:

    1B—MICKEY VERNON
    2B—JOE GORDON
    3B—BROOKS ROBINSON
    SS—LUIS APARICIO
    OF—JOE DiMAGGIO
    OF—MICKEY MANTLE
    OF—AL KALINE
     C—JIM HEGAN
    RP—ALLIE REYNOLDS
    LP—WHITEY FORD

Deserve Cooperstown: Reynolds and Ken Keltner.
Toughest Pitcher: Ford.
Most Underrated: Vernon.
Strongest Team: 1949–54 Yankees.

WHITLOW WYATT

Wyatt, a righthanded pitcher, bounced around the American League for nine years with the Tigers (1929–33), White Sox (1933–36), and Indians (1937). Then, after a year in the minor leagues, the Dodgers purchased his contract and he became a big winner, including a league-leading 22 victories in 1941 and league-leading totals of five and seven shutouts in 1940 and 1941. His lifetime record was 106–95 with a 3.78 ERA, but during his tenure with the Dodgers (1939–44), he won 80 and lost 45. He finished his career with the Phillies in 1945. Wyatt picks:

```
1B—LOU GEHRIG
2B—BILLY HERMAN
3B—BROOKS ROBINSON or EDDIE MATHEWS
SS—PEE WEE REESE
OF—BABE RUTH
OF—JOE DiMAGGIO
OF—TED WILLIAMS
 C—BILL DICKEY
RP—BOB FELLER
LP—WARREN SPAHN
```

Toughest Batters: Stan Hack and Lonny Frey. "The slap hitter gave me more trouble than the guy who swung the bat hard. The slugger leads the ball. He has a tendency to guess with you and I could always outguess him. The guy who slaps the ball, though, you don't want to change speeds on him."

Strongest Team: Yankees of the late 1930's.

Comments: "Herman was the smartest player I ever saw. Reese was a good hitter, a good baserunner, and a great shortstop. Williams followed the ball at the plate as well as anyone I ever saw. Feller had the best stuff I ever saw, but Spahn had the best control."

EDDIE YOST

Yost played third base for the Senators (1944, 1946–58), Tigers (1959–60), and Angels (1961–62). A modest hitter, .254 lifetime, he did tie for the league lead in doubles with 36 in 1951 and topped all AL batsmen with 115 runs scored in 1959. But his main offensive asset was a sharp eye, which helped him earn 1614 bases on balls, the seventh highest total in history. All those walks gave him a career on-base percentage over .390 and made him an excellent leadoff hitter. Yost, who led the AL in walks six times, selects:

1B—HARMON KILLEBREW
2B—NELLIE FOX
3B—BROOKS ROBINSON
SS—LOU BOUDREAU or PHIL RIZZUTO
OF—TED WILLIAMS
OF—MICKEY MANTLE or JOE DiMAGGIO
OF—AL KALINE
C—YOGI BERRA
RP—EARLY WYNN
LP—WHITEY FORD

Deserve Cooperstown: Mickey Vernon and Richie Ashburn.

Most Underrated: Vernon.

Strongest Team: Yankees of the late 1940's and 1950's.

Comments: ''The players I've picked are those I played with or against. However, in those days black players were just breaking into the major leagues. There have been many black players who belong on a team such as this, players I have seen play over my twenty-two years as a coach.''

GUS ZERNIAL

Zernial, a power hitting righthanded outfielder, slugged 237 home runs in an 11-year career with the White Sox (1949–51), Athletics in Philadelphia (1951–54) and Kansas City (1955–57), and Tigers (1958–59). In 1951 he led the AL in both homers (33) and RBI's (129). He hit more than 20 homers in six seasons, achieving his personal high of 42 in 1953. Zernial, whose lifetime batting average was .265, chooses:

    1B—FERRIS FAIN
    2B—NELLIE FOX
    3B—BROOKS ROBINSON
    SS—PHIL RIZZUTO
    OF—TED WILLIAMS
    OF—MICKEY MANTLE
    OF—JOE DiMAGGIO
     C—YOGI BERRA
    RP—BOB LEMON
    LP—WARREN SPAHN

Deserves Cooperstown: Fox.
Toughest Pitcher: Lemon.
Most Underrated: Fox.
Strongest Team: 1949–53 Yankees.

ADDENDUM

Several players declined, for one of a variety of reasons, to select an all-time all-star team position by position but did offer opinions about the other categories in the survey.

BOB ALLISON hit 256 home runs and batted .255 in 13 seasons (1958–70) with the Senators-Twins. Eight times he hit over 20 homers. The toughest pitcher for him was "any pitcher who made over $20,000 a year, Whitey Ford, Sam McDowell, Jim Palmer, and anybody else who wore a Baltimore uniform."

MARK BELANGER was the defensive criterion for American League shortstops for most of his 17 years (1965–81) with the Orioles. Although he batted only .228 with Baltimore and (for one final season) with the Dodgers, he took home eight Gold Gloves during his career and was considered an indispensable part of Earl Weaver's Oriole teams. According to Belanger, the most underrated player in recent years has been Buddy Bell, "who makes all the plays and then some, and who also happens to be a very good hitter." The single strongest team? "Baltimore between 1969 and 1971."

EWELL BLACKWELL was for a few seasons the toughest pitcher in baseball until injuries damaged his career, which spanned the years 1942, 1946–53, and 1955, with the Reds, Yankees, and Athletics. Although he ended with a record of only 82–78, he pitched 12 shutouts in two years (1946–47) and won 22 and lost only eight with a 2.47 ERA and a league-leading 193 strikeouts in 1947. According to Blackwell, the toughest batter was "None of them. I had pretty good success against everyone." If the testimony in this volume is any indicator, he is correct.

JIM BUNNING won more than 100 games in both the American and National Leagues while pitching for the Tigers, Phillies, Pirates, and Dodgers between 1955 and 1971. He also pitched a no-hitter in each league and compiled a lifetime record of 224–184. He tied for the AL lead in wins with 20 in 1957 and led the league in strikeouts three times. The toughest batter he faced was Ted Williams. "He had no defined weakness. Usually when you get two strikes on a hitter he has a defined weakness. Williams didn't. If you kept the ball down and away on Williams, all you had was a good chance to keep it in the ballpark."

LEW BURDETTE won 203 and lost 144 in 18 seasons with the Yankees, Braves, Cardinals, Cubs, Phillies, and Angels between 1950 and 1967. He won 20 or more games twice. He led the NL in ERA in 1956 (2.70) and tied for the league lead in won–lost percentage (.667) in 1958 and in wins (21) in 1959. In the 1957 World Series he won three complete games and compiled an 0.67 ERA against the Yankees. "Orlando Cepeda was the toughest for me. I was a low ball pitcher and he was a low ball hitter. He stood way back in the batter's box and stepped in."

FRANK CROSETTI played shortstop for the Yankees from 1932 until 1948 and batted .245 while anchoring the infield for seven pennant-winning teams. He volunteers the opinion that "Tony Lazzeri and Ernie Lombardi should be in the Hall of Fame."

ALVIN DARK played shortstop (and later third base) for the Braves, Giants, Cardinals, Cubs, and Phillies in 1946 and from 1948 to 1960. A lifetime .289 hitter, Dark batted over .300 in three consecutive seasons for the Giants. He also later managed the Giants and Athletics. Dark thinks the toughest pitcher was Ewell Blackwell, because he "threw the ball from down beneath and he threw it hard," and that the 1972–74 Oakland A's were the best team he ever saw.

LARRY DOBY, the first black player in the American League, batted .283 with 253 home runs in 13 seasons (1947–59) with the Indians, White Sox, Indians again, Tigers, and White Sox again. His best seasons were in 1952, when he led the American League in home runs, runs scored, and slugging percentage, and in 1954, when he led in homers and runs batted in. Doby, who managed the White Sox in 1978, thinks that eligibility for Cooperstown has been "watered down ever since they started letting in players who were only good in one facet of the game. Once upon a time you had to be good offensively *and* defensively." As for the toughest mound opponent he ever faced, "that would have to be Allie Reynolds, not only because he was a good pitcher but because I think I used to press more when I'd play the Yankees in the Bronx. The reason for that was that, since I was from Paterson, there would always be a lot of people I knew in the stands and I didn't want them to go home disappointed in the 'home-town boy.' " The single best team? "1954 Indians, who else?"

TAYLOR DOUTHIT hit .291 in 11 seasons with the Cardinals, Reds, and Cubs. He was the center fielder on three Cardinal pennant winners (1926, 1928, and 1930). His highest batting average was .336 in 1929. "Any all-time all-star team would have to include old teammates of mine like Jim Bottomley, Frankie Frisch, Rogers Hornsby, Chick Hafey, and Grover Cleveland Alexander," he says.

BIBB FALK batted .314 as an outfielder for the White Sox (1920–28) and Indians (1929–31). He had two spectacular seasons—1924, when he batted .352, and 1926, when he hit .345. "You can't pick a team like that," he says, "but if you did, it would have to have Lou Gehrig, Eddie Collins, Babe Ruth, and Ty Cobb." As for the most underrated player, "Well, Ted Lyons says that I was and I played against him in college and with him with the White Sox."

BOB FELLER was elected to the Hall of Fame in 1962 after an 18-year (1936–41, 1945–56) career with the Indians during which he compiled a record of 266–162 (3.25 ERA). Among the fireballing righthander's numerous accomplishments were winning 20 games six times and hurling three no-hitters. His single best season was undoubtedly 1946 when he had a record of 26–15 with 36 complete games, 348 strikeouts, 10 shutouts, and an ERA of 2.18. For Feller the toughest batters were "Tommy Henrich and Taft Wright as lefthanders and Joe DiMaggio as a righthander, though overall I'd have to say that Rogers Hornsby and Ted Williams were the greatest hitters in an absolute sense I ever saw." Regarding the most underrated player of his time, Feller picks Ernie Lombardi and adds that the Reds catcher should also be in the Hall of Fame. The strongest single team? "No doubt about it—the Yankees of the 1930's. If you want to get down to a single season rather than a period of several years, however, I don't think you can overlook the 1954 Indians, either."

WHITEY FORD, a Hall of Famer since 1974, was the ace lefty of the Yankees pitching staff for 16 seasons (1950, 1953–67). With a 2.75 lifetime ERA he won 236 and lost only 106 to establish a record for the highest career won–lost percentage (.690) for pitchers with 200 or more victories. He led the AL (or tied for the lead) in wins three times, in won–lost percentage three times, and in shutouts twice. In 1961 he won the AL Cy Young Award for his 25–4 record. He holds World Series records for most Series played (11), most victories (10), most games (22), most strikeouts (94), and consecutive scoreless innings (33 ⅔). His toughest hitter was Nellie Fox. The strongest team he saw was the 1961 Yankees.

BILL FREEHAN caught for the Tigers for 15 years (1961, 1963–76) and batted .262 while hitting 200 home runs. He batted as high as .300, in 1964, and hit as many as 25 homers, in 1968. An excellent defensive catcher, Freehan won five consecutive Gold Gloves (1965–69). The toughest pitcher he faced was Luis Tiant. The most underrated players were Dick McAuliffe and Earl Wilson. "Everybody talks about McLain and Lolich, but Wilson turned us around a number of times, winning big games when the Tigers were on the verge of collapse." The strongest team was the 1968–71 Orioles. "The A's were great in the early seventies but I'll take the Robinsons' Orioles over them."

JOE GARAGIOLA batted .257 in nine seasons (1946–54) with the Cardinals, Pirates, Cubs, and Giants. Currently a popular network broadcaster, he says, "No pitcher was the toughest. I was an equal opportunity out."

BOB GIBSON, a Hall of Famer, won 251 and lost 174 with an astonishing 2.91 ERA in 17 years (1959–75) with the

Cardinals. Among his mound accomplishments were winning 20 games five times, striking out at least 200 batters nine times, hurling 56 career shutouts, and retiring with 3117 strikeouts. In 1968 he enjoyed one of the finest seasons in pitching history, posting a record of 22–9 with 13 shutouts and 268 strikeouts and a nearly invisible 1.12 ERA. Gibson, who collected two Cy Young awards, an MVP trophy, and a no-hitter during his career, picks out Al Oliver as a player "generally overlooked" even though "he's always been one of the most consistent .300 hitters in the game." As for the batters who gave him trouble, he says that "almost all of them were the banjo hitters who just slapped at the ball." The strongest team? "That would have to be the Giants of the sixties. Those teams with Mays, McCovey, and Marichal."

BILLY GOODMAN was a lifetime .300 hitter while playing all four infield positions plus the outfield for the Red Sox, Orioles, White Sox, and Colt .45's between 1947 and 1962. In 1950 he won a batting championship with a .354 average. Curiously, he did not have a regular position for the Red Sox that season and played no more than 45 games at any one spot. Goodman thinks Tommy Henrich and Charlie Keller belong in the Hall of Fame and that the greatest team ever was the Yankees in the 1950's. "There was nobody else like them."

CARMEN HILL pitched for the Pirates, Giants, and Cardinals in a 10-year career (1915–16, 1918–19, 1922, 1926–30) punctuated by stretches in the minor leagues. In 1927 he won 22 games and lost 11 for the pennant-winning Bucs. Lifetime he was 49–33 with a 3.44 ERA. "Bill Terry was the toughest batter for me to get out. Catcher Earl Smith was the most underrated player. The strongest team I ever saw was the 1927 Pirates, although overall the Cardinals had the strongest teams of that era." Smith, a lefthanded batter, batted .303 in 12 seasons (1919–30) with four NL teams.

JUDY JOHNSON, a Hall of Famer since 1975, was the premier third baseman in the old Negro Leagues. Between 1921 and 1937 he played for Hilldale, the Homestead Grays, Darby Daisies, and Pittsburgh Crawfords. "There were too many great players to pick one team," he says, "but Josh Gibson was the best hitter I've ever seen, Dizzy Dean and Satchel Paige were the two greatest pitchers, and the Homestead Grays in the thirties was the greatest team.

MICKEY MANTLE, who was elected to the Hall of Fame in 1974, patrolled center field for most of his 18 seasons (1951–68) with the Yankees. He batted .298, hit 536 home runs (to place him sixth on the all time list), and drove in 1509 runs. He led the AL in batting and RBI's once each, in slugging three times, and in homers four times. His personal highs were a .365 batting average (1957) and 54 homers (1961). Three times the AL MVP (1956, 1957, 1962), he won the Triple Crown in 1956 (.353, 52, 130). In 12 World Series he hit 18 homers, scored 42 runs, and drove in 40 runs—all records. "You can't pick a whole team like that, but if we were choosing up sides and every player was in a pool, my first pick would be Whitey Ford and my second would be Ted Williams. Beyond that there would be just too many. The toughest pitcher I ever faced wasn't even in my league. That was Sandy Koufax. But I would also have to single out Herb Score from the left side. From the right side there is no question; it was Dick Radatz. I read in a Dallas newspaper that I faced Radatz sixty-six times in my career and he struck me out forty-five times. If he wasn't the toughest, I don't want to remember who was. For me 'underrated' describes a guy who will do anything to win a game, and Billy Martin and Pete Rose come to mind. The pitching on the 1961 Yankees may not have been as great as when we had Reynolds, Raschi, and Lopat, but the 1961 Yankees were the best team that ever was."

MARTY MARION spent his entire career (1940–50, 1952–53) with St. Louis teams, the Cardinals and Browns. The slick-fielding, rangy shortstop batted .263 and played in four World Series. He also managed the Cardinals, Browns, and White Sox. "An All Star team won't always win games for you. There is a very fine line between a superstar and a good everyday player and you would probably do better with teamwork among good regulars than you would with individual superstars. The toughest pitcher for me was Ewell

Blackwell. He threw sidearm and I think he stepped on third base to throw home. The strongest team I saw was the 1942 Cardinals.''

BILLY MARTIN batted .257 over 11 seasons (1950–53, 1955–61) with the Yankees, Athletics, Tigers, Indians, Reds, Braves, and Twins. In five World Series he batted .333. In the 1953 Series he established or tied records for batting (.500) and hits (12), and in 1952 he made a dramatic catch off Jackie Robinson in the seventh inning to clinch the Series. Equally dramatic have been his comings and goings as Yankee manager, as which he has won two pennants and a World Series. ''I had trouble with a lot of pitchers but especially with Herb Score, who had a terrific fastball and an outstanding curve. There have been hundreds of underrated players who played in the shadow of a Musial or a DiMaggio. I don't know who the *most* underrated was, but I can tell you how you get to be underrated. I hit the longest home run of my career in old Griffith Stadium and I figured I'd finally get the headlines. So Mantle comes up and hits the longest home run ever hit in Griffith. The headlines the next day say 'Mantle Blasts Ball' in great big letters and 'Martin Also Homers' in little letters underneath. Another time I was on third base and Mickey hits one of his tape-measure shots. Crosetti's coaching at third and he's yelling at me to tag up. I always listened to my coaches so I go back to third and there I am with my picture in the papers the next day heading back to third base while the ball is sailing a mile away. That's how you get to be underrated.''

EDDIE MATHEWS was elected to the Hall of Fame in 1978. He played for the Braves (1952–66) in Boston, Milwaukee, and Atlanta, the Astros (1967), and the Tigers (1967–68). He hit 512 home runs, including 40 or more in a season four times. He led the league in homers twice, scored over 100 runs eight times, and drove in over 100 five times. He played in the 1957 and 1958 World Series for the Braves. The toughest pitcher for him was Juan Marichal. (''I hit my five hundredth home run off him, but he usually got me out.'') The strongest team he remembers is the 1957–59 Braves. (''We had it all—speed, defense, power, pitching.'') As far as underrated players go, "Let's just put it this way. I hit more than five hundred home runs and I am in the Hall of Fame, so then why doesn't American Express want me to do commercials for them?" And of Cooperstown, Mathews says, "Baseball has been very slow in recognizing people who belong there. Even in my case. Ernie Banks and I ended up with the exact same number of home runs, but it took me about five years longer to get in than it did him. Nothing against Ernie, but I even look better in a lobby."

LOU PINIELLA, who opened the 1986 season as the Yankees' manager, was a clutch hitting outfielder and designated hitter with the Orioles, Royals, and Yankees in 1964 and from 1968 to 1984. The American League Rookie of the Year in 1969, he batted .291 in his 18 seasons, .305 in five AL Championship Series, and .319 in five World Series. "The most underrated player was Bobby Murcer. The toughest pitchers were Geoff Zahn and Nolan Ryan. One was slow and the other was fast. Anybody can hit the stuff in between."

PHIL RIZZUTO, "The Scooter," was a Yankee shortstop for 13 seasons (1941–42, 1946–56). He batted .273 and played in nine World Series. He won the American League Most Valuable Player Award in 1950 on the strength of a .324 batting average, 36 doubles, 125 runs scored, and 91 walks. Today he is a popular Yankee announcer. "The toughest pitcher I ever faced was Bob Feller. The most underrated player was Tommy Henrich. The single strongest team was the 1941 Yankees. The last time I was asked to pick an all-time all-star team, I forgot to put in Babe Ruth. I said then, in 1957, that I would never try to pick another. So, I'll just say Ruth, Lou Gehrig, Joe DiMaggio, and Bill Dickey would have to be on it and leave it at that."

ROBIN ROBERTS, elected to the Hall of Fame in 1976, won 286 and lost 245 in 19 seasons (1948–66) with the Phillies, Orioles, Astros, and Cubs. He won 20 or more for six consecutive years (1950–55), topping the NL in the last four of those seasons and reached a high of 28 victories in 1952. The toughest batter he had to face was Ernie Banks. "He hit about fifteen home runs against me in key games and key situations. But the worst blow of my career was when Joe DiMaggio hit a home run in the tenth inning to beat me 2–1 in my only World Series appearance." The most underrated player was Del Ennis. "He was a productive, solid hitter, but he was from Philadelphia and it's tough, for some reason, to be recognized in your home town."

PREACHER ROE posted a record of 127–84 over a 12-year career that began slowly with the Cardinals (1938), puttered along with the Pirates (1944–47), and then exploded with the Dodgers (1948–54). For the Dodgers he led the National League in winning percentage in both 1949 and 1951, turned in an astonishing mark of 22–3 in 1951, and went 44–8 over the 1951, 1952, and 1953 seasons. According to the lefthander, his toughest batters were "righthanders and lefthanders, but especially Monte Irvin and Del Ennis." The most underrated player, in Roe's view, was one-time roommate Billy Cox, who "got overlooked because he didn't hit home runs like the other Dodgers did" but who "won as many games with his glove as some of the others did with their bats." Roe also thinks it's a good sign that brilliant fielders like Luis Aparicio and Brooks Robinson have entered the Hall of Fame "because it's a recognition that you have to win games in the field as much as in the batter's box."

EDD ROUSH went into Cooperstown in 1962, almost half a century after he began an 18-year (1913–29, 1931) career with three Federal League teams, the Giants, and the Reds. A lefthand-hitting outfielder with a career mark of .323, he led the National League in batting twice and in slugging percentage, doubles, and triples one season each. Says Roush: "I don't know who was tough and who was easy. All of them were about the same to me, and they knew that, too. They all knew that if they got in my way, they got hurt. . . . As for an underrated player, I'll take Jake Daubert. The man won batting championships in the National League, but you'd never know it. As far as I'm concerned, Daubert belongs in the Hall of Fame ahead of a lot of others in there today. Same thing for Heinie Groh. Daubert and Groh, they went out to the field to play, not like these modern players who walk out there, dig a hole in the batter's box, get in to hit, call time to dig another hole, then take a pitch, then dig some more. . . . More hole digging than baseball playing going on these days.''

RED SCHOENDIENST was a switch-hitting second baseman for the Cardinals, Giants, and Braves from 1945 to 1963. His lifetime average was .289 and his season high was .342 in 1953. A bout with tuberculosis limited his activity in his last five seasons. He returned to St. Louis to manage the Cardinals from 1965 to 1976 and for part of 1980. As player, manager, and coach he has spent more years in a Redbirds uniform than anyone else. Carl Erskine and Johnny Podres were the toughest pitchers for him. ''I couldn't pick up their ball.'' Whitey Kurowski and Dal Maxvill are his selections as most underrated. And the Dodgers of the 1950's and 1960's was the strongest team.

HAL SCHUMACHER was the righthanded complement to Carl Hubbell on the Giants pitching staff in the 1930's. Prince Hal spent his entire career (1931–42, 1946) with the Polo Grounders, for whom he won 158 and lost 128 while compiling an ERA of 3.36. For three seasons (1933–35) he was as good a righthander as any in the game, compiling records of 19–12, 23–10, and 19–9 and ERA's of 2.16, 3.18, and 2.89. ''Ripper Collins, Phil Cavarretta, and Tony Cuccinello were the toughest batters for me to get out. I'd say Jo-Jo Moore was the most underrated player of my time. The strongest team would have to be the 1936–37 Yankees.''

PAUL SPLITTORFF chalked up a record of 166–143 in 15 seasons (1970–1984) with the Royals. The southpaw's best years were 1973 (20–11), 1977 (16–6, league-leading .727 percentage), and 1978 (19–13). According to Splittorff, ''any dream team for one game would have to include George Brett, Joe Rudi, and Thurman Munson and have Catfish Hunter, Dave McNally, and Rollie Fingers ready to pitch.'' For an underrated player, he picks Carney Lansford. As for the toughest batter against him, he selects Dick Allen because ''he could hit both my fastball and my breaking pitches and more than that I just didn't have.''

BIRDIE TEBBETTS was a .270 hitter and an excellent defensive catcher in 14 seasons (1936–41, 1946–52) with the Tigers, Red Sox, and Indians. He has spent over 50 years in baseball as a player, manager, and scout. He managed the Reds, Braves, and Indians for 11 seasons. "The pitcher I couldn't hit was someone nobody remembers, Thornton Lee of the White Sox. I don't know why to this day. If I knew, I would've hit him."

BILL TERRY went into the Hall of Fame in 1954 on the basis of a 14-year (1923–36) career with the Giants during which he batted a lofty .341. The lefthand-hitting first baseman, whose .401 in 1930 marked the last time a National Leaguer reached the .400 hitting level, also managed the Giants to three pennants during his 10 years (1932–41) at the helm of the Polo Grounders. Asked whom he considered an underrated player, Terry said "me—It took them almost twenty years to elect me to the Hall of Fame, and the reason for that was that I wasn't too well liked by all those newspapermen who really decide such things." As for the players who have been inducted into Cooperstown in recent years, he subscribes to the criticism that "a lot of them were just good at one thing—hitting, fielding, or running—and I always thought the idea was that you had to be a great player overall." The strongest team? "1935 Giants. We won everything, didn't we?"

LUIS TIANT won 227 and lost 170 with a 3.28 ERA in 19 seasons (1964–81) with the Indians, Twins, Red Sox, Yankees, and Pirates. A burly righthander with an unorthodox, herky-jerky motion, he led the AL in ERA twice (1968 and 1972) and won two World Series games in his only Fall Classic (1975). "I just couldn't get Tony Oliva and Rod Carew out. I had a lot more trouble with contact hitters than with power hitters."

TED WILLIAMS, one of the greatest hitters in baseball history, was elected to the Hall of Fame in 1966 after batting an astonishing .344 and belting 521 home runs for the Red Sox in 19 seasons between 1939 and 1960. The last major leaguer to bat .400, the lefthand-hitting outfielder's long list of achievements include winning the Triple Crown in 1942 and 1947, being elected American League MVP in 1946 and 1949, and leading the league in important offensive categories no fewer than 40 times. For Williams, the toughest pitcher was "also the greatest I ever saw—Bob Feller." He also cites Bob Lemon, Hoyt Wilhelm, and Whitey Ford for "a combination of their delivery and the liveliness of their ball." As for an underrated player, he names Eddie Joost, "who was the backbone of the Athletics for about three or four years." Strongest team? "I'd have to say that the Yankees, Indians, and Red Sox all had great twenty-five-man units between 1946 and 1950, and that's why there was always a pennant race right down to the wire." With regard to the Hall of Fame, Williams names Phil Rizzuto, Joe Gordon, and Bobby Doerr as players "who should have been in there a long time ago."

EARLY WYNN was inducted into the Hall of Fame in 1971 on the basis of a 23-year (1939–1963) pitching career during which he posted a record of 300–244. Originally a member of the Senators, the big righthander had his greatest seasons (including five 20-game years, two league leaderships in strikeouts and one in ERA) in subsequent stays with the Indians and White Sox. For Wynn the toughest batter was Yogi Berra "because he hit everything, including one time when I bounced a curve six inches in front of the plate and he slammed it for a double." Concerning his numerous failures before obtaining his three hundredth win, Wynn says that "it became important to me as soon as I reached my two hundredth win. I was going to get that three hundredth game no matter what it took. My manager at the time, Birdie Tebbetts, thought I was crazy. He said I would have been better off winning two hundred ninety-nine because nobody had ever done that before and I would've become more famous for failing than succeeding."